ROMAN SOCIETY AND ROMAN LAW IN THE NEW TESTAMENT

ROMAN SOCIETY AND ROMAN LAW IN THE NEW TESTAMENT

BY

A. N. SHERWIN-WHITE

THE SARUM LECTURES
1960–1961

OXFORD
AT THE CLARENDON PRESS
1963

Oxford University Press, Amen House, London E.C.4

GLASGOW NEW YORK TORONTO MELBOURNE WELLINGTON
BOMBAY CALCUTTA MADRAS KARACHI LAHORE DACCA
CAPE TOWN SALISBURY NAIROBI IBADAN ACCRA
KUALA LUMPUR HONG KONG

PRINTED IN GREAT BRITAIN
AT THE UNIVERSITY PRESS, OXFORD
BY VIVIAN RIDLER
PRINTER TO THE UNIVERSITY

PREFACE

THESE lectures are about the Hellenistic and Roman setting, and especially the legal and administrative and municipal background, of Acts and the synoptic gospels, if I may use so old-fashioned a term. Finally, and more briefly, in Lectures Six and Eight, I have something to say about the social and economic background. This is no new subject. Some might term it a well-ploughed field. But time marches on in scholarship as in other things. I was led into this reopening of old inquiries partly by my own interest in the strictly judicial questions, and partly after observing how relatively old-fashioned is a good deal of the scholarship still commonly cited, particularly about the city life of the eastern provinces, in the more obvious commentaries and histories of the early Church. William Ramsay was a very learned and intelligent man—but 'vixere fortes *post* Agamemnona'. I observed also—what is common to all zones of scholarship—how out of focus can be the vision of even the acutest New Testament historian, although he is acquainted with the latest trends in the study of the Roman empire, just because inevitably he has not been able to immerse himself in the Roman evidence and the Roman aspect until its understanding becomes a second nature. It may be useful if someone from the Roman side looks again at the old evidence, even where there is no new material, and appraises the New Testament setting in terms of modern Romanist developments. No doubt I in turn will be quickly found to suffer from just that same lack of focus in dealing with Judaic and Christian material which is outside my sphere. Scholars attempting to deal with two worlds of this magnitude need two lives. We must appear as amateurs in each other's field. A Roman public law and administration man such as myself cannot be fully acquainted with New Testament scholarship and bibliography over so great an area as I must venture to trespass on. But one may learn what are the questions requiring answers, and one may show how the various historical and legal and social problems raised by the Gospels and Acts now look to a Roman historian. That, and only that, is the intention of these lectures.

Another apology. At this stage of the evolution of classical and biblical studies a great deal of material has to be re-examined, often for only a small result. You are bound to say from time to time 'we have heard this before', though perhaps you will not always say 'we have heard *all* this before'. I hope to put a new shine on some of the old lamps. Recent Roman researches of scholars other than myself should give a new look to some familiar biblical materials by the mere act of presentation.

My first investigations concern the account of the trials of Christ and of Paul, in three lectures. I must warn you— and this is not an apology but a caution—that the first lecture, today's,—there is no escape—will be almost pure Roman history. This is intended to provide the basis of the following two discourses, in which I will come to grips with biblical texts. Preliminary questions arise about the powers of Roman governors and the nature of their jurisdiction. To answer these adequately it is necessary to restate the basic evidence and to reconstruct a story which has been much modified by particular studies, but not reconsidered as a whole, since Mommsen wrote his history of Roman public law some seventy years ago.

I must add a note of gratitude first to the fidelity of the audience which sustained my enthusiasm during Michaelmas and Hilary terms 1960–1, and second to those members of it who helped me subsequently with discussion and criticism, especially Professor C. E. Dodd, Mr. P. A. B. Brunt, the Rev. J. R. Porter, and Professor A. H. M. Jones, to whom it is due that the grosser errors of judgement and understanding have been purged in some measure from the original draft, which has not, however, been substantially rewritten. To my colleague Mr. D. A. F. M. Russell I have at all times owed a great debt, not only in matters literary and philological, but generally for the cautionary scepticism with which he faces doubtful problems.

A. N. S. -W.

July 1961

CONTENTS

ABBREVIATIONS

AE	*Année Épigraphique.*
Am. J. Theol.	*American Journal of Theology.*
Ant.	Josephus, *Antiquitates Iudaicae.*
A–J	F. F. Abbot and A. C. Johnson, *Municipal Administration in the Roman Empire*, Princeton, 1926.
BG	Caesar, *De Bello Gallico.*
BGU	*Berliner griechische Urkunden.*
BJ	Josephus, *Bellum Gallicum.*
BSR	*Papers of the British School at Rome.*
CAH	*Cambridge Ancient History.*
Charlesworth	M. Charlesworth, *Documents Illustrating the Reigns of Claudius and Nero*, Cambridge, 1939.
Cicero, *II in Verr.*	Cicero, *Secunda Actio in Verrem.*
CIG	*Corpus Inscriptionum Graecarum.*
CIL	*Corpus Inscriptionum Latinarum.*
Cl. Phil.	*Classical Philogy* (Chicago).
Cl. Rev.	*Classical Review.*
Cod. Iust.	*Codex Iustinianus* in *Corpus Iuris Civilis.*
Collatio	*Collatio Legum Mosaicarum et Romanarum* in *FIRA.*
D.	*Digesta iuris Romani* in *Corpus Iuris Civilis.*
Dio	Cassius Dio, *Historiae.*
Dio Chrys.	Dio Chrysostomus, *Orationes.*
Ditt. *Syll.*	W. Dittenberger, *Sylloge Inscriptionum Graecarum.*
D. Pen. R.	Th. Mommsen, *Droit pénale romaine*, Paris, 1903.
DPR	Th. Mommsen, *Droit publique romaine*, Paris, 1897.
E–J	V. Ehrenberg and A. H. M. Jones, *Documents Illustrating the Reigns of Augustus and Tiberius*[2], Oxford, 1955.
Eph. Epigr.	*Ephemeris Epigraphica.*
FIRA	S. Riccobono, *Fontes Iuris Romani Antejustiniani*, ii, Florence, 1941.
Greek Coins	*Catalogue of Greek Coins* (*British Museum*), London.
GS	Th. Mommsen, *Gesammelte Schriften*, iii, Berlin, 1907.
IEJ	*Israel Exploration Journal.*
IGRR	*Inscriptiones Graecae ad Res Romanas pertinentes*, Paris, 1911.

ILS	H. Dessau, *Inscriptiones Latinae Selectae*, Berlin, 1892.
Inscr. BM	*Ancient Greek Inscriptions in the British Museum*, Oxford, 1874.
Jackson–Lake	F. J. Foakes-Jackson and Kirsopp Lake, *The Beginnings of Christianity*, London, 1920.
Jones, *Cities*	A. H. M. Jones, *Cities of the Eastern Roman Provinces*, Oxford, 1937.
Jones, *Greek City*	A. H. M. Jones, *The Greek City*, Oxford, 1940.
JRS	*Journal of Roman Studies*.
JTS	*Journal of Theological Studies*.
Juster	J. Juster, *Les Juifs dans l'empire romain*, Paris, 1914.
L–S	Liddell and Scott, *Greek–English Lexicon*.
Num. Zeit.	*Numismatische Zeitschrift*.
OGIS	W. Dittenberger, *Orientis Graecae Inscriptiones Selectae*.
Phil. *VS*	Philostratus, *Vitae Sophistarum*.
Pliny, *Ep.*	Plinius, *Epistulae*.
Pliny, *NH*	Plinius, *Naturalis Historia*.
RC	A. N. Sherwin-White, *The Roman Citizenship*, Oxford, 1939.
Rev. Hist. droit fr.	*Revue historique de droit français et étranger* (Paris).
Rev. Int. droits de l'ant.	*Revue internationale des droits de l'antiquité* (Brussels).
SEG	*Supplementum Epigraphicum Graecum*.
Sent. Pauli	*Sententiae Pauli* in *FIRA*
Sitzb. Berlin. Akad. Wiss.	*Sitzungsberichte der Preußischen Akademie der Wissenschaften zu Berlin*.
Suet.	Suetonius, *Vitae Caesarum*.
Tac. *Ann.*	Tacitus, *Annales*.
Z–S	*Zeitschrift der Savigny-Stiftung für Rechtsgeschichte*.

emperor instead of the Roman Senate about particular problems, and for the emperor to advise them by a rescript which had the force of law.[1] Numerous examples from the time of Trajan and Hadrian onwards can be extracted from the *Digest*.[2] But this is a development of the second century of the Principate. Earlier, such intervention arose less directly when a provincial community addressed itself immediately, as it was free to do, to the Princeps. He might then address a letter of firm advice to the proconsul, or refer the whole or part of the business back to him for consideration.[3] The earliest example of a proconsul treating a recommendation of the Princeps as an order comes, characteristically, from the time of the autocratic Domitian.[4] His principate probably forms the divide between the earlier period of independence and the later period of increasing control. But in the Julio-Claudian period the proconsuls were remarkably independent figures. Few bounds were set to the free exercise of their *imperium*. Unless the proconsul offended the wealthy magnates of his province, he was unlikely to be called to account at Rome for abuse of power when his proconsulship was over. He was under no compulsion to consult the Senate, which was his nominal director, and still less the Princeps, about the problems of his province. Having the *imperium*, the proconsul had the total power of administration, jurisdiction, defence—in so far as that arose —and the maintenance of public order.[5]

[1] Mommsen *DPR*, iii. 287 f., v. 133 ff. for basic discussion. Mommsen is cited in the French edition for the convenience of those who lack German.

[2] e.g. *D.* i. 16. 10.xlviii, 18. 1. 11–12, 19; 19. 5 pr., 20. 6—if all are proconsuls; but cf. 48. 22. 7. 10 and 14 for term *praesides* in Ulpian, *De off. procons.*

[3] The four 'edicts' of Augustus from Cyrene are the best example of this way of using the language of 'advice' and *auctoritas* instead of command. Later, cf. the edict of Claudius to the proconsuls of Asia summarized in *SEG*, iv. 516. In general M. Grant, *From Imperium to Auctoritas*, 430 ff., and articles cited ibid.

[4] Ditt. *Syll.*[3] ii. 821 D.

[5] Mommsen, op. cit. iii. 302 f., 308 f.

LECTURE ONE

'Coercitio', 'cognitio', and 'imperium' in the first century A.D.

THE starting-point of this investigation must be the definition of the power of the provincial governor. In the New Testament we have to do with proconsuls and procurator-governors but not with the imperial legates. The proconsul in the first century of the Principate was still very much the independent administrator that he had been in the Republican period. He held the *imperium*, and was limited in his use of it over ordinary provincials only by certain statute laws, notably the law of extortion and the law of treason or *maiestas minuta*. These gave little protection to the common man in the provinces against the tyrannical abuse of power, because their operation depended upon an elaborate and expensive procedure of accusation, though the provincial Roman citizen was protected against summary execution by clauses of the *lex Iulia* concerning riots, or *vis publica*. By the latter part of the second century A.D. the proconsuls had fallen under the control of the emperors, who issued them with directives, known as *mandata*, just like the imperial legates before they set out for their provinces. This is apparent from, for example, texts of the lawyer Ulpian, who speaks in his *De officio proconsulum* of the imperial *mandata*. This situation can be traced back to the time of the emperor Antoninus Pius at least.[1] Earlier than this it had become customary for proconsuls to consult the

---

[1] *D.* i. 16. 6. 3. Cf. 48. 3. 6, 1; 6. 6 (Pius).

The extent of the governor's power over the ordinary provincial subject, or *peregrinus homo*, is best seen from the only law that limited it, the extortion law or *lex repetundarum*. A proconsul could be as harsh and arbitrary as he liked, so long as he did not take money or property, 'things', *res*, from a provincial, even with the provincial's consent. Then, and only then, did a suit for extortion lie, down to A.D. 6. In that year the notorious Volesus Messala, a proconsul of Asia, executed 300 provincials in a single day and walked about among the bodies exclaiming 'ecce regale factum'.[1] It needed an act of retrospective legislation to bring his misdeeds under the cognizance of the extortion law. It is probable that henceforth extreme cruelty, or *saevitia* as the sources call it, could be brought as a charge against a governor, even if not accompanied by financial extortion. But this remedy still remained only the remedy of the wellto-do, the *potentes*; their power to look after themselves is attested by a set-piece example from the time of Nero in the *Annals* of Tacitus.[2]

No ancient authority defines *imperium*. The best documentation of its effects is to be found in the fifth of Cicero's *Verrines*, where he enlarges upon all those misdeeds of Verres which Cicero had been unable to bring as specific charges against him because they did not involve the taking of money.[3] The wide sweep of the proconsul's power is summed up by the plea advanced in the year A.D. 100 by certain persons charged with aiding and abetting an extortionate proconsul. They claimed that they were men of provincial status, and compelled by fear to obey every command of the proconsul,[4] 'Esse se provinciales et ad omne

---

[1] For Messala, Tac. *Ann.* 3. 68. Sen. *Dial.* iv. 5. 5. Cf. A. N. SherwinWhite, 'Poena Legis Repetundarum', *BSR*, xvii. 5 ff., and *JRS*, 1952, 43 ff. criticized in part by M. I. Henderson, ibid. 1951, 71 ff.

[2] Tac. *Ann.* xv. 20.   [3] Cf. A. N. Sherwin-White, art. cit., 1952, 54.

[4] Pliny, *Ep.* iii. 9. 15. Below, p. 73.

proconsulum imperium metu cogi'. You must do what the
proconsul bids, or you will be punished for a what the
lawyers called *contumacia*. The classical lawyers of the late
second and early third centuries make it clear enough that
the proconsuls still held the *imperium*, however much it had
come by then to be fettered about by imperial legislation.
From the *imperium* stems the basic power of criminal jurisdiction: designated by the terms *coercere* and *animadvertere*. The
proconsul, says Ulpian, and only the proconsul, is com-
petent to do this. The power resides in him alone, and he
cannot delegate it.[1] This is not merely the doctrine of the
'classical' lawyers, but is valid for an earlier age. So much is
shown by a text of Pomponius writing in mid-second century, and by a rescript of Trajan to Pliny, who was then
imperial legate of Bithynia with Pontus.[2] Two slaves had

[1] *D.* i. 16. 6. pref. 'solent etiam custodiarum cognitionem mandare lega-
tis ... sed hoc genus mandati extraordinarium est: nec enim potest quis gladii
potestatem sibi datam *vel cuius alterius coercitionis* ad alium transferre, nec
liberandi igitur reos ius, cum accusari apud eum non possint.' This refers
to the whole field of criminal jurisdiction and not just to the more limited
form of *ius gladii*, *pace* A. H. M. Jones, art. 'I appeal', 923, cited below,
p. 10 n. 1. The addition of the italicized words makes this clear. The
classical lawyers are positive that the *legatus proconsulis* had no independent
potestas of his own. Venuleius, *D.* i. 15. 11, confirms the text of Ulpian, should
this be suspected of interpolation: 'si quid erit quod maiorem animadver-
sionem exigat reicere legatus apud proconsulem debet: neque enim animad-
vertendi coercendi vel atrociter verberandi ius habet.' This extends far
below the level of *ius gladii*. Marcian and Ulpian insist that the legate re-
ceives the civil jurisdiction only by mandate from the proconsul (ibid. 4, 6. 5.
6, 1) and lacks some aspects, such as the power of conducting manumissions,
which the proconsul possessed in virtue of his *imperium* even outside his
province (*D.* i. 16. 2, confirmed earlier by Pliny, *Ep.* vii. 16. 32). The proconsular legates were inferior in this respect to the assistants (*legatus iuridicus*)
of the imperiall egates. *D.* 1. 16. 3 and 20. 1. Pomponius, writing in the
mid-second century, clinches the issue briefly for the earlier period: 'legatus
proconsulis nihil proprium habet.' (ib. 13). Hence the title of the proconsular
legates—*legatus propraetore*—must be honorary and not technical.

[2] Pliny, *Ep.* x. 30. 1. 'secundum mandata mea fecit Sempronius Caelianus
mittendo ad te eos de quibus cognosci oportebit an capitale supplicium
meruisse videantur.' For Pomponius see note 1 above.

been discovered masquerading as recruits in the Roman forces. The officer in charge of the provincial levy had sent them to Pliny, and Trajan remarked that he did right in referring to the governor a case involving the capital penalty. Even the trial and execution of slaves was reserved for the holder of *imperium*. What applies to the emperor's legate in a matter such as this applies *a fortiori* to the proconsuls. Pomponius makes it quite clear that only the proconsul, and not his legate, holds *imperium*. This strict limitation of the capital jurisdiction can be taken back to the time of Augustus. In an instruction of Augustus addressed to the proconsul of Cyrene in 7–6 B.C. provision is made for the use of delegated jurisdiction except in capital cases, which are to be kept in the hands of the proconsul himself.[1] The independent character of the *imperium* even in the later Empire is shown by a discussion in two third-century lawyers about the effect of the formula used when an emperor referred a petitioner back to the provincial governor. The formula was 'eum qui provinciae praeest adire potes'. Both lawyers agree that this did not mean that the governor was then obliged to hear the case himself. He was left free to handle the matter as he chose.[2]

The unfettered quality of the governor's *imperium* is very relevant to the judicial problems of the Gospels and of the Acts of the Apostles. But first it must be established whether the equestrian governors of Judaea had the same powers as proconsuls and imperial legates.[3] This must be done without using the evidence of the scriptural books themselves, or the argument will be circular. The governors

[1] The proconsul is to hear the cases himself with or without the use of a jury as he thinks fit. For this jury system see below, p. 15. E–J, 311, iv. 65 ff.

[2] *D.* i. 18. 8–9.

[3] The *imperium* of the imperial legate is in itself as absolute and independent as that of the proconsul, Mommsen, *DPR*, iii. 280. See below, pp. 7–9.

of Judaea belong to a rather special group of imperial administrators, to whom some attention has been given in recent years, though the question of their technical powers has not been widely discussed.[1] These are men of non-senatorial rank, technically Roman 'knights', a class of men owning a moderate minimum of property, who were used to supplement the senatorial proconsuls and legates by taking over the government of relatively small areas that required special treatment; mostly these were military governments over rebellious or newly acquired areas. Such were the various Alpine districts known as Rhaetia, Noricum, and the Cottian and Maritime Alps, the island of Sardinia, and of course Judaea. The greatest of them was Egypt. Their title in the period before Claudius was not *procurator* but *praefectus*.[2]

The key passage concerning the powers of these prefects comes from the *Annals* of Tacitus for the year A.D. 53. The emperor Claudius that year secured by means of a formal decree of the Senate an extension to the powers of his financial agents, the officials properly called *procuratores Augusti*. They were to acquire the power of civil jurisdiction in certain financial matters.[3] Tacitus goes on to explain that the equestrian governors or 'prefects' of Egypt had from the

[1] Mommsen, *DPR*, iii. 283, treated the question inadequately, regarding all the procuratorial provinces, on the false analogy of Egypt (below, p. 11), as annexed kingdoms in which the Princeps ruled as the heir of the former kings. A. H. M. Jones, 'Procurators and Prefects', *Studies in Roman Government*, 117 f., is the most recent and formal discussion. The present essay was written independently of Jones's article, but reaches similar conclusions.

[2] Sherwin-White, *BSR*, xv. 12 f. H. G. Pflaum, *Les Procurateurs équestres*, &c. (Paris, 1950), 22 f. Cf. Jones, art. cit. 119, but the point was noted briefly by Mommsen *DPR*, loc. cit.

[3] Tac. *Ann*. 12. 60. Tacitus continues with a somewhat oblique reference to the criminal jurisdiction of the Republic. The relevance of this to the procurators is not certain, since the passage contains an ambiguous change of emphasis at this point. Cf. Sherwin-White, art. cit. 21, nn. 65, 67. D. Stockton, *Historia*, 1961, 116 ff.

time of Augustus been given the full judicial powers of a Roman magistrate. He adds: 'mox alias per provincias et in urbe pleraque concessa sunt quae olim a praetoribus noscebantur'. This obscure phrase must refer to the category under discussion—the prefects. Gradually, in the period between Augustus and Claudius—*mox*—as the equestrian provinces came into being, their governors were given power on the analogy of the Prefect of Egypt. Ulpian, in a passage from his book *Ad edictum*, clinches the matter, by saying that the Prefect of Egypt had been given powers similar to those of proconsuls, *imperium ad similitudinem proconsulis*, by a law, *lege*.[1] The reference to a law of the Roman people is most unusual, in such a context, and evidently refers to the institution of the office in the early years of Augustus. In the restored republican system of the Augustan age only a law of the people could confer *imperium*.

When in A.D. 6—the very year that Judaea became a province—an equestrian military governor was sent to Sardinia in place of the annual proconsul, it is very unlikely that he was given powers notably inferior to his predecessor.[2] In a document of A.D. 67 from Sardinia which gives the history of certain administrative disputes in the island, the same terms are applied to the equestrian governor's jurisdiction and that of the proconsul.[3] The term *procurator* came into use for these equestrian governors under Claudius, and the first governor of Mauretania under Claudius is styled *procurator pro legato*. It indicates that his position was akin to that of an imperial legate. A somewhat similar title had been

---

[1] *D.* 1. 17. 1. Cf. Jones, art. cit., 121, for the rejection of the view that this passage is interpolated.

[2] Dio, 55. 28, 1. Pausanias, vii. 17. 2

[3] *FIRA*, i, no. 59, or Abbot and Johnston, *Municipal Administration of the Roman Empire*, no. 58, henceforth cited as A–J. Sardinia was governed by *praefecti* or *procuratores* from A.D. 6 until proconsular rule was restored in A.D. 67.

given to the equestrian governor of Sardinia,[1] *praefectus pro legato*.

The next witness is Josephus. In a well-known passage of his *Jewish War* he states that Coponius, the first governor, was sent with power μέχρι τοῦ θανάτου 'unto death'.[2] This is ambiguous. At first sight it seems to refer to what the lawyers call *ius gladii*, the right of the sword, which at this date meant that its holder had the power of death over Roman citizens who were soldiers in his forces. But the parallel passage in the Jewish Antiquities only says: 'Coponius was sent . . . to have the supreme power . . . over the Jews.' In the context of the establishment of the new Roman administration it is much more likely that Josephus means, in his *Jewish War* also, that the governor was given the equivalent of proconsular *imperium*, so far as criminal and political jurisdiction was concerned. The equestrian governors had military forces under their command. Though their troops were not normally legionary troops, but local auxiliaries, their commanders and often their centurions were Romans. Hence the prefects needed the powers of discipline, normally derived from the *imperium*, to exercise their command effectively, but hardly that of executing Romans.

It might be thought that the many facts given by Josephus' full account of the equestrian administration of Judaea suffice to prove the point. But Josephus' narrative is mostly concerned with insurrections, and hence is seldom evidence for the routine and civil administration. The early evidence outside Josephus sufficiently suggests that from the beginning the equestrian provincial governors had the equivalent of *imperium*, and hence that the governors of Judaea could do what an imperial legate or a proconsul could do.[3] By some

---

[1] *AE*, 1924, no. 66. Cf. *ILS*, 105, 'obtinente T. Pompio (P)roculo pro leg(ato)'.

[2] Jos. *BJ*, 2. 8. 1. *Ant.* 18. 1. 1.   [3] *DPR*, iii. 280–1.

chance it happens that the classical lawyers have little to say specifically about the powers of equestrian governors except for the fortunate statement about the Prefect of Egypt used above.[1]

A word of caution is necessary about the relationship of the *imperium* and jurisdiction of the legates and procurators to that of the emperor himself. Their powers are not mandatory in the sense that they are the substitutes or deputies of the Princeps, or that their subjects can normally appeal from their decision to that of the emperor. Mommsen defined this matter very clearly in the *Staatsrecht*: 'they are the mandatories of the Princeps in the sense that they are appointed by the emperor at his will . . . and are discharged by him at his will. Their *imperium* belongs to them only because of their appointment and lasts as long as it.'[2] But it is a separate *imperium* for all that, and the governor's actions are only subject to cancellation by the Princeps, if he chooses to intervene from above in virtue of his *imperium maius*, or overriding power. This is not so much of a legal quibble as it may sound to modern ears. It means that there was no automatic right for the provincial subject to appeal from the tribunal of the governor to that of the Princeps. He could only do so if he possessed some special privilege.

In this discussion the term *ius gladii* has not been used in a technical sense for the power of the governor over either Roman citizens or *peregrini*, though the text of Josephus about the powers of Coponius brought the matter up. The term has confused commentators on *Acts*, because it has two

---

[1] Callistratus, *D.* i. 19. 3, where the text is uncertain, probably refers to the criminal jurisdiction of procurator-governors and implies that it was equal to that of other governors. The late *Sent. Pauli*, v. 26. 2, notes that the equestrian military officers had the military *coercitio* over citizen troops. The title *De officio praesidis* in *D.* i apparently refers only to senatorial governors.

[2] *DPR*, iii. 280 f.

distinct meanings in legal and historical texts. Professor
A. H. M. Jones has clarified the evidence, which was left in
a state of some uncertainty by Mommsen in the *Strafrecht*.[1]
Jones has shown that it is a question of dates. For the first
two centuries of the Empire the term referred only to the
power given to provincial governors who had Roman citizen
troops under their command, to enable them to maintain
military discipline without being hampered by the provisions of the laws of *provocatio*. The army commander had
the power of execution, and the secondary officers had the
power of severe castigation, over their soldiers. When in the
third century A.D. the *constitutio Antoniniana* turned all provincials into Roman citizens, it became necessary to modify
the former exemption of Roman citizens from the capital
jurisdiction of the governors. Hence the lawyers invented
a distinction between the *imperium* which conferred the capital power over citizens, and that necessary for other jurisdiction. In some texts *ius gladii* is now equated with *merum
imperium*, as the full power. But titles in inscriptions show
that the narrower technical meaning of *ius gladii* also continued to be used after this date. The matter need not be
pressed further. Paul and his Roman associates were not
soldiers, and hence the question whether the procurator of
Judaea held the *ius gladii* is irrelevant for present purposes.
They may have done so, since they had some troops of
citizen status, though no legionaries, under their command.
In the passage from Josephus already discussed, where Josephus speaks of the power of life and death, he may have
misunderstood the technical Latin term, if the procurator
had the *ius gladii* in addition to his ordinary powers. There
is a passage from Philostratus where the term 'holding the

[1] A. H. M. Jones, 'I appeal unto Caesar', *Papers presented to D. M.
Robinson*, 918 ff. Mommsen, *D. Pen. R.* i. 289 ff. Cf. also J. L. Strachan-
Davidson, *Problems of Roman Criminal Law* (Oxford, 1912), ii. 167 ff.

sword' is used similarly of the ordinary power of a proconsul over provincials.[1]

The discussion of *imperium* demonstrates usefully the answer to a much-discussed question about the status of Roman Judaea. There has been a tendency, countenanced even by the authority of Mommsen, to speak as though Judaea were not a true province or even technically part of the Roman empire.[2] This is coupled with a similar tendency to speak of the client kingdoms as outside the Roman empire. The previous discussion should show that there is no difference between the status and conditions of Judaea and of the other early equestrian administrations. The confusion arose from something that Tacitus said about the status, not of Judaea, but of Egypt. In the *Histories* he remarked metaphorically of Egypt that Augustus 'kept it within the household'—*domi retinere*—but this did not mean that Egypt was the private property of Augustus.[3] Roman historians are now satisfied that Egypt was part, as Augustus said in the *Res Gestae*, of the *imperium populi Romani*, into whose coffers, as Velleius Paterculus remarked, its tribute was poured.[4] The same holds good for Judaea. The strict usage of the term *provincia* in the late Republic and early Principate is elastic. In the time of Augustus himself it is unlikely that the different parts of Syria and adjacent Asia Minor were thought of as separate provinces: they were all part of the single great eastern *provincia* assigned to Augustus by the various settlements of his power made in 27 B.C., and subsequently different methods of management were employed at various times for various areas, including the use of client kings. But this did not mean that some districts lay outside

[1] See Lecture Four, p. 76.

[2] Above, p. 6 n. 1. Cf. K. J. Cadbury, in Jackson–Lake, *Beginnings of Christianity*, v. 300, n. 2.　　　　　　[3] Tac. *Hist.* i. 11.

[4] *Res Gestae* (E–J, no. 1), 27. 1. Velleius, ii. 39. 2. Cf. U. Wilcken, *JRS*, 1938, 138 ff., esp. 142.

the Roman empire.[1] Basically the term *provincia* is relevant
to a man, not a territory. When Judaea is administered by
Augustus or his prefect, it is his *provincia*. The term that
comes nearest to the modern idea of an administrative terri-
torial province is *forma provinciae stipendiariae*. Texts ranging
from Caesar's *Commentaries* to the *Annals* of Tacitus show
that the decisive elements are three: permanent military
occupation, regular taxation, and Roman supervision of
public order, including jurisdiction and municipal government.[2] By all these tests Judaea was a province.

This digression may fitly be concluded by the observation,
which is only of technical interest, that it is probable, from
what was said a little earlier, that the correct contemporary
title for at least the pre-Claudian governors of Judaea was
praefectus rather than *procurator*. Tacitus, in the well-known
reference, naturally used the normal term of his own times.[3]
Of the scriptural sources, Acts and Matthew never use the
Greek equivalent of *procurator*, ἐπίτροπος, but the more
military ἡγεμών.[4] The rest use only the name of Pilate,
though the term ἐπίτροπος is used by Luke and Matthew in
its basic sense.[5] Luke once has ἡγεμών.[6]

Having established the equestrian *imperium* by sources
independent of the Scriptures, one may turn to the actual
exercise of criminal jurisdiction in the early Principate.

---

[1] Strabo, xiv. 5. 6, p. 671, remarks that Cilicia Tracheia was left to a king
instead of a legate for reasons of convenience.

[2] Caesar, *BG*, ii. 1. 3, v. 41. 5, vii. 77. 14–16; Velleius, ii. 37. 5, 117. 3–4;
Tac. *Ann*. xi. 18. 3, xv. 6. 6. For the sum cited see Velleius, ii. 97, 4.

[3] Ibid. xv. 44. 4.

[4] Cf. p. 6 n. 1. Matt. xxvii 2, 11, 16, 21, 27; Acts xxiii. 25, 27, 33,
xxiv. 1, 10. Josephus uses ἡγεμών and ἔπαρχος—the normal rendering of
praefectus—in *Ant*. 18. 2, 2, and ἐπίτροπος of the Claudian period, ibid.
xx. 5, 1. Philo uses the first and last of these terms writing in the Claudian
period; cf., e.g., *In Flaccum*, 2. 74. 163. *Leg*. 132. The newly found inscription
of Pilate from Caesarea in fact calls him '[Praef]ectus Iud[aea]e', *Rendiconti
Ist. Lombardo 1961*.

[5] Matt. xx. 8; Luke viii. 3.   [6] Luke xx. 20.

Cadbury, in his Appendix to the Jackson–Lake *Commentary on Acts*, remarked with some justice that the difficulty of assessing the value of the evidence in Acts was that Acts itself is the chief source of evidence for the technique of provincial criminal jurisdiction, *cognitio*, in the early Principate.[1] There is no formal description of criminal trials by provincial governors between the brief evidence of Cicero's *Verrines* and that of Pliny's Letters from Bithynia–Pontus, including the account of the trial of the Christians, in about A.D. 110. From the evidence of the classical lawyers and of imperial rescripts in the *Digest* an account can be constructed of the developed forms of *cognitio* in the later second and early third centuries. The standard exposition of this procedure is to be found still in Mommsen's *Strafrecht*, with modern amendments.[2] But the question remains how far this system is valid for the period of Acts.

A preliminary sketch of the early development of provincial jurisdiction here becomes necessary. Mommsen was satisfied to observe briefly in a masterly footnote that the later procedure can be detected fully fledged in documents of the Flavio-Trajanic period, A.D. 70–117.[3] But more is needed than that. The Roman State itself only acquired a formal system of criminal jurisdiction in the period of the late Republic, and this system was still expanding in the time of Augustus. The major offences against persons, society, and the government, were defined by a number of detailed statutes—*leges publicae*—concerning, for example, adultery, forgery, murder, bribery, and treason. The whole system was known as the *ordo iudiciorum publicorum*—the List of National Courts, perhaps. This was a tidy system, but even

[1] Op. cit. v. 299.
[2] *D. Pen. R.* i. 274 ff., ii. 10 ff. Also Strachan-Davidson, op. cit. ii. 159 ff. Below, p. 17 n. 2, for the moderns.
[3] *D. Pen. R.* i. 278 n. 1.

so it was not complete. Rare offences, such as offences against the State religion and incendiarism, and the offences of the common man, such as burglary and robbery, were not covered by the *ordo*. Essentially the *ordo* dealt with the offences of high society and the governing personnel. The crimes of the common man were left to the summary jurisdiction at Rome of the annual magistrates. This was fairly soon replaced—in the latter years of Augustus—by the jurisdiction of more permanent officers of State—the *praefectus urbi* and *praefectus vigilum*. These were police-court magistrates, and their jurisdiction was, as the lawyers put it, 'outside the List', *extra ordinem*. They dealt with the offences not covered by the *ordo*. They had no formal juries in their courts, unlike the praetors who preside over the *ordo* and its jury-courts or *quaestiones*. They were bound by no specific criminal laws. Their powers depended upon the *imperium* which they held either as deputies of the Princeps, or like the Prefect of Egypt by special enactment. They dispensed justice by personal *cognitio*, and they determined their own punishments. This basic pattern can be detected in outline from the early Principate, though detailed information comes only from the classical lawyers.

Such was the dual system of criminal jurisdiction at Rome, where the central criminal courts of Italy held their sessions. None of this applied compulsorily in the provinces of the Empire to the jurisdiction of governors over the mass of provincial subjects, or *peregrini*, though it exercised some influence over their arrangements. The governor left a great deal of minor jurisdiction to the local municipal courts. His special concern was with matters affecting public order. These were largely but not solely the capital crimes of the Roman *ordo*. But since the traditions of provincial government were established long before the *ordo* was completed, provincial jurisdiction was based on the *imperium* and the free exercise of the governor's judgment. He might follow local custom if he liked, and in the period of the Principate he was also free to adopt the rules of the *ordo* where this was appropriate. There was no compulsion to do so, particularly in the proconsular provinces whose proconsuls received no general instructions from the central government. The lawyer Proculus, active in the mid-first century A.D., dryly remarks that a provincial governor should consider not what is done at Rome, but what *ought* to be done in general.[1] Besides, for all those crimes not covered by the *ordo* the governor was bound to fall back on local custom and his own ingenuity. A provincial *peregrinus* had no claim to be tried by the rules of the *ordo*, and the emperor's legate or procurator was only bound to apply them if the emperor laid it down in his *mandata*.

Sudden light is cast on the criminal jurisdiction in the provinces by the documents known as the Edicts of Augustus addressed to the proconsuls of Cyrene in 7–6 B.C.[2] From these it appears that at that date charges less than capital were left in the control of local courts, but that for the trial of *peregrini* on capital charges there existed in Cyrene a system of juries analogous to the courts of the Roman *ordo*. These juries were manned, on the advice of Augustus, by a mixture of *peregrini* and Roman citizens. Yet though Augustus in his edicts paid a good deal of attention to the improvement of these juries, he left their use optional in capital cases. In his fourth edict, dealing with other types of cases, he remarks: 'this does not apply to capital charges, which the governor must hear and decide either by himself or by providing a jury'. That is, the jury court was only an alternative to personal *cognitio*. This jury system disappears

---

[1] *D.* i. 18. 12. For his date, W. Kunkel, *Herkunft . . . der r. Juristen*, 123.
[2] Conveniently in E–J, no. 311, and iv. See on them especially F. de Visscher, *Les Édits d'Auguste* (Louvain, 1940), ch. v, esp. 172 ff.

without trace after Augustus, and there is no certain indication of its use in any other province, though there is a bare possibility that it existed for a time in Asia. An inscription of the time of Tiberius names an equestrian official—*praefectus fabrorum*—whose duty was connected with jurisdiction and included the function defined as *sortiendis iudicibus in Asia*. It is possible that this refers to the drawing up of a list of persons for service as the *iudex privatus* of the civil law. But it could with rather more probability refer to the choice of criminal juries, in whose selection the lot had commonly been used in Roman practice.[1]

After the Cyrene edicts there is very little evidence in the first century A.D. about provincial jurisdiction over *peregrini*. But there is a certain amount of evidence concerning the trial of Roman citizens by proconsuls and legates, which were of greater interest to Roman historical writers. These cases, which fall between A.D. 65 and 100, have been recently studied by Professor A. H. M. Jones in connexion with the rules of *provocatio*, or appeal.[2] They are remarkable in that they suggest that there were certain exceptions to the rules which forbade the capital sentence and execution of a Roman citizen by a provincial court. This aspect must be examined later. But these cases are also relevant to the investigation of *cognitio*, in that on each occasion the governor proceeded by personal *cognitio* and inflicted punishments that were *extra ordinem*. There is no indication of the use of juries, and in the notorious case of Marius Priscus, a proconsul of Africa *c.* A.D. 98 who accepted bribes from the prosecutors, the fairly full account of Pliny makes this plain.[3] The bribes were given to the proconsul and his legate; the intervention of a jury would have altered the nature of the transaction. Some thirty years earlier, in the period 65–68,

---

[1] *ILS*, 6286. Cf. A. H. J. Greenidge, *Legal Procedure of Cicero's Time*, 438.
[2] Jones, 'I appeal', 921 f.   [3] Pliny, *Ep.* ii. 11. 8; 23.

a legate of Spanish Tarraconensis and a legate of Lower Germany were similarly hearing capital charges against Roman citizens from their tribunal (*pro tribunali*) in personal jurisdiction.[1] If this was the method of trying Roman citizens, it must apply all the more to the trial of *peregrini* in the period of Nero and the Flavians. It is also noticeable that there is no distinction in the matter between proconsuls and imperial legates.

But how did the system work in detail? The characteristics of the later jurisdiction *extra ordinem* were three in number. First, there is the free formulation of charges and penalties, summed up in the lawyer's phrase *arbitrium iudicantis*.[2] The second is the insistence on a proper formal act of accusation by the interested party. Third, cases are heard by the holder of *imperium* in person on his tribunal, and assisted by his advisory cabinet or *consilium* of friends and officials. Of these elements the Cyrene edicts at the beginning of the Julio-Claudian period testify only to formal accusation by private accusers, and to the trial by the holder of *imperium*. All the elements except the *consilium* can be detected in Pliny's account of his own and his predecessors' jurisdiction in Bithynia–Pontus at the beginning of the second century. There is the variation of penalties—*damnatio ad metallum* in varying forms and sentences of relegation replace the uniform death penalties of the *ordo*; this is a sure sign of the free working of *imperium* and of the principle of *arbitrium iudicantis*. Equally, the determination of new offences unprescribed by statutes points to jurisdiction *extra ordinem*.

---

[1] Suet. *Galba*, 9, 1; Dio, 63. 2, but details are lacking. Cf. also Pliny, x. 58. 2–3.

[2] On *arbitrium iudicantis*, originally Mommsen, *D. Pen. R.* iii. 399 ff. More recently it is the theme of U. Brasiello, *La Repressione penale in. d. romano* (Naples, 1937), e.g. 191 f., 292 f.; F. de Robertis, 'Arbitrium iudicantis', *Z-S. Sav. St.* 1939, 219–60; G. Cardascia, 'L'Apparition dans le droit etc.', *Rev. hist. droit. fr. étranger*, 1950, 305 ff.

Pliny was prepared to punish the Christians with death,
though uncertain of the precise nature of the offences
charged against them, on the grounds of what lawyers called
contumacia, where others might have been satisfied to administer a beating or lock them up.[1] There is one case of
particular interest. The well-known rhetorician and philosopher Dio of Prusa, who was a Roman citizen, had buried
his wife in the precinct of a statue of the emperor.[2] He was
accused by a private enemy, but not formally under the *lex
maiestatis*, as might have been done since both parties were
Roman citizens. The accuser simply alleged the facts against
Dio, and invited Pliny *ut cognoscerem pro tribunali*. This is the
essence of the procedure *extra ordinem*. The accuser alleges
a misdeed, and the judge decides how to deal with it. In
this case Pliny could construe the charge as a *crimen maiestatis* but was not bound to do so.[3] Had the charge been
made under a statute law of the *ordo* he would have had no
option but to deal with the charge precisely as formulated.
Finally there is the insistence upon independent prosecution
by third parties. The system is not inquisitorial. There must
be a prosecutor. This comes out well in the affair of the
Christians. Trajan insists in his well-known reply to Pliny
that all charges must be properly made by the usual process
of *delatio*.[4] The business had indeed begun in this very
manner, when the Christians were haled before Pliny by
independent accusers.[5]

[1] Pliny, *Ep.* x. 96. 3. Cf. *Sent. Pauli*, v. 26. 2. On *contumacia*, below, p. 19.
[2] Pliny, *Ep.* x. 81, 2, recently studied at immense length by G. Sautel,
Rev. int. droits de l'ant. (sec. 3), 1956, 422 ff.
[3] 'adiecit etiam esse in eodem positam tuam statuam et corpora sepul-
torum uxoris Dionis et filii, postulavitque ut cognoscerem pro tribunali.'
There is no mention of the term *maiestas* in Pliny's letter, which treats the
charge as an open problem, s. 8. Trajan, equating it with *maiestas*, dismisses
it out of hand, *Ep.* 82.
[4] Pliny, *Ep.* x. 97. 1. 'conquirendi non sunt. si deferantur et arguantur
puniendi sunt.'   [5] Ibid. 96. 2. 'ad me tamquam Christiani deferebantur.'

The basic elements of the *cognitio* system can thus be brought down to the opening years of the second century. So far as the proconsuls of Bithynia–Pontus are concerned there is reasonable implication for the preceding generation also. Pliny makes it clear that in his administration he was following, and was expected by Trajan to follow, the *exempla proconsulum*, the precedents of his predecessors.[1] But earlier evidence can be secured by considering two closely parallel forms of *cognitio*: the administrative *cognitio* of proconsuls, and the personal *cognitio*, both criminal and administrative, of the Princeps himself. Cadbury, in his Appendix to the Acts *Commentary*, takes too narrow a view of the evidence, on the silent assumption that *cognitio* fell into watertight compartments. But this is not the case, as is shown by considering the proceedings of the proconsul of Sardinia in A.D. 69. This case illuminates several aspects of the procedure of governors in the New Testament, and of the workings of *imperium*.[2]

There was a long-standing dispute about boundaries between two municipalities in Sardinia. No less than three governors, a procurator and two proconsuls, had repeatedly ordered one of the two parties to withdraw from territory occupied in defiance of a former settlement. The defiance continued despite strong threats that the governor would severely punish—*severe animadversum*—what he called the authors of sedition—*auctores seditionis*—if they persisted in their wilful disobedience, or *contumacia*. After various evasions by the offenders the proconsul held an administrative court, took the advice of his *consilium*, which included his legate, his quaestor, and six other gentlemen, and issued a last warning: if the Galillenses did not withdraw by a fixed date he would execute the long-threatened punishment for their

[1] Ibid. 69–72.
[2] *FIRA*, i, no. 59, or A–J, no. 58, with bibliography.

persistent disobedience. This document very clearly illustrates the free working of the governor's power, *arbitrium
iudicantis*, and the use of the *consilium*. It also illustrates how
difficult it was for a Roman governor to enforce his will even
in so small a province as Sardinia, and even when he had
some forces at his disposal, as was the case in Sardinia.

There is a nice parallel to the Sardinian document in the
edict of a legate of Galatia in *c.* A.D. 93 which shows how
slight is the difference between administrative and criminal
cognitio. The legate is dealing with corn-hoarding in a period
of famine.[1] He lays down rules for the compulsory sale of
corn by the farmers to the municipality, and invents a sanction: 'if any one does not obey, let him know that I will
exact punishment in full measure for whatever [corn] is retained against my edict'.[2] The document also stresses the
use of private accusers in the enforcement of the edict:
'those who bring charges shall receive an eighth part [of
what is discovered]'.

The evidence can be brought right down to the dramatic
date of Acts by using the accounts of imperial *cognitiones*.
The technical pattern of *cognitio* before the emperor, whether
administrative or judicial, whether *pro tribunali* or *in cubiculo*,
did not differ from that of provincial governors. For a detailed discussion Dr. Crook's recent book *Consilium Principis*
supersedes the previous investigations of the French scholar
Cuq and others.[3] Pliny's account, in three letters, of the
imperial tribunal of Trajan shows all the technical elements
that are found elsewhere both in criminal and administrative jurisdiction.[4] The accounts in Tacitus of the trials of

[1] A–J, no. 65 a; *JRS*, xiv. 180.

[2] 'quod si quis non paruerit sciat me quidquid contra edictum meum
retentum fuerit, in commissum vindicaturum.'

[3] J. A. Crook, *Consilium Principis* (Cambridge, 1955).

[4] *Ep.* iv. 22, vi. 22. 31: delation, vi. 22. 2, 31. 3–5–6–9, *arbitriumi udicantis*,
vi. 22. 5, 31. 12, use of *consilium*, iv. 22. 3, vi. 22. 5, 31. 12.

conspirators before the tribunal of Claudius and Nero do not help greatly, because either these were extraordinary occasions or the trials are too briefly and too untechnically described. But *arbitrium iudicantis* is obvious in the free variation of penalties, which depart widely from those prescribed by relevant statute laws.[1] The preference for accusation rather than inquisitorial methods is apparent, and the use of the *consilium* can be detected.[2] In the middle of Claudius' reign, at the trial of the senator Valerius Asiaticus before the Princeps, the use of *accusatores* and of the *consilium*, and the arbitrary stiffening of penalties, can be traced.[3]

So far Tacitus. But the best documentation for the Julio-Claudian period comes from Philo, and from those odd documents known as the Acts of the Pagan Martyrs. Philo, in his account of the famous Jewish embassy to the emperor Gaius, very clearly indicates the normal use made by an emperor of his *consilium*.[4] But this description, though often used, is not of a trial, not even an administrative one. More to the purpose is the papyrus version of the trial of Lampon and Isidore before Claudius. Dr. Musurillo, in his edition of the *Acta*, showed the strong probability that there was a hard core of historical narrative behind these documents, possibly in the form of a summary of the actual trials derived from official archives, though written in their present form in a later age.[5] There was then discovered the genuine record of a minor administrative inquiry held before the emperor

---

[1] *Relegatio* and *deportatio* in varying degrees replace the death penalty, which was the *poena legis* for *maiestas*, Tac. *Ann.* xiv. 50, xv. 71.

[2] In the Pisonian trials the method seems mostly to be inquisitorial, with *indices*, informers, taking the place of *delatores*, accusers, ibid. xv. 56, 66, 67. 1. But in 69. 1: 'non crimine non accusatore existente, quia speciem iudicis induere non potest, ad vim dominationis conversus.'

[3] Ibid. xi. 1. 1 and 3. 1–2. The penalty of adultery was not capital under the *lex Julia*.

[4] Philo, *Legatio*, 349 f. Cf. Crook, op. cit. 39.

[5] H. A. Musurillo, *Acts of the Pagan Martyrs* (Oxford, 1954), 249 ff.

Caracalla at Syrian Antioch.[1] The remarkable freedom of language which the advocates use towards and in the presence of a not very patient emperor goes far, as Dr. Crook has noted, to confirm the historicity of the *Acta* in what had been thought to be their most improbable feature—the abusive language with which the parties address the Princeps.[2] No one is likely to pretend that the *Acta* are more than a mixture of party journalism and historical novelette. But it is likely that their historical framework is sound. Hence they provide possible evidence for the usages of *cognitio principis* in a provincial affair in the time of Claudius. Their salient feature for the present purpose is the informality of the procedure, and its general similarity to that revealed in Pliny's account of Trajan's tribunal. This similarity suggests that they present the legal forms of the earlier period. The method is accusatorial, and the different parties conduct their cases freely and at length.[3] The *arbitrium iudicantis* appears dimly, in that what begins as an accusation against King Agrippa ends with the condemnation of the leaders themselves; possibly this happened, as in one of the cases heard before Trajan in Pliny's account, because Claudius turned the tables on the accusers by finding them guilty of vexatious prosecution, or *calumnia*.[4] However that may be, the *Acta Isidori* help to fill the gap in the documentation of the *cognitio*-procedure in the Julio-Claudian period, though their evidence, even if free from obvious anachronisms, should not be pressed too far.

The conclusion is, that a provincial governor, whether a proconsul, an imperial legate, or an imperial procurator, would deal with serious criminal or political or administra-

---

[1] P. Roussel and F. de Visscher, *Syria*, xxiii. 173 ff.

[2] Crook, op. cit. 83 f., 142 f.

[3] *Acta Isidori* in Musurillo, op. cit. 18, col. i. 15 ff., col. ii. 1 ff.

[4] Ibid. 125. 137; Pliny, vi. 31. 12.

tive jurisdiction affecting *peregrini* just as he thought fit, in regard to the formulation of charges and penalties. He would probably follow the lead of the *ordo* in the field covered by the statutory criminal laws, *leges publicae*, though more in the formulation of charges than of penalties. Outside that field he would follow the examples of his predecessors, or use his own invention and the advice of his *consilium*. The form of judicial trial was the personal *cognitio* of the governor, who alone had the capital power, assisted by his *consilium*, which as its name indicates was more a body of assessors than of jurors. Initiation of charges and the presentation of the case ordinarily depended upon private prosecutors. All this is adequately documented throughout the second half of the first century A.D., and can now be carried back into the middle of the first century A.D. and the Claudio-Neronian era.

LECTURE TWO

The Trial of Christ in the Synoptic Gospels

BEFORE discussing the great controversy about the nature of the investigation before the Sanhedrin, and its bearing on the precise charges against Christ, the evidence should be considered in the light of the Roman criminal procedure *extra ordinem*. In the account of the trial of Christ before Pilate two of the three synoptic gospels, Mark and Matthew, are decidedly more synoptic than the third, Luke. But this applies more to the phases of the story before the hearing at the tribunal of Pilate than to the account of the latter. In the hearing before Pilate the synoptic narrative fits the Roman framework remarkably well, considering that it was written with an entirely different purpose in mind. The trial is *pro tribunali*, the actual *bema* of Pilate being mentioned in Matthew.[1] Accusations are duly made by *delatores*, the chief-priests and the elders of the people acting as such.[2] The account of this is generalized. In practice there must have been not more than two or three spokesmen. The charge is clearly indicated, not as a charge against a particular Roman law, but as a charge of particular undesirable actions on which Pilate is asked to adjudicate. Mark and Matthew merely hint at the nature of the charge by giving Pilate the question: 'Are you a king of the Jews?' That this means 'a leader of the resistance' is shown by a parallel from Josephus, who in his anti-resistance

[1] Matt. xxvii. 19.
[2] Matt. xxvii. 12; Mark xv. 3; Luke xxiii. 1, 4.

fashion remarks of the troubles after the death of Herod: 'as the several companies of the seditious lighted upon anyone to head them, he was created a king immediately, in order to do mischief to the public'.[1] Luke is explicit: 'we found this fellow disturbing our people, telling them not to pay tribute to Caesar, and calling himself a king'.[2] This fits very well the workings of *cognitio*. The accusers allege facts, and the judge decides what to make of them. Since there was no defence, Pilate had no option but to convict. That was the essence of the system.

The story of the reluctance, or at least the surprise, of Pilate, however much it may have been worked up for the propaganda purposes of the authors, is not without Julio-Claudian analogies. The Roman criminal courts were more familiar with the absentee accuser than with the defendant who would not defend himself. A series of ordinances beginning with a well-known decree of the Senate inspired by the emperor Claudius sought to protect defendants against defaulting accusers who left their victims, as Claudius complained, *pendentes in albo*, swinging idle on the court lists.[3] But a better comparison comes from the procedure in the early martyr trials, first testified, but not first employed, seventy years later. Those who did not defend themselves were given three opportunities of changing their minds before sentence was finally given against them. This was an early technique already established as the regular thing before Pliny's investigations in *c.* A.D. 110, his letter about the

[1] Jos. *Ant.* xvii. 10, 8. He continues: 'they were in some small ways hurtful to the Romans'.

[2] Matt. xxvii. 11; Mark xv. 2; Luke xxiii. 2.

[3] *BGU*, 611, col. ii. For the *Sc. Turpilianum*, *D.* 48. 16. 7, see below, 52, 113 ff. Absentee defendants are in a different category. In an Egyptian *cognitio* of A.D. 89 the Prefect gives them a second chance of appearance before condemnation in absence, *FIRA*, iii, no. 169. The lawyers were tender towards them, a year's grace being allowed them by a rule not later than Trajan, *D.* 48. 17. 5. See further Lecture Five, p. 114 n. 3.

Christians being the earliest evidence for it. The triple citation appears also as a usage of the second century in dealing with absentee accused persons. The method had been established before Pliny suggested, for the first time, that there was any reason to be tender towards the accused Christians.[1] That means that this was a device invented for the protection of the *reus*, the defendant, as such, because Roman judges disliked sentencing an undefended man as much as an inadequately accused man. The remark of Festus in Acts, of which the justice should be apparent after Lecture One, is in the same spirit: 'It is not the custom of the Romans to make away with a man until the accused has had his accusers face to face, and has had an opportunity of defending himself against the charge.'[2] In Mark and Matthew the question is twice put to Christ by Pilate, in Luke once only to Christ, and thrice, instead, to the importunate prosecutors.[3]

One may here leave aside the worked-up sections concerning the release of Barabbas, and other material, such as the story of Pilate's wife in Matthew, and the sending of Christ to Herod in Luke, none of which is part of the *cognitio* proper. There follows the decision itself. This is given in virtually identical terms in Matthew and Mark φραγελ-λώσας παρέδωκεν ἵνα σταυρωθῇ, 'Pilate had Christ scourged and handed him over to be crucified'. Luke is rather less precise at this point: 'Pilate gave sentence that what they asked should be done . . . and delivered Jesus up to their will.' Matthew and Mark are correct.[4] The trial by *cognitio* gives not merely a verdict but a condemnation to a particular punishment. Matthew and Mark give the substantial

---

[1] Pliny *Ep.* x. 96. 3. For the triple citation see *D.* 48. 1. 10, discussed in Lecture Five, p. 117 n. 3.   [2] Acts xxv. 16.

[3] Mark xv. 2–4; Matt. xxvii. 11–15; Luke xxiii. 3. 13–22.

[4] Mark xv. 15; Matt. xxvii. 26; Luke xxiii. 25.

equivalent of the technical *duci iussit* of Latin texts.[1] The jurors of the Roman *ordo* gave a verdict of 'guilty' or 'not guilty', *fecisse videtur*, and the sentence prescribed by a statute law automatically followed.[2] But the proconsul or procurator with *imperium* orders an execution. The authors are correct also in the minor point of the beating. The jurists recognize a gradation of beatings: *fustes, flagella, verbera*. The severer beating was never a punishment in itself but was associated with other punishments.[3] The lightest form, *fustigatio*, is frequently associated with a magisterial warning, when the governor reckons that the situation did not require a formal *cognitio*. Thus in the case of fires caused by negligence, the *Praefectus Vigilum* at Rome might give the negligent party a severe warning with a beating or the threat of a beating by *fustes*.[4] This was technically an act of *coercitio* pure and simple. The same was done by provincial governors when dealing with the ancient equivalent of juvenile gangs.[5] Luke has this technique in mind when he represents Pilate as saying: 'You have brought this man to me as disturbing the people. But he has done nothing deserving the death penalty. So I will give him a warning and let him go', παιδεύσας οὖν αὐτὸν ἀπολύσω.[6] This is close to Callistratus' remark on those who stir up *turbulentas acclamationes popularium*. Of these Callistratus says: 'si amplius nil admiserint nec ante sint a praeside admoniti, fustibus caesi dimittuntur.' In Luke the term παιδεύσας is ambiguous, like the English 'give him a lesson'. Though commonly translated 'after a beating' it need mean no more than *cum*

---

[1] Cf., e.g., Pliny, *Ep.* x. 96, 3.

[2] Greenidge, *Legal Procedure in Cicero's Time* (Oxford, 1901), 498.

[3] *D.* 48. 19. 7; 10 pr. Brasiello, op. cit. 390 ff.

[4] Paulus, *D.* i. 15. 3. 1.

[5] Callistratus, *D.* 48. 19. 28. 3. Cf. *Sent. Pauli*, v. 21. 1: 'primum fustibus caesi civitate pelluntur. perseverantes autem in vincula publica coniciuntur aut in insulam deportantur.'   [6] Luke xxiii. 14–22.

admonuerim.[1] But the cautionary beating is likely enough, as in the similar cases of St. Paul at Philippi and at Jerusalem when first arrested by the military tribune.[2] The synoptic writers thus get their technicalities right in this small matter —the severe beating accompanies the capital sentence, and the lighter whipping goes with the proposed act of *coercitio*.[3]

Something must be said about the incident in Luke of the dispatch of Christ to Herod, as the ruler of Galilee. Pilate did this 'because Christ came from the region of Herod's power', in the words of Luke. There is a similar incident in Acts when the procurator Felix asked Paul from what province he came.[4] Neither Pilate nor Felix nor Gallio in Achaea hesitated to deal with a defendant whose place of origin was *outside* their own province when the man was charged with a crime *inside* their province. Why then the question? A rather fine point of Roman criminal law is involved. The answer given by Mommsen was that strictly a man was supposed to be tried by the governor of the province of his permanent home, wherever the offence was committed, and that this was the custom of the earlier Principate. Later, according to Mommsen, this usage was changed for practical reasons by a series of ordinances to allow trial in the province where the crime was committed; *forum delicti* replaces *forum domicilii*, as the lawyers say.[5] Mommsen was rather unhappy about this notion of *forum domicilii*, which does not fit the nature of *coercitio* and *cognitio extra ordinem*. One does not expect a governor of the late

[1] Liddell and Scott quote only Hosea vii. 2 (Sept.) for the sense of 'punish' and the noun form in Hebrews xii. 9. Arndt–Gingrich, *Lexicon of the N.T.* s.v. 'B', quote no N.T. parallel for sense 'whip'.

[2] Acts xvi. 22–24, xxii 24; below, pp. 70 ff.

[3] For the association of beatings with the severer penalties, cf. *Sent. Pauli*, v. 18. 1, 21. 1.

[4] Luke xxiii. 7; Acts xxiii. 35.

[5] Mommsen, *D. Pen. R.* ii. 23 f.; *GS*, iii. 442.

Republic and early Principate, when faced by a malefactor, to bother about the very fine question whether his *imperium* allowed him to deal with a man who was *in* but not *of* his province. But since certain legal texts seemed to indicate this doctrine, Mommsen put it forward with reservations.

These texts were to a certain extent misinterpreted by Mommsen in his old age, when he wrote the *Strafrecht*. The basic passage is a text of Celsus belonging to the time of Trajan or Hadrian: 'non est dubium quin cuiuscumque est provinciae homo qui ex custodia producitur cognoscere debeat is qui ei provinciae praeest in qua agitur.'[1] That is clear enough, and should give the doctrine of the earlier Principate. Here *agitur* clearly either means 'where the man is active' as contrasted with *cuiuscumque est provinciae* or 'where the crime is being done'. One may compare a passage of Macer in which the term 'ubi factores agere dicuntur' means 'where the criminals are said to be living'.[2] Celsus adds that some governors have the habit of sending such offenders back to their province of origin for trial after a preliminary investigation. And he concludes with the comment: 'quod ex causa faciendum est.' Assuming that none of this is affected by interpolations, it would seem that Mommsen has reversed the historical development. *Forum delicti* was the ordinary practice of the early Principate, but with the development of theory and bureaucratic notions the custom of *forum domicilii* began to arise. Another text, from Ulpian, also suggests that there was a good deal of argument in the later second century about questions of overlap in provincial jurisdiction.[3] Finally, the practical disadvantages of *forum domicilii* led to the assertion of a general

---

[1] Celsus, *D.* 48. 3. 11.   [2] *D.* 48. 3. 7.

[3] *D.* 48. 22. 7. 11–13. He raises the nice question: 'an interdicere quis alicui possit provincia in qua oriundus est cum ipse ei provinciae praesit quam incolit.'

rule in the empire of *forum delicti*. The texts cited by Mommsen support this order. They deal with examples of transferred jurisdiction as though they were unusual and exceptional. That is just what the last part of Celsus' above statement asserts. 'ex causa faciendum est' means that this should be done only for special reasons. Mommsen, to make the phrase fit his interpretation, wished to delete the words *ex causa* as a gloss or interpolation. A statement of Paulus makes sense at any period: 'praeses in suae provinciae homines tantum imperium habet et hoc dum in provincia est. . . . habet interdum imperium et adversus extraneos homines si quid manu commiserint . . . nec distinguuntur unde sint.'[1] The general principle of *forum delicti* is asserted by Papinian, and implied by Ulpian in a passage of his *De officio proconsulis*.[2] A passage of Macer—a third-century lawyer—refers to the extradition of offenders, of whatever origin, who have fled the province of their crime.[3] So the general statements of jurists of the early third century assert the principle of *forum delicti* clearly enough.

The idea of *forum domicilii* really belongs to the jurisdiction of the *ordo*, not to the realm of *cognitio extra ordinem*. The difficult cases in the evidence are connected with offences defined by *leges publicae*. For example, in an anecdote of Philostratus a man of Tyre is tried in Achaea on a charge of murder because he was an honorary citizen of Athens, though a Syrian by province. Evidently he might have claimed to be tried in Syria; in Roman law murder

---

[1] *D*. i. 18. 3. Mommsen made too much of *interdum*. There were other matters apart from criminal offences in which a man was subject only to his proper authority. A rescript of Pius, *D*. 48. 2. 7. 4, concerns slaves of a *dominus* who is refused *revocatio in provinciam suam* in order to exercise the usual right to defend them. But this provides no parallel for *ingenui*, who were not pieces of property.

[2] Papinian, *D*. 48. 2. 22. Ulpian, *D*. 48. 22. 7. 11–13. Cf. also Modestinus, *D*. 49. 16. 3. pref. [3] *D*. 48. 3. 7.

belonged to the *ordo*.[1] Eventually an enactment of Severus, in the *Codex*, dated A.D. 196, specifically asserts the principle of *forum delicti* both for cases under the *ordo* and for those *extra ordinem*.[2] This confirms the opinion of the jurists of the same period, cited earlier.

Returning now to the Scriptural examples, one observes that Pilate, Felix, and Gallio did not feel bound to refuse jurisdiction over extraneous defendants and to send them back to their provinces of origin for trial, as on Mommsen's view one would expect. But either they, or the narrator, were aware of the possibility, which was certainly establishing itself in some areas by the beginning of the second century. By the third century the suggestion could not have occurred to anyone who knew the system that then prevailed. The point of the question put to Paul, in mid-first century, was not to protect the rights of the accused, or those of another governor, but to enable the procurator or proconsul in question to avoid a tiresome affair altogether, if he felt inclined, either by expelling an accused person from a province to which he did not belong, or by a refusal of jurisdiction. As for Herod and Pilate, it is worth observing that Herod the Great, according to Josephus, had the abnormal privilege of extraditing offenders who had fled from his kingdom to other parts of the Roman empire. Possibly some remnant of this privilege underlay the sending of Christ to the second Herod: most of the activities of Christ had taken place in Galilee.[3]

---

[1] Philostratus, *VS*, ii. 19. 3. Cf. also a ruling of Septimius Severus concerning the *lex Fabia de plagiariis*, *Cod. Iust.* iii. 15. 2.

[2] *Cod.* iii. 15. 1.

[3] *BJ*, i. 24. 2. Cf. Juster, *Les Juifs dans l'Empire Romain* (Paris, 1914), ii. 145. There is an alternative explanation, often adopted, that Pilate was trying to pacify Herod for a supposed infringement of his rights in the obscure affair of the massacre of the Galileans at Jerusalem (Luke xiii. 1). But this falsely assumes that Galileans were not justiciable in Judaea.

So much for the procedural aspects of the synoptic accounts of the trial. It is noteworthy that though Luke at first reading gives the most intelligible account of the trial as a whole, and Mark the least, yet by no means all the advantages lie with Luke. On certain technical points, such as the reference to the *tribunal* and the formulation of the sentence, Mark and Matthew are superior. But Luke is remarkable in that his additional materials—the full formulation of the charges before Pilate, the reference to Herod, and the proposed acquittal with admonition—are all technically correct.

So far, by confining discussion to the synoptic account, the most contentious issue concerning the trial of Christ has been avoided. This is the question of the charge. Lietzmann, in his well-known paper *Der Prozeß Jesu,*[1] more cogently than any other scholar put the view that the only charge before Pilate was that of insurrection. Lietzmann, of course, rejected as unhistorical the version of John, in which the offence against the Jewish law is twice made the principal charge,[2] Pilate is represented as finding Christ innocent of any political crime,[3] and authorizes the Jews to execute the judgment of the Sanhedrin for the religious offence. John xviii. 31 is the crux: 'Pilate said, "Take him and judge him according to your law." The Jews replied, "We are not allowed to put any man to death".' This puts firmly what is only implicit in two of the three synoptic narratives, and absent from the third—the notion that the Sanhedrin, having condemned Christ for blasphemy, then sought the fiat of Pilate for the execution. In Mark and Matthew, whose

[1] *Sitzber. Preuss. Akad. Wiss.*, 1931, 313 ff. with bibliography, ibid. For the earlier bibliography of the trial of Christ from 1676 to 1912 the curious may consult Juster, ii. 137. For a parallel but briefer criticism of Lietzmann, see G. D. Kilpatrick, 'The Trial of Jesus', *Friends of Dr. Williams Library, Sixth Lecture* (Oxford, 1953). P. Winter, *On the Trial of Jesus* (Basel, 1961), follows Lietzmann.   [2] John xviii. 30–31, xix. 7.   [3] John. xix. 4–7, 12.

narratives cohere very closely, there is no doubt that the Sanhedrin passes sentence for blasphemy: 'κατέκριναν αὐτὸν ἔνοχον εἶναι θανάτου. Then, in Matthew, 'they take counsel to put him to death [θανατῶσαι], bound him and took him before Pilate'.[1] The Judas narrative is inserted at this point in Matthew, beginning with the significant words 'Judas, seeing that Jesus was condemned'.[2] This interpretation is anticipated by Matthew in the prophetic passage set before the journey to Jerusalem: 'The son of man shall be handed over to the high priests and scribes, who will condemn him and hand him over to foreigners to scourge and crucify him.'[3] This interpretation, according to Lietzmann, is lacking in Mark's account of the arrest and trial. Mark certainly gives no clear explanation of the connexion between the Sanhedrin session and the trial before Pilate. In the otherwise practically identical sentence—Mark xv. 1—linking the two scenes, Mark has the phrase συμβούλιον ποιήσαντες, corresponding to Matthew's σ. ἔλαβον, but he omits the vital words ὥστε θανατῶσαι.

In Luke the whole business is worked out systematically. There is a plot to trick Christ into treasonable utterances, so as to hand him over to the 'government and the power of the governor'.[4] After the arrest there is a somewhat incoherent and allusive account of the session of the Sanhedrin, without a clear statement about a condemnation: merely 'What need have we of further witness? We have heard it from his own mouth'.[5] Then comes the transfer to the tribunal of Pilate on explicit charges of treason. Later, in the epilogue to Luke's Gospel, Cleophas says to the risen Christ, before the recognition: 'Our priests and rulers handed him over to judgement of death and crucified him.'[6]

---

[1] Mark xiv. 64; Matt. xxvi. 66–67, xxvii. 1. [2] Matt. xxvii. 3.
[3] Matt. xx. 17–19. [4] Luke xx. 20.
[5] Luke xxii. 71. [6] Luke xxiv. 20.

The solution of Lietzmann is simple—that Mark contains the kernel of historic fact which has been well elaborated in Luke, and that the narratives of Matthew and John tendentiously try by their account of the Sanhedrin trial to transfer the blame from the Roman governor to the Jews, for political reasons connected with the early mildness of the Roman government in the Apostolic age towards the Christians. Lietzmann seeks to clinch this by a formal argument. He poses a dilemma : either the Sanhedrin sentenced Christ and carried out the sentence in the Jewish fashion, by stoning, or Pilate sentenced Christ and carried out the sentence in Roman fashion, by crucifixion. Since all the evidence agrees that the execution was in Roman fashion by Romans, then the trial and condemnation by the Sanhedrin is a fabrication. He then presents an alternative proof. The Sanhedrin had the power of capital punishment, and had no need of a fiat from the procurator to carry out its execution. He puts rather less weight on this second argument, which is primarily aimed at the credit of Matthew and John, of whom the latter explicitly asserts that the Sanhedrin could put no man to death.

Lietzmann's analysis of the differences between Mark and the others is somewhat weakened by an omission. He failed to observe that Mark, by including the anticipatory prophecy of the trial and death of Christ in the same terms as Matthew, followed exactly the same tradition as the trial story of Matthew: 'they shall condemn him to death and hand him over to foreigners and *they* shall scourge him and kill him, . . . '.[1] It is also mildly unfortunate for Lietzmann that there is some doubt about the reading of κατακρινοῦσιν αὐτὸν θανατῷ in the prophecy in Matt. xx. 19, where θανατῷ has been bracketed, but there is no apparent doubt about the same words in the parallel passage in Mark. This seems

[1] Mark x. 33–34.

to cast general doubt on the attempt to distinguish between the source value of the narratives in these two Gospels and to diminish the supposed superiority of Mark. But this is a question of techniques in source criticism, which is not our immediate concern.

Lietzmann's formal argument has considerable logical force, but it seems to involve three false historical assumptions. The first two concern the powers of the Roman governor, and the third those of the Sanhedrin. A Roman historian could maintain, against Lietzmann, that if the Roman governor is asked to carry out an execution he will do it according to his own usage, and not according to that of the particular *peregrini* with whom he is dealing. This proposition is hardly susceptible of direct proof, because of the lack of parallel incidents. It simply lies in the nature of things, that is, the nature of *cognitio*. Pliny, for example, did not understand the charges against the Christians in Pontus, but he condemned them to a Roman execution without hesitation. If Pilate accepted a theological charge in his court, it would not occur to him to give sentence in non-Roman terms. Again, there is an assumption in Lietzmann's theory that two different kinds of charge could not be made against the defendant at the same time. This happens to be true of jurisdiction under the *ordo*. But the trial of Christ is a *cognitio extra ordinem*, where the judge is free to proceed as he likes. Multiple charges were common enough in the extraordinary jurisdiction of the capital in the Flavian period.[1]

But the third is the vital question. Did the Sanhedrin or did it not possess capital jurisdiction at this period? The

[1] The Augustan *lex iudiciorum publicorum* and a supporting *SC* forbade multiple charges, while in the Flavian period the jurisdiction of the Princeps and of the Senate, which were *extra ordinem*, allowed them. *D*. 48. 2. 12. 2. Quintilian, *Inst.* iii. 10. 1. Cf. Suet. *Titus*, 8. 5.

starting-point is the statement in the trial narrative of John:
'We are not allowed to put any person to death.' On this
point depends the historicity of the narrative of the Sanhedrin trial in Matthew, Mark, and John. Lietzmann, of
course, wishes to eliminate the Sanhedrin trial altogether.
Hence he makes much of the remarkable attempt of Juster,
in his great book about the Jews in the Roman empire, to
prove that the Sanhedrin possessed this power.[1] Indeed, the
kernel of Lietzmann's main argument is derived from Juster.
But the truth is, to speak generally, that all that the learned
Juster did was to make out a case which would have some
probability if it were the common practice of the Roman
government to allow capital jurisdiction to local municipal
or ethnic tribunals. When we find that the capital power was
the most jealously guarded of all the attributes of government, not even entrusted to the principal assistants of the
governors, and specifically withdrawn, in the instance of
Cyrene, from the competence of local courts, it becomes
very questionable indeed for the Sanhedrin.[2] Significantly,
in Cyrene the local courts were not municipally but pro-
vincially organized, and the rule was laid down that even in
their limited jurisdiction a man should not be tried by judges
from his own city. The only exceptions, in the Empire at
large, to these limitations, were the highly privileged communities known as *civitates liberae* or 'free states', communes
which for past services to the Roman State were made
independent of the authority of Roman magistrates in local
administration, and enjoyed unrestricted jurisdiction over
their own citizens.[3] A contemporary example is the city of

---

[1] Juster, ii. 128–52.

[2] Above, pp. 3 f. 15 f. Cf. especially the fourth edict from Cyrene, l. 65.

[3] On *civitates liberae* see, conveniently, A–J, ch. v.; Sherwin-White, *Roman
Citizenship*, ch. vi. Independent jurisdiction is testified at Chios, A–J, no. 40
(Ditt. *Syll.*[3] 785), *c.* A.D. 5 14, and Cnidos, A–J, no. 36 (Ditt. *Syll.* no. 780),
6 B.C. Cf. Strabo, iv. 1, 5 (p. 181), on the jurisdiction of Massilia.

Rhodes, which was deprived of its technical freedom by the emperor Claudius for exceeding its powers in the treatment of Roman citizens.[1]

Jerusalem was quite certainly not a 'free city', but very much the opposite. Public order was in the hands of a Roman military unit stationed in the heart of the city. The general permission given to the Jews to follow their own customs, in a series of decrees and edicts from the time of Julius Caesar onwards, and the reaffirmation of this by Augustus and Claudius for the province of Judaea, is very far from proving that the Sanhedrin was allowed capital jurisdiction after the establishment of the Roman provincial régime. This is the loosest and the most audacious of the arguments of Juster.[2] Very strong evidence is necessary to prove so remarkable an exception to the general custom of the Empire, which was largely based upon the necessity of preventing anti-Roman groups from eliminating the leaders of the pro-Roman factions in the cities by judicial action. Traditionally, municipal *libertas* was a reward for loyalty to Rome. Turbulent Judaea is the very last place where we would expect any extraordinary concessions. Hence the evidence needs to be strong, where it is in fact weak. But one *may* expect to find some limited concession intended to lessen the difficulty of dealing with this very troublesome people. Juster gives a large part of his case away by the necessary admission that the procurator took the place of the kings. He has himself shown that Herod and his successors jealously kept the ordinary capital jurisdiction in their own hands.[3]

[1] Dio, 60. 24. 4.

[2] Op. cit. ii. 132 ff. Cf. especially *BJ*, ii. 11. 6; *Ant.* xvii. 11. 1–2. The former passage merely states that Tiberius Alexander 'made no alterations in the ancient laws', and the latter gives the Jewish request, granted by Augustus, that they 'might live by their own laws . . . under a Roman governor'. Juster, op. cit. ii. 153, admits that the edicts affecting the Diaspora concerned only questions of religious practice (*Ant.* xiv. 10. 10–21 and 19. 5. 2–3).

[3] Op. cit. ii. 128 ff.

The positive evidence cited by Juster to prove that the Romans allowed the Sanhedrin capital jurisdiction, including the power of execution, consists of the story of the execution of Stephen in Acts, and of James in Josephus' *Antiquities*, and the rule about pagan trespassers inside the precinct of the Temple.[1] This last is very clearly a special case. A speech of Titus, Vespasian's son, in Josephus, confirmed in part by a well-known inscription, proves that the Sanhedrin was allowed to execute violators of the Temple including, remarkably, Roman citizens.[2] But if the Sanhedrin had the general right to execute offenders against the religious law, this special concession would not have been necessary. At best it proves nothing about its ordinary jurisdiction over Jews, because the concession concerns police powers over 'gentiles', not over Jews. The remarkable clause about Roman citizens is known only from the somewhat rhetorical passage in Josephus—a speech of Titus, not part of the factual narrative. Josephus is quite capable of suppressing any limiting conditions in the matter. The purpose of the concession, as Mommsen noted, was to prevent unfortunate behaviour by the 'drunken soldiery' from precipitating a riot in the tender heart of Jewry.[3] There is no evidence here for a general capital jurisdiction of the Sanhedrin.

The story of the execution of James in Josephus, as the text stands, explicitly disproves the thesis of Juster. It is

[1] Op. cit. ii. 138–42. Of his four other arguments, two concern texts of the Mishna and Talmud, below, pp. 40–41. Two others indicate that the Sanhedrin possessed some power of jurisdiction, but not that it was capital— the arrests and beatings in Acts iv. 1–21, v. 17–40, and vague statements in Jos. *Ant.* 13. 10. 6, 18. 1.4. *BJ*, ii. 8. 9. The latter merely refers to the private practices of the Essenes.

[2] *BJ*, vi. 2, 4. *OGIS*, 598; for a second copy see *SEG*, viii, n. 169. But the wording is very curious and suggests lynchings rather than executions. See below p. 43 n. 1.

[3] *GS*, iii. 441 n. 6.

represented as an action of the extremist element in the Sanhedrin, and as being *ultra vires*, undertaken in the interval between the retirement of the procurator Festus and the arrival of his successor Albinus. The moderate faction report the conduct of the High Priest to Albinus, and shortly after he is deposed. Accordingly, it becomes necessary for Juster to amend this troublesome text,[1] which is one of those sections of Josephus suspected of interpolation because they mention the name of 'Jesus who is called Christ'. Juster is at remarkable pains to retain just so much of the story as proves his case, while omitting the phrases and sentences which suggest that the execution was illegal without the fiat of the procurator. It is amusing to see the sceptical Juster commending the Christian Origen and Hegesippus, who have different versions of the story, as sources superior to Josephus. Juster mocks at the notion that there was no one to represent the governor during an interregnum. But the hard core of the story is just what we would expect in the Jewish situation and from the workings of *imperium*. The capital jurisdiction was precisely what the governor could not delegate, least of all when he had left his province.[2] In a later age rules were designed to prevent the existence of interregnal periods. Governors were not supposed to leave their provinces until the arrival of their successors.[3] Ulpian comments in his day: 'utilitas provinciae exigit esse aliquem per quem negotia sua provinciales explicent.'

One may recall here the long and successful disobedience —*contumacia*—of the Sardinian landholders recounted in the edict of the proconsul Helvius Agrippa.[4] Provincials could maintain a good many irregularities if they were determined. The efficacy of the Roman provincial control is apt to be over-estimated by those not closely in touch with the

---

[1] *Ant.* xx. 9. 1 ; Juster, ii. 140 f.
[3] *D.* i. 16. 10.
[2] Above, p. 4.
[4] Above, pp. 7–8.

sources. This consideration leads on to the case of Stephen, which Juster is compelled to use, rather reluctantly, because he likes to make fun of the supposed accuracy of Acts. The story is there told as of a trial and an execution.[1] There is no formal sentence, and the actual wording has been widely interpreted as a lynching: 'They rushed upon him in a general impulse, drove him out of the city and stoned him.' It is perhaps fair to admit that this impression may be due to the bias of the source. It is possible that the Sanhedrin, which before the Herodian period had been the sovereign court of Judaea, tried to exercise its full power whenever there was a chance of doing so unchecked.[2] The activities of Paul after the death of Stephen, not noticed by Juster, are an example.[3] This evidence should be considered with the story of the arrest and examination of John and Peter by the Sanhedrin, given in two versions in Acts.[4] The basic elements common to both the narratives are: (1) the arrest of the apostles in the Temple area where they had been preaching,[5] (2) threats of severe punishment or death,[6] (3) examination by the Sanhedrin, (4) dismissal of the accused after either a warning or a beating.[7] This suggests either that the Sanhedrin lacked the executive power of severe punishment, or, more probably, that it possessed the power in a restricted form for offences within the Temple precinct.

That the Sanhedrin had powers of jurisdiction as the supreme court of Jewish law, short of the death penalty, is not in dispute. That is all that the Hebraic evidence, of which Juster makes much, seems to prove. There is a vague and indirect claim in an allusive Talmudic text, of apparently the fourth century, that the capital jurisdiction of

---

[1] Acts vi. 12–15, vii. 57–59.

[2] For the origins of the Sanhedrin, see briefly Pauly–Wissowa, *RE*, (ii) iv. 1346 ff.

[3] Acts xxvi. 11.

[4] Acts iv. 1–21, v. 17–40.

[5] Acts iii. 1–11, iv. 1–3, v. 21.

[6] Acts iv. 21, v. 40.

[7] Acts iv. 21, v. 40.

the Sanhedrin survived until the year 70. Even Juster does not put great weight on this text, which naturally is not drafted from the Roman juridical point of view, and is quite in accord with the situation suggested by John.[1] Juster makes more of a text of the Mishna, derived from Rabbi Eleazer ben Zadeh, who lived, it seems, in the early second century.[2] Eleazer quoted the case of the daughter of a priest condemned for adultery and executed by burning after trial before a Jewish tribunal. Juster supposes this case to have occurred before the destruction of Jerusalem in 70.

The Mishna evidence should be considered with that of the curious passage from Origen's *Letter to Africanus*, first noted by Mommsen and later utilized by Juster.[3] Origen describes the power enjoyed by the Jewish patriarch in his own day, which made him, by imperial concession, συγχωροῦντος τοῦ βασιλέως, a virtual king of the Jewish folk. He continues: 'There even take place trials according to the law of Moses, secretly [or 'quietly', λεληθότως] and men are condemned to death, neither entirely openly, nor yet without the knowledge of the emperor.' Juster exalted this into a proof *a fortiori* of unfettered jurisdiction before 70. But he paid no attention to the qualification λεληθότως. Mommsen saw that this suggests a situation, which is equally possible for the pre-70 period, in which the municipal government took as much rope as it dared.

The most likely solution is that the Sanhedrin was allowed in the procuratorial period a limited criminal jurisdiction, both for police purposes in the Temple area and for

---

[1] Juster, ii. 138 n. 1. It is not the purpose of these lectures, or within the province of a Roman historian, to examine Rabbinical material as such in critical detail. But the texts certainly seem to lack any of the precision that is offered by the Graeco-Roman evidence, and which is essential to an exact evaluation of the legal situation. Cf. also the remarks of G. D. Kilpatrick, art. cit. 17 f.   [2] M. Sanhedrin 7. 2.

[3] Mommsen, *D. Pen. R.* i. 139 n. 3, 279 n. 1. Juster, ii. 151 n. 2.

the maintenance of the Jewish law. The scriptural tradition, both in Acts and the Gospels, suggests that the Roman procurators objected to capital sentences for theological offences. But the fairly well-attested question of adultery is different. Juster oddly makes no use of the story in John of the stoning of the woman taken in adultery.[1] Even if this story is not textually canonical it is historically good material. Perhaps it is too ambivalent for Juster: no Sanhedrin is mentioned and the story suggests a lynching. Yet here is an offence of which the Roman public law itself had recently taken cognizance in the *lex Iulia de adulteriis*, though not as a fully capital crime. This is the sort of local custom which might be ratified under the Roman system of toleration. But, as the evidence stands, the only certain exception to the general rule that the municipal authorities of the Empire were refused capital jurisdiction is that the Sanhedrin possessed certain powers of this sort in connexion with the maintenance of public order in the Temple area. Anything else should either belong to the jurisdiction of the procurator or require his sanction. If the Sanhedrin, under a strong high-priest, occasionally overstepped these limits, it was not unparalleled in other parts of the empire. One may recall the curious passage in Philostratus, as late as the time of Hadrian, where the sophist Polemon warns the city of Smyrna not to occupy itself with charges such as murder, sacrilege, and adultery, because these require a δικαστὴς ξίφος ἔχων, a judge with a sword, and only the proconsul had that.[2]

Josephus, describing Jewish customs in his *contra Apionem*, implies that capital penalties were in common use for sexual offences in his own day. Possibly the civic lynching was the traditional method of execution, and remained in use not only in the considerable territories of the tetrarchies, but

[1] John viii. 7–11.
[2] Phil. *VS*, i. 25. 2 (p. 532). Mommsen, op. cit. i. 278 n. 1.

was tolerated or surreptitiously practised in those areas of the province not under the immediate eye of the procurator. Apuleius, in the Golden Ass, could represent his characters as in danger of death from a civic tribunal.[1] But a casual reference in Josephus shows that though the local city councils and sanhedrins could arrest and punish robbers and brigands with imprisonment, execution for these offences depended on the procurator.[2]

Perhaps one of Juster's more sweeping arguments needs a word of correction. He holds that Augustus must have restored the full power of the Sanhedrin because Josephus speaks of the first, or 'good', procurators as not disturbing the customs of the Jews, whereas most of our information concerns the 'bad' procurators, who behaved illegally or tyranically. Hence when they are found taking over the function of the Sanhedrin it does not count as evidence of the norm. This is an absurd distinction, ignoring the fundamental nature of *imperium*, which justified the actions of 'good' and 'bad' governors alike.[3] There is also a crushing argument against the notion of Augustus restoring what Herod had taken away, in the experience of the city of Alexandria in Egypt and its town council; it had lost this under the Ptolemies, and nothing would induce Augustus and his successors to restore it.[4]

[1] Apuleius, *Met.* x. 5–10. Jos. C. *Ap.* ii. 25. 31. This latter solution of the capital problem was developed in a discussion with the Rev. J. R. Porter, who suggested that lynching is the proper explanation of the very curious wording of the Wall inscription: 'if a man is taken, it is his own fault. Death follows at once.' For the survival of lynching among Jewish communities even in the late Empire see *Cod. Iust.* i. 9. 3. Philo approves it, *De Spec. Leg.* i. 54–58.

[2] Jos. *BJ*, ii. 14. 1. 'Festus destroyed a great many of them . . . but Albinus . . . permitted the relations of such . . . as had been laid in prison for robbery, either by the senate of every city or by the former procurators, to redeem them for money.' Cf. *Ant.* xx. 9. 5. *BJ*, ii. 13. 2 for their execution by the procurator.   [3] Op. cit. ii. 132 n. 5. Cf. above, pp. 3 ff.

[4] Cf. *Cambridge Anc. Hist.* x. 294 with *P. Lond.* 1912 and *PSI*, 1160.

The specific problem of the Sanhedrin and the trial of Christ can now be faced. Lietzmann and his followers sought to reject the trial before the Sanhedrin as unhistorical on the ground that, in the shape which it takes in Matthew, Mark, and John, it is based on the false assumption that the Sanhedrin lacked the capital jurisdiction. The sentence of the Sanhedrin can only be carried out by the procurator, but the procurator executes a different sentence. If Juster's attempted proof of the Sanhedrin's capital powers is not sound, then the story of the Sanhedrin trial requires fresh consideration. There is one detail on which Lietzmann pours a good deal of scorn, which can be shown instead to be the best proof of the soundness of the tradition. This is the description of the trial taking place during the night and of Christ being sent to Pilate 'early in the morning'. It is one of the weaknesses in Lietzmann's paper that, while seeking to demonstrate the superiority of the Marcan narrative, he yet has to prefer Luke's version of the meeting of the Sanhedrin and the reference to Pilate. In Luke Christ is arrested when it is night, and the Sanhedrin meets 'when it was day': the first investigation then takes place, and necessarily a good deal later they take Christ before Pilate.[1] But in Mark and Matthew the night is occupied by the interrogation before the Sanhedrin, and Christ is taken before Pilate as soon as it is morning, εὐθὺς πρωί or πρωίας γενομένης, when the Sanhedrin has made its decision.[2]

It may be noted in passing that the phrase which Matthew and Mark use at this point—in slightly different forms, συμβούλιον ἔλαβον ὥστε θανατῶσαι and συμβούλιον ποιήσαντες —certainly cannot mean 'held a council meeting' but must bear the same meaning of 'taking a decision' or 'forming a plot' that the phrase has elsewhere in the two Gospels.[3]

---

[1] Luke xxii. 66, xxiii. 1.   [2] Mark xv. 1; Matt. xxvii. 1.
[3] Cf. Mark iii. 6; Matt. xii. 14, xxii. 15, xxvii. 7, xxviii. 12.

This συμβούλιον cannot be constituted into a second, matutinal, meeting of the Sanhedrin, which was the only historical meeting according to Lietzmann.[1]

On Luke's time-table the reference to Pilate cannot take place until several hours after dawn. One can tell, from our ample evidence about the arrangement of the upper-class Roman official's daily round, that the tactless Jews would have arrived, on this scheme, at a moment when Pilate was enjoying the elaborately organized leisure of a Roman gentleman. There is plenty of information about the Roman daily round. The emperor Vespasian was at his official duties even before the hour of dawn, and the elder Pliny, most industrious of Roman officials, had completed his working day, when Prefect of the Fleet, by the end of the fourth or fifth hour.[2] In Martial's account of daily life at the capital, where two hours are assigned to the protracted duty of *salutatio*, the period of *labores* ends when the sixth hour begins. Even a country gentleman at leisure begins his day at the second hour.[3]

The detail of the time-table may seem trivial, but it is like the button that hangs the murderer. Mark and Matthew have the time-table right, where Luke is less probable. The Jews, because of the festival, were in a hurry. Hence there was every reason to hold the unusual night session if they were to catch the Procurator at the right moment. The quite unessential detail of the fire, which is common to both Mark and Luke, in the story of Peter's denial, supports the Marcan version.[4] Why light a fire—an act of some extravagance—if everyone was sleeping through the night? By way

---

[1] Lietzmann, art. cit. 315 f.

[2] Pliny, *Ep.* iii. 5. 9–11, vi. 16. 4–5. The elder Pliny (ibid.) finished work, bath, *gustatio*, and siesta, by the seventh hour.

[3] Martial, iv. 8. 5–8; Pliny, *Ep.* iii. 1. 4, ix. 36. 1. Cf. also Mommsen, op. cit. ii. 33 n. 2, on the limitation of hours of jurisdiction in the later Empire.   [4] Mark xiv. 54; Luke xxii. 55–56.

of analogy—it is not an exact parallel—one may quote the younger Pliny's astonishment at his uncle's habit of studying at night, and the way he underlines it as an exceptional circumstance when a protracted session of the Senate was concluded by lamplight.[1] Lietzmann, who makes much of the evidence of Peter and its limitations, cannot have things both ways. If this story is part of the basic tradition, from Peter's eye-witness, then there was a nocturnal session, and the historicity of the Sanhedrin trial is confirmed.

The detail about the time-table is like that of the soldiers sharing out the clothing of Christ. Given the relevant prophecy from the Old Testament, there is every reason to assume that this is one of the evolved myths dear to the form-critics. But, as has been familiar since Mommsen, legal texts confirm that it was the accepted right of the executioner's squad to share out the minor possessions of their victim. The custom, which must derive ultimately from the custom of plunder on the field of battle, became the subject of a legal dispute on which the emperor Hadrian pronounced a solution.[2]

The objection that the Sanhedrin had no need to have recourse to Pilate for the execution of Christ has already been eliminated. The trial before the Sanhedrin and the condemnation for blasphemy regain historical probability. There is nothing in the Roman background to make the older solution improbable: that the Jewish leaders, finding or knowing that Pilate was unwilling to confirm an execution for a purely theological offence, added or substituted an alternative charge of sedition, which Pilate ultimately accepted as the basis of his sentence. But it is equally possible, in Roman usage, that when Pilate refused a verdict on the political charge, they fell back on the religious charge,

---

[1] *Ep.* ii. 11. 16, 18, iii. 5. 8–9, iv. 9. 14.
[2] Mommsen, *D. Pen. R.* i. 280 n. 2.

which Pilate finally accepted under the sort of political pressure that is indicated in a convincing technicality by John. The telling phrase—'If you let this man go, you are not Caesar's friend'—recalls the frequent manipulation of the treason law for political ends in Roman public life, and uses a notable political term—*Caesaris amicus*—to enforce its point.[1]

It is not the purpose of this lecture to examine critically the difficulties involved in John's version of the trials of Christ. But after the survey of the legal and administrative background, it is apparent that there is no historical improbability in the Johannine variations of this sort from the synoptic version. The framework of the trial is not notably inferior to that of Luke. It begins with a formal delation— 'What accusation bring ye against this man?'—and ends with a formal condemnation *pro tribunali*.[2] The elaboration of what takes place between these two terminals—and the motives of this elaboration—is another matter. But the principal novelty—the implication that Pilate adopted, or was willing to adopt, the sentence of the Sanhedrin—is entirely within the scope of the procurator's *imperium*.[3]

[1] John xix. 12. Crook, *Consilium Principis*, 23 f. The connotation, originally political rather than personal in Republican usage, becomes markedly official in imperial documents, with the suggestion that so and so is the official representative of the Princeps. Cf. A–J, nn. 49, 59: 'Plantam Iulium amicum et comitem meum'. The term 'friend of Caesar' is used in a very similar way to that of the Gospel in passages of the contemporary Philo. Cf. *In Flaccum*, 2. 40.

[2] John xviii. 29, xix. 13.

[3] P. Winter's book on the trial of Jesus, cited 32 n. 1, appeared after the delivery of this lecture. His legal argument, here refuted, is merely a summary of Leitzmann's, and hence of Juster's, as indeed his whole thesis is an expansion of Leitzmann. Its legal foundations are equally fragile. Much more accurate, if old-fashioned, in its Roman background, is J. Blinzler, *Der Prozess Jesu*[2] (Regensburg, 1960), esp. 163 ff., 198 ff., 248 ff.

LECTURE THREE

Paul before Felix and Festus

THE account in Acts of the trial of Paul before the procurators Felix and Festus bristles, or is commonly supposed to bristle, with problems. Yet it long ago satisfied Mommsen himself, who labelled it briefly, in the *Strafrecht*, as an exemplary account of the provincial penal procedure *extra ordinem*, comparable to that of Apuleius in his *Apologia*.[1] The basic elements of this procedure, enumerated in the first lecture, and demonstrated for the earlier Principate, are all there. The charge is made and sustained by private prosecutors, first certain Jews from the province of Asia, and later the leading clerics of Jerusalem, who appear before the governor with an advocate to represent them.[2] The narrative insists on formal prosecution both in the letter of Claudius Lysias to Felix and in Felix's preliminary inquiry: 'I shall hear you when your accusers are present.'[3] The same is true of the trial before Festus, where the clerics duly appear as accusers, this time without an advocate.[4] There is also the very correct remark of Festus to the Jews at Jerusalem: 'It is not the custom of the Romans to allow the condemnation of a man until the accused has had his accusers face to face, &c.' After this, Festus bade the Jewish leaders bring their charges in due form.[5]

The governor appears formally on his tribunal, *pro*

---

[1] Mommsen, *D. Pen. R.* i. 278 n. 1.

[2] Acts xxi. 27–28, xxiv. 1–2.

[3] Acts xxiii. 30, 35.   [4] Acts xxv. 6–7.

[5] Acts xxv. 5, 16. χαρίζεσθαι in s. 16 repeats the idea of αἰτούμενοι χάριν in s. 3.

tribunali, and acts with the assistance of his *consilium*.[1] These details appear only in the trial before Festus. The detail about the advocate is of interest. In the imperial *cognitiones* before Trajan, described by the younger Pliny, the parties appear with or without advocates as they please.[2]

The moderns make a great difficulty about the charges against Paul, which they say are never made precise. The unfriendly critics have the support of Mommsen in this, and make much of the issue.[3] This is very surprising. The charges are perfectly clear when related to the system *extra ordinem*, and any supposed difficulty arises from a misunderstanding of this. In the first session at Jerusalem the Asian Jews accuse Paul of speaking against the People, the Law, and the Temple, and of bringing Hellenes—that is the man Trophimus—into the Temple area.[4] Paul, be it noted, was arrested within the precinct.[5] In the scene before the Sanhedrin Paul defends himself rather sophistically from charges of what one may call heresy, κατὰ τὸν νόμον . . . περὶ ἀναστάσεως νεκρῶν κρίνομαι.[6] This agrees with the letter of Lysias, περὶ ζητημάτων τοῦ νόμου αὐτοῦ.[7] Then in the accusation before Felix, Tertullus charges Paul with 'stirring up a plague of discord among all the Jews throughout the world, and being the leader, or founder, of the sect of the Nazarenes'.[8] Paul, in his defence, denies that he 'made speeches to anyone' or caused any 'excitation of the mob', either in the Temple or the synagogues or the city, and challenges his accusers to produce any evidence of this.[9]

---

[1] Acts xxv. 6, 10, 12.   [2] Pliny, *Ep.* iv. 22. 2, vi. 31. 9–11.
[3] Cadbury's appendix 'Roman Law and the trial of Paul' in Jackson–Lake, op. cit. v. 297 f., is the most accessible modern discussion. Mommsen, *GS*, iii, 'Die Rechtsverhältnisse des Apostels Paulen', 441 f.
[4] Acts xxi. 27–29.   [5] Acts xxi. 30.
[6] 'My trial is under the Law . . . and concerns resurrection.'
[7] 'concerning questions of his Law. Acts xxiii. 3, 6, 29.
[8] Acts xxiv. 5.   [9] Acts xxiv. 12–13.

He then passes on to the religious question, but rubs in the point that in this too he had been present in the Temple 'without mobs or disturbances'.[1] In the hearing before Festus the account of the charges and of Paul's defence is much briefer. This is summed up in the words: 'I never did anything against the law of the Jews or the temple or Caesar.'[2]

Cadbury, in his appendix to the *Acts Commentary* of Jackson and Lake, came close to the true explanation when he remarked that the charge of stirring up strife was *constructive*.[3] This could be expanded. The Jews were trying to induce the governor to construe the preaching of Paul as tantamount to causing civil disturbances throughout the Jewish population of the Empire. They knew that the governors were unwilling to convict on purely religious charges and therefore tried to give a political twist to the religious charge. This reluctance is brought out several times by the author of Acts, notably in the letter of Lysias: 'He was charged with questions of their law, and had done nothing worthy of death or imprisonment.'[4] So too in Festus' account of his own preliminary inquiry: 'The accusers brought no charge against him of any evil act that I could understand',[5] ὧν ἐγὼ ὑπενόουν. The word is pejorative, and at its strongest means 'suspect'. This phrase may well correspond to the formula 'any act of which I was prepared to take cognizance', 'de quibus cognoscere volebam'. Claudius, in his well-known letter to the people of Alexandria, uses the term in the sentence: 'Let them not do things compelling me to take serious notice.'[6] Perhaps *animadversio* in the judicial sense is the nearest equivalent.

---

[1] Acts xxiv. 18.   [2] Acts xxv. 7–8.

[3] Op. cit. 306. The term *Acts Commentary* will be used henceforth for this great book.   [4] Acts xxiii. 29.   [5] Acts xxv. 18–19, cf. 25.

[6] ἐξ οὗ μείζονας ὑπονοίας ἀναγκασθήσομαι λαβεῖν. P. Lond. 1912 *ad fin.* in M. Charlesworth, *Documents Illustrating the Reign of Claudius and Nero* (Cambridge, 1939), C. n. 2.

Compare also the language of the anonymous edict about the violation of tombs in Palestine: 'Let nobody disturb any tomb at all. Otherwise I wish such a person to be condemned to death on the charge of tomb-robbery.'[1]

Under the procedure *extra ordinem* the constructive charge was not only permissive but normal, as was demonstrated in the first lecture. The facts are alleged, and the governor is expected to construe them as he thinks fit. The complication and prolongation of the trial of Paul arose from the fact that the charge was political—hence the procurators were reluctant to dismiss it out of hand—and yet the evidence was theological, hence the procurators were quite unable to understand it. Not surprisingly, Festus called in King Agrippa as an assessor, to help him to draft the explanation which had to be sent with the prisoner to Rome.[2]

This interpretation of the charge against Paul is confirmed by the parallel evidence of the letter of Claudius to the Alexandrines, which was unknown to Mommsen and Juster. F. Cumont[3] first noticed its relevance to Acts xxiv. 5. Claudius there sums up his objection to certain political actions of the Jews as: 'stirring up a universal plague throughout the world', κοινήν τινα τῆς οἰκουμένης νόσον ἐξεγείροντας. The similarity to the formulation of the charge against Paul is startling, 'stirring up a plague and disturbances for the Jews throughout the world', λοιμὸν καὶ κινοῦντα στάσεις πᾶσι τοῖς Ἰουδαίοις κατὰ τὴν οἰκουμένην.[4] The similarity is deliberate. It is evident that the narrative of Acts is using contemporary language. The charge was precisely the one to bring against a Jew during the Principate of Claudius or the early years of Nero. The accusers of

[1] Ibid., C. no. 17, or *FIRA*, i, no. 69.
[2] Acts xxvi. 24–27.
[3] F. Cumont, *Rev. Hist. Rel.* xci (1925), 1 ff.
[4] Acts xxiv. 5. Though there is no impossibility in taking λοιμόν after κινοῦντα, the text reads as if a participle had been omitted before it.

Paul were putting themselves on the side of the government. The procurator would know at once what the prosecution meant. Chronologically, of course, the texts are in the right order. Claudius' letter to the Alexandrines belongs to the first years of his reign, and it was not the only occasion on which he had to fulminate against Jews.

A subsidiary point is worth noting. The original charge was made by certain Asian Jews who disappear from the case. In the hearing before Felix, Paul objects, rightly, that they ought to be present to make their charges.[1] The Roman law was very strong against accusers who abandoned their charges. Claudius himself had been busy with legislation aimed at preventing accusers within the system of the *ordo* from abandoning their charges. He made a speech about the matter in the Senate, and his proposals were later completed by the SC. Turpilianum of A.D. 61, under Nero.[2] This laid down penalties for the offence which the lawyers call *destitutio*. There is an example of this principle in a trial *extra ordinem* which took place before the tribunal of Trajan in A.D. 106–7.[3] Once again, the author of Acts is well informed. But there is more to it than that. The disappearance of one set of accusers may mean the withdrawal of the charge with which they were particularly associated. The Asian Jews had accused Paul of two things: one, preaching everywhere, i.e. throughout the 'world', the *oikoumene*, against the Hebraic law, and, two, of bringing Hellenes into the Temple. Charge one was taken over by the Jewish clergy. Charge two, according to Acts, could not be substantiated: 'They had *seen* Trophimus with Paul in the city, and *thought* he had been taken into the Temple.'[4] Hence when the Asian Greeks

---

[1] Acts xxiv. 18–19.

[2] *BGU*, 611, cols. ii–iii (Charlesworth, C. n. 3); *D.* 48. 16 at length. See *RE*, iii, 1414 ff.

[3] Pliny, *Ep.* vi. 31. 9–12.   [4] Acts xxi. 29, cf. xxv. 19.

withdrew from the case, Paul had a sound technical objection to put forward.

Hence, too, it is not surprising that Felix adjourned the case for the arrival of Lysias the tribune, the only independent witness as to the fact of any civil disturbance.[1] That the case was put into cold storage by Felix, and left for his successor, creates no difficulty.[2] Josephus regarded it as unusual when a later procurator, Albinus, on hearing of his supersession, dealt with all the charges or executions which were pending.[3] Mommsen remarked that there was no means of compelling a governor to give judgment *extra ordinem*, though the rules of the *ordo* tried to prevent judicial delays in that sphere.[4] The delay suited the parties. Felix, departing for Rome, tried to ensure that no accusation would be brought against himself for maladministration, under the extortion law, by the Jewish leaders; he leaves Paul 'on a charge', to please them.[5] Some years later, under Nero, there was a great to-do at Rome about the undue influence which provincial politicians exerted on governors by the threat of a prosecution for extortion.[6] It is remarkable that though charges had been made against both Pilate and Cumanus, the predecessors of Felix, no general charge was made against him, despite the troubles of his administration.[7] The collocation in Acts of the departure of Felix and this attempt to secure the favour of the Jews is thus in historical perspective. Josephus does, however, record that the Jews of Caesarea, but not those of the rest of the province, made

---

[1] Acts xxiv. 22.　　　[2] Acts xxiv. 25–27.　　　[3] Jos. *Ant.* xx. 9. 5.
[4] Mommsen, *GS*, 444. Cf. *D. Pen. R.* ii. 176–7. *D.* 48. 16. 15. 5 mentions *occupationes praesidum* as a ground for the law's delay, but the Roman law was more concerned to prevent *destitutio* by accusers than to speed up the courts themselves. See Lecture Four, pp. 112 ff.
[5] Acts xxiv. 27.　　　　　　　　　[6] Tac. *Ann.* xv. 20–22.
[7] Jos. *Ant.* xviii. 4. 2, xx. 6. 3; *BJ*, ii. 12. 6–7. For Felix's troubles see *BJ*, ii. 13.

a complaint against Felix, which Nero's adviser, the excellent Burrus, quashed.[1] This was very different from the treatment given to Cumanus and his assistants earlier.

The activities of Claudius Lysias raise no special difficulty. Juster, in his book on the Jews in the Roman empire, objected to the statement that Lysias, wanting to know what was the charge made by the Jews against Paul, bade the high-priests and all the Sanhedrin meet.[2] It is true no doubt that the Sanhedrin did not need the permission of any Roman official to hold its meetings, any more than any other municipal council. But all that the Acts means here is that the tribune requested the Sanhedrin to hold a special meeting for his convenience. This meeting is not represented as a judicial trial in the narrative description, or in the letter of Lysias. It is only in Paul's own speech to the Sanhedrin that the verb κρίνεις κρίνομαι is used of the attitude of the Sanhedrin to him.[3] The main narrative regards the occasion as an inquiry made necessary when Paul revealed his Roman citizenship, and thus precluded more direct methods.[4] Even if Paul had not been a Roman citizen, the tribune lacked the necessary *imperium* to deal judicially with prisoners of provincial status, once he had restored public order. It is not clear why Cadbury suggests that Lysias might have tried the case himself.[5] In dispatching the prisoner to the governor with a *libellus* of explanation, and instructing the accusers to make their charge before the governor's tribunal, Lysias was acting very much as was enjoined by rescripts of Hadrian and Pius later, in the case even of brigands arrested by municipal police, who in most provinces had the role filled by Lysias in Judaea. They were

---

[1] *Ant.* xx. 8. 9.   [2] Juster, op. cit. ii. 141 n. 1.
[3] Acts xxiii. 3, 6.
[4] Cadbury, op. cit. 304–5, is correct here, though he very oddly calls the incident an *anquisitio*, a term proper to the Republican procedure of *iudicium populi*.   [5] Op. cit. 306.

not only required to send a written account of the preliminary interrogation of the prisoner to the governor, but
to turn up and substantiate their charges. This held, even in
the field of summary jurisdiction over vulgar crimes.[1] This
procedure may be brought a little nearer the age of Acts by
the account in the younger Pliny of a certain runaway slave
who was brought before the municipal magistrates of Nico-
media.[2] The sergeant in charge of a small detachment in
that city dispatched the man with a written report to Pliny.
The parallel is not exact, because of the status of the prisoner
and certain peculiar circumstances. But it is in accord with
the later procedure that Felix should adjourn the case before
him 'until Lysias comes'.

There is the matter of the question put to Paul by Felix:
'From what province do you come', and the surprising fact
that when he heard that Paul came from an alien province,
Cilicia, Felix declared that he would hear the case, where we
expect the opposite.[3] It was argued earlier that the custom
of *forum domicilii*, that is, of referring an accused person
back to the jurisdiction of his native province, was never
more than optional, and that it was not firmly established in
the early Principate.[4] But in the case of a Roman citizen,
and of a Jewish imbroglio, the procurator might well have
been glad to avail himself of any such usage. Why, then, did
Festus not do so, having asked the question itself? The
answer may well lie in the status of Cilicia, which even
more than Judaea, though a separate administrative area,
was a dependency, of the Legate of Syria in the early Principate. By the Flavian period all Cilicia had become a separate
province under its own imperial legate.[5] Earlier the mountainous areas were in the hands of local kings, but under the

---

[1] *D.* 48. 3. 6. Marcian, quoting Hadrian and Pius.
[2] Pliny, *Ep.* x. 74.   [3] Acts xxiv. 34–35.
[4] Above, pp. 28 f.   [5] Cf. *CAH*, xi. 603.

general supervision of the Legate of Syria, who was apparently in direct control of the coastal lowland where Tarsus lay.[1] The change may have taken place in the early years of Nero. The Legate of Syria is found exercising military authority in Cilicia, conjointly with local kings, under Tiberius and as late as A.D. 52 under Claudius, and possibly in the second year of Nero.[2] In the fourth year of Nero the Cilicians accuse a senator of extortion, who is either the first separate governor of the province, or less probably one of the assistants of the Legate of Syria.[3]

If Cilicia at the time of the incidents of Acts xxiv did not have a separate imperial legate, Felix's decision is explained. The Legate of Syria was not to be bothered with minor cases from Judaea, though it was his duty to intervene in times of great crisis, and the status of Cilicia did not require that its natives should be sent back to it for trial, even if the later usage of *forum domicilii* was in vogue. Yet another complication lay in the fact that Paul's city, Tarsus, was a *civitas*

---

[1] The kingdoms are well documented chronologically from Augustus to Claudius, e.g. Dio, 54. 9. 2, 59. 8. 2, 60. 8. 2. Tac. *Ann.* ii. 42, vi. 41, xii. 55. Strabo, xii. 1. 4 (p. 535), xiv. 5. 6 (p. 671), and ibid. 18 (p. 676), shows that they were confined to the mountainous sector of Cilicia Tracheia in the west and the Amanus in the east, excluding the maritime plain from the river Lamus (west of Soli and Pompeiopolis) eastwards to the Amanus. The existence of a provincial regime in Cilicia is not well documented, though implied by Strabo, xiv. 5. 6, and more directly indicated (ibid. 14, p. 675) in a reference to Athenodorus of Tarsus as 'honoured by the governors (ἡγεμόσι) and in the city'. Cf. also Tac. *Ann.* ii. 58 for another implication of a provincial régime. J. G. Anderson, *Cl. Rev.* (1931), 190. *CAH*, loc. cit. and x. 261, 279, 745. The 'coast' which Antiochus ruled in A.D. 52 is evidently that of Cilicia Tracheia (Tac. *Ann.* xii. 55, cf. Dio, 59. 8. 2), which he must have held until his deposition in A.D. 72; cf. *CAH*, xi. 603 f.

[2] Tac. *Ann.* ii. 78, 80, vi. 41, xii. 55. In xiii. 8 Quadratus legate of Syria meets Corbulo at Aegeae in Cilicia Pedias, presumably within his own province, though the passage is ambiguous: 'illuc progressum ne si ad accipiendas copias Syriam intravisset Corbulo omnium ora in se verteret'. Cf. H. Furneaux, *Annals of Tacitus*, ad loc.

[3] Ibid. xiii. 33. Cf. Furneaux, ad loc.

libera, and hence its citizens were exempt from normal provincial jurisdiction.[1]

One minor point arises. If the author of Acts has made a slip in implying that Cilicia was already a separate province, the slip is venial, because within two or three years that was the situation. But the implication is not real. Felix asked 'from what province do you come?'; Paul replied 'from Cilicia', which technically was not a province, but a part of a province. The narrative in fact shows remarkable familiarity with the provincial and juridical situation in the last years of Claudius. An author familiar with the later situation of Cilicia, and the final form of the judicial custom of *forum delicti*, would have avoided altogether the question of Paul's *patria*, or place of origin.

The Citizenship of Paul

There remains the question concerning the Roman citizenship of Paul and its legal consequences. The author of Acts has been accused of all sorts of obscurities and inaccuracies in this matter, though in fact the precise legal situation of Roman citizens in provincial jurisdiction is not well documented at this period. For the early Principate the starting-point is the citation of a clause of the *lex Iulia de vi publica*, from Ulpian's *De officio proconsulis*, and from the *Sententiae Pauli*, a compendium compiled not earlier than the mid-fourth century. The law itself belonged to the period of the Principate of Augustus.[2] The text runs in Ulpian: 'lege

[1] Pliny, *NH*, v. 92. Cf. Strabo, xiv. 5. 14, p. 674. For 'free states' see Lecture Two, p. 36 n. 3.

[2] A. H. M. Jones (art. cit. below) left the question of date open. But careful consideration of the privileges granted with the Roman citizenship by Octavian to Seleucus of Rhosus before 31 B.C. shows that provincial *provocatio* did not then exist. If any provincial brought a capital charge against Seleucus or his descendants, they were given the right to send a special envoy to the Roman Senate about the matter. After the *lex Iulia* this cumbrous procedure became unnecessary. *FIRA*, i. 55, ii, 9 (E–J, no. 301, ii, 9).

Iulia de vi publica tenetur qui cum imperium potestatemve haberet civem Romanum adversus provocationem
necaverit verberaverit iusseritve quid fieri aut quid in collum
iniecerit ut torqueretur.'[1] This text is a summary of something much longer, but uses the terminology of Republican
legislation. A citation from Marcian adds: 'lege Iulia de vi
cavetur ne quis reum vinciat impediatve quominus Romae
intra certum tempus adsit'.[2] The text in the *Sententiae Pauli*
substitutes the terminology of a later age in some places, but
adds in what seems convincingly early phraseology: 'qui
. . . condemnaverit inve publica vincula duci iusserit' among
the forbidden acts. It also adds a list of exceptions, beginning 'qui artem ludicram faciunt, iudicati etiam et confessi'.[3]
These are unlikely to belong to the original law, but the
first item, the exclusion of actors, should belong to the early
Principate. Police action of the kind forbidden by the
original law was taken on several occasions under Tiberius
and Nero.[4] The latter occasion may fix the date of the
exception. A praetor at Rome had arrested and enchained
certain supporters of the buskin, when a tribune intervened
to protect the actors. Finally the Senate passed a decree
approving the action of the praetor. One at least, then, of the
exceptions belongs to the Julio-Claudian period.

These clauses of the *lex Iulia de vi* protected the Roman
citizen who invoked the ancient right of *provocatio*, from
summary punishment, execution or torture without trial,
from private or public arrest, and from actual trial by
magistrates outside Italy.[5] They are to be understood in

[1] *D.* 48. 6. 7. [2] Ibid. 8. [3] *Sent. Pauli*, v. 26. 1–2.
[4] Tac. *Ann.* iv. 14. 4, xiii. 25. 4, 28. 1.
[5] For the earlier discussion see Mommsen, *DPR* iii. 309 ff., and for the
Republican origins see Greenidge, *Legal Procedure of Cicero's Time* (Oxford,
1901), 318 ff. Strachan-Davidson, *Problems &c.*, ii, ch. 19, 166 ff. and ch. 20,
who is inadequate on the *lex Iulia*, A. H. M. Jones has clarified several
issues in his articles 'Imperial and senatorial jurisdiction in the early

connexion with the *ordo* system, which had created for Roman citizens a method of trial by jury at Rome for statutory offences. Against this there was no *provocatio*. The citation from Ulpian proves only the protection against physical punishment, whether as an act of *coercitio* or by way of executing sentence. But the fragment in the *Sententiae Pauli* indicates that *provocatio* protected a man from trial and sentence: 'qui . . . condemnaverit'.

That these clauses are especially concerned with the position of Roman citizens outside Italy is suggested, though not quite proved, for the early Principate, by the fact that Ulpian cites the law in his *de officio proconsulis*, and by the description of the magistrates affected as 'qui cum imperium potestatemve haberet'.[1] The passage from Marcian indicates that the general intention was that accused persons who invoked the right of appeal should be tried at Rome by the courts of the *ordo*. Without delving into the history of *provocatio* under the Republic, it may suffice to remark that there had never been any appeal against the authority of the *quaestiones publicae*, the jury courts established by statute law.[2] They had been created to provide a refuge for those threatened by the personal jurisdiction of magistrates. It would seem that Professor A. H. M. Jones in his recent study of *provocatio* is probably right in the conclusion that from the date of the *lex Iulia* the Roman citizen was protected throughout the Roman empire from the capital jurisdiction and violent *coercitio* of provincial governors.[1] At any rate,

Principate', *Historia*, 1955, 478 ff., and 'I appeal unto Caesar' in *Studies presented to D. M. Robinson*, 918 ff. Both are conveniently reprinted in his *Studies in Roman Government*, iv–v. 51 ff., 67 ff.

[1] Cf. Jones, 'I appeal', 920. The distinction between annual magistrates and 'persons holding *imperium*' appears explicitly in Ulpian's citation of the *lex Iulia maiestatis*, *D*. 48. 4. 1.

[2] Strachan-Davidson, op. cit. ii. 48, cf., e.g., Cic. *pro Flacco* 4. *Phil.* i. 21. Mommsen, *D. Pen. R.* i. 323, ii. 155.

late in the reign of Augustus there is a clear instance, in the
second edict of Augustus from Cyrene, not used by Professor
Jones, which shows that by that date the *lex Iulia* was being
applied to actions in provinces.[1] A certain Sextius Scaeva,
who appears to be a private citizen rather than a magistrate,
had caused three Roman citizens to be sent in chains from
the province to Rome for a judicial inquiry. Augustus
declares that: 'no blame or ill-feeling should attach to
Scaeva for this act . . . which was in order and proper'.
Augustus was protecting Scaeva in advance against any
charge made against him under the clause of the *lex Iulia*
quoted by Marcian, which forbade anyone to bind a Roman
citizen.

The effect of this formal extension of the citizen's right of
appeal throughout the Empire was that, by the time of
Trajan, Roman citizens charged with certain offences were
automatically sent by provincial governors to Rome for
trial. The governors make no attempt to try these cases
themselves.[2] The *locus classicus* is Pliny's handling of Romans
accused of Christian practices in Pontus.[3] Another example
may be found in the trial before Trajan's tribunal in Italy
of a Roman citizen and local magnate of Ephesus, one
Claudius Aristion, for seditious activity in his own province;
this case may well have originated from an appeal against
the proconsul's jurisdiction.[4] An earlier example not hither-
to noticed may be obscurely detected in the year 64 from
the *Annals* of Tacitus, where a Roman citizen was sent in
chains for an unknown offence to the tribunal of Nero by the
proconsul of Asia.[5]

There are, however, a certain number of cases in which
a provincial governor tried, sentenced, and executed, or

---

[1] E–J, no. 311, ii. 42–47.   [2] Jones, loc. cit.
[3] Pliny, *Ep.* x. 96. 4, 'quia cives Romani erant, adnotavi in urbem re-
mittendos'.   [4] Ibid. vi. 31. 3.   [5] Tac. *Ann.* xvi. 10. 2.

severely punished Roman citizens for capital offences without any suggestion that such action was contrary to the law of *provocatio*. Some of these cases were considered in the discussion of *cognitio*;[1] they have long troubled historians because it is difficult to explain them all away as the abuse of power. In some of these instances one would expect the accused to protect himself against the corruption of a governor by invoking the *ius provocationis*, and in one instance we are told that the governor, the just but severe Sulpicius Galba, the future emperor, ignored the act of appeal.[2] These various instances have led Professor Jones to suggest, with the ambiguous support of certain obscure texts from the classical lawyers, that by the Flavian period, if not earlier, a distinction had arisen in the matter of appeal between two classes of crimes—those of the *ordo* defined by statute laws, and those which fell *extra ordinem*.[3] He has argued that provincial governors were given special authority to deal with certain crimes of Roman citizens covered by the *ordo*, and that the right of appeal was no longer allowed in such cases. There were reasons of practical utility for this change—notably the growing number of Roman citizens in certain provinces, which could lead to great inconvenience, or even to a breakdown of jurisdiction, if all cases of murder, forgery, and adultery were referred to Rome. This new theory seems to have a great deal to recommend it. Jones is unduly cautious over some of the evidence. He is inclined to treat the examples of Galba from Tarraconensis and Gessius Florus from Judaea as instances of abuse of power. This reduces the chronological extent of the evidence, because these are the only pre-Flavian examples. Both are Neronian, and from the hey-day of political delation at Rome, a time when a governor was unlikely to court wantonly a prosecution

---

[1] Above, pp. 16 f.   [2] Suet. *Galba*, 9, 1.
[3] 'Jurisdiction', 480 f., and 'I appeal', 921 f.

by his enemies, who would take advantage of any such lapses. Suetonius quotes the incident involving Galba as an example, not of contravention of the laws, but of exceptional severity of punishment. The condemned man appealed, not against his trial, but against sentence of crucifixion, when he expected the normal execution by the sword. The disciplinarian Galba may well have been acting within his rights. Again, Josephus disapproved of Gessius Florus for executing for active sedition Jews who were Roman citizens, but this does not prove that the action was illegal.[1] Hence the date of this innovation may be carried back into the Neronian period. The examples, it may be noted, come from governorships of all three categories, imperial legates, equestrian procurators, and proconsuls.[2] But this particular distinction does not matter much for our purposes. The charges against Paul were either *extra ordinem*, as is probably the case, or if they could be subsumed under any statutory crime of the *ordo* it would be one of those, such as the treason law, which were not left to the authority of the provincial governors. In the instance from Pliny cited earlier, the magnate of Ephesus, Claudius Aristion, had been sent to Rome for trial on just such a charge of subversion.

There is always the possibility, which is too often forgotten, that a Roman citizen of mean estate might prefer not to invoke his right of appeal. If he was satisfied with the honesty of his judge and had a sound defence, it might well be to his disadvantage to transfer his trial to Rome, where his witnesses might not be able to follow him. There is good

[1] Jos. *BJ*, ii. 14. 9. That they were men of equestrian standing strengthens the argument in the text. The action of a legate of Germania Inferior in the disturbed period of 68 is more doubtful, Dio, 63 (64) 2. 3.

[2] The Flavian examples are limited to proconsuls, Pliny, *Ep.* ii. 11. 8, x. 58. 3. But the evidence for the Flavian period on political and judicial history is notably thin compared to the Julio-Claudian period, with the loss of most of Tacitus' *Histories* and the ending of Josephus.

evidence of this kind of difficulty. The emperor Augustus had the extortion law amended, by limiting the number of witnesses required at Rome, precisely to reduce this difficulty.[1]

Just how, then, does the narrative of Acts fit what is known of the usage of *provocatio* in the provinces? Neither Felix nor Festus had any hesitation in giving a formal hearing at his tribunal *pro tribunali* to the charges against Paul, although in the narrative Paul made it clear from the beginning that he was a Roman citizen, and the charges against him in the opinion of his accusers were capital.[2] He had remained in some form of custody, if not in actual chains, for some two years. Acts uses the word δεδεμένον of this period,[3] but possibly this refers to the sort of military custody by which he was later dispatched under escort to Rome, and which meant that he lived under military surveillance in a private house.[4] None of this was illegal according to the strict wording of the known fragments of the *lex Iulia*, since Paul did not exert his right of appeal until the end of the narrative of the trial before Festus; thereafter he was in course of dispatch to Rome. The law only applied to acts *adversus provocationem*. A cautious governor such as the younger Pliny might prefer to ship his citizen charges off to Rome, but he was not compelled to do so if there was no formal appeal.

Cadbury suggested that the procurator had the power to disallow an appeal, and that he might himself have tried the prisoner, merely seeking confirmation of sentence if he found the man guilty.[5] This is clean contrary to the evidence of the *lex Iulia* and of Pliny. Cadbury had in mind the trial

[1] Cf. the preamble to the SC. Calvisianum, E–J, no. 311 v.
[2] Acts xxii. 25. Lysias understood the charges to be capital, Acts xxiii. 29.
[3] Acts xxiv. 27, cf. xxvi. 29.
[4] Acts xxvii. 1, xxviii. 16; 30. Cf. Mommsen, *GS*, 444.
[5] Appendix, op. cit. v. 311, 317–18.

of Herod's son Antipater, who was a Roman citizen, before the Legate of Syria.[1] But that was a very different affair involving high politics and the rights of client kings over their own families.[2] The procedure followed by the Legate of Lugdunensis in the time of Marcus Aurelius is more relevant; he hesitated even at that date to try Roman citizens without prior reference to Rome.[3] But this will not serve for the exact evaluation of procedure in the time of Claudius. Festus certainly discussed the appeal of Paul with his advisory cabinet before announcing: 'to Caesar thou hast appealed. To Caesar thou shalt go.'[4] But that does not mean that the procurator could ignore the *lex Iulia* at will. Paul had made his appeal in order to avoid the transfer of the investigation to Jerusalem. Festus had to decide whether to send him to Rome forthwith, or to carry his investigation further. The *lex Iulia* merely forbade the passing of sentence and execution: *condemnaverit* is the operative word. It is unlikely that such appeals were common in Judaea, where Roman citizens were not numerous. The governor would need to check the technical question with his cabinet. Besides, the charges against Paul originally included the one capital crime that lay within the jurisdiction of the Sanhedrin itself—that of violating the sanctuary by the introduction of strangers.

The remark of Festus to Agrippa 'When this man appealed to Augustus I decided to send him' should not be pressed to imply that the procurator had discretion contrary to the *lex Iulia*.[5] Acts, however sound in these parts, is not derived from a shorthand copy of court proceedings. The remark of Festus is parallel to his earlier and more explicit statement to Agrippa: 'When Paul made an appeal that he should be

---

[1] Jos. *Ant.* xvii. 5. 7–8, 7. 1. For the citizenship of Antipater, ibid. xvi. 2. 4.
[2] *BJ*, i. 23, 5.
[3] Eusebius, *Hist. Eccles.* v. i. 207. See pp. 69 f. below.
[4] Acts xxv. 12.
[5] Acts xxv. 25.

kept for the judgment of Caesar, I bade him be kept in custody until I send him to Caesar.'[1] Equally when Agrippa remarked: 'this man could have been released if he had not appealed to Caesar', this does not mean that in strict law the governor could not pronounce an acquittal after the act of appeal.[2] It is not a question of law, but of the relations between the emperor and his subordinates, and of that element of non-constitutional power which the Romans called *auctoritas*, 'prestige', on which the supremacy of the Princeps so largely depended. No sensible man with hopes of promotion would dream of short-circuiting the appeal to Caesar unless he had specific authority to do so. This could only be the case if Professor Jones's theory about capital charges of the *ordo* is correct, and correct for the Julio-Claudian period. In that case the appeal could be disallowed in certain types of cases. It may be that Festus had to discuss with his advisers, not whether to allow an appeal in general, but whether the charges against Paul were or were not *extra ordinem*, and if they were not, whether they belonged to the special category of crime for which appeal could be refused. Since the charges were *extra ordinem* in large part, the appeal was automatically valid. Festus was naturally only too glad, politically, to rid himself of the prisoner. To have acquitted him despite the appeal would have been to offend both the emperor and the province.

A similar political solution applies to the difficulty that Mommsen made over Paul's statement at Rome: 'I was compelled to appeal to Caesar when the Jews resisted [my acquittal], but it was not because I wanted to accuse my own people.'[3] This does not contradict the earlier account of the act of *provocatio*, where there is no suggestion of compulsion. The compulsion was not legal, but political. Mommsen

---

[1] Acts xxv. 21.   [2] Acts xxvi. 32.
[3] Acts xxviii. 18-19. Mommsen, *GS*, 443 n. 5.

rightly remarked elsewhere about this passage that a Jew who was a Roman citizen might well be reluctant, on ethnical grounds, to insist overmuch on his Roman privileges.[1] Paul is here defending himself from an implied criticism.

Mommsen remarked that the texts in Acts which mention the appeal of Paul—there are no less than six—do not connect it explicitly with his Roman status.[2] That is true, but there was no necessity to reassert what had been established very circumstantially at the beginning of the inquiry. It is absurd to go further, as Cadbury does, and doubt whether Paul did in fact appeal. He had in mind Paul's assertion when Festus invited him to accept trial at Jerusalem: 'I stand at the tribunal of Caesar, where I ought to be judged.'[3] It is only after this that Paul makes his formal appeal: Καίσαρα ἐπικαλοῦμαι. Mommsen took the earlier statement for a rhetorical version of the appeal formula, but wrongly. The tribunal of the emperor is not the tribunal of the procurator. Festus is more accurate in his statement to Agrippa: 'Paul appealed to be kept for the judgment of Augustus.' Cadbury took the sentence about the tribunal of Caesar literally, to mean that the procurator was the deputy of Caesar and held power as a delegate. Technically that is not true, either in the terminology of the classical lawyers, or in the usage of the late Republic and early Principate. The governor's *imperium* is his own; unlike that of the assistant legate, it is not a *mandata jurisdictio*, though it is subordinate

---

[1] Art. cit. 440.

[2] Ibid. 443. Acts xxv. 10, 11–12, 21, 25–26, 32, xxviii. 19.

[3] Cadbury, Jackson–Lake, v. 319. Acts xxv. 10. Juster, ii. 163 n. 1. went so far as to doubt the appeal of Paul, on the strange ground that Acts does not name the emperor. But why should it? *Caesar* was in common popular usage as the imperial title in this period in the East, as, e.g., Charlesworth, ɪɪɪ. C. 1, 17, N. 13, E–J, nos. 322, 360A, 118, and the usage of Philo indicate; cf. *In Flaccum*, 35, 40, 42, 105.

to the *maius imperium* of the Princeps in the sense that his acts can be cancelled by the latter.[1]

But Cadbury was more right than Mommsen. Paul is objecting not to the jurisdiction of Festus, but to his apparent intention of giving the Jewish clergy excessive influence in his court by transferring the hearing to Jerusalem, even though it is to be ἐπ' ἐμοῦ, i.e. before Festus.[2] A provincial might well regard the governor's tribunal as the tribunal of the Princeps, just as, in the Gospel narratives, the tribute is the tribute of Caesar, though in law it was the tribute of the SPQR. Festus could not hand over his capital jurisdiction, either in earlier or in later usage, to a provincial tribunal such as the Sanhedrin, or to any third party.[3] But nothing prevented him from using the Sanhedrin, or members of it, as his own *consilium*. That is what Paul feared. To avoid it he invoked the right of trial before a court at Rome. One may compare the way in which the younger Pliny very evidently took his cue, in the trial of the Christians, from their enemies.[4]

The transfer of the place of trial is itself quite in order. When first Festus visited Jerusalem after his arrival as governor, the Jewish clergy renewed the complaint against Paul, and requested that he be summoned to Jerusalem. Festus replied that as he himself was going at once to Caesarea, the charges should be made there.[5] Then during the hearing at Caesarea, Festus, presumably prompted by the prosecutors—though the text does not say so precisely— himself suggested a transfer of the case back to Jerusalem.[6]

---

[1] Above, p. 9. Cf. Ulpian, *D.* 1. 18. 4: 'praeses provinciae maius imperium in ea . . . habet omnibus post principem.' Ulpian and others contrast the independent powers of the proconsul with that of the assistant legates 'qui nihil proprium habent', ibid. 13. Cf. i. 16. 1–2; 7. 2; 11–13.

[2] Acts xxv. 9.   [3] Above, p. 4.

[4] Cf. Pliny, *Ep.* x. 96. 5, on the test of malediction: 'quorum nihil cogi posse *dicuntur* qui sunt re vera Christiani.' He himself was totally ignorant of the procedure in these matters, 1, ibid.

[5] Acts xxv. 1–6.   [6] Acts xxv. 9.

This recalls an incident in Pliny's governorship of Bithynia. The philosopher Dion was accused by his political enemies in his native city of Prusa. The accusers asked Pliny to stage the trial in another city for the evident reason that Dio had many friends in Prusa. Pliny at once transferred the case to Nicaea.[1]

The account of the trial before Festus and Felix is then sufficiently accurate in all its details. In its references to *provocatio* it is in accord with what is otherwise known of the practice in the first century A.D. What is equally important is the fact that the author does not confuse *provocatio* with the procedure of the late Empire known as *appellatio*, which is a very different business. In this the author has the advantage over some modern critics. Professor Jones's summary of the difference between the two systems cannot be bettered : 'The lawyers of the third century write of a world in which everyone except a slave is a Roman citizen. Appeal to the emperor is universally allowed—except in the case of notable brigands . . . and ringleaders of sedition—but this appeal is something very different from the old *provocatio*. It may be exercised in either civil or criminal cases in exactly the same form, and is normally made after sentence within two or three days. The judge now tries the case and gives his sentence, and then the condemned party appeals, whereas in the earlier period the judge either did not try the case at all, or at most made a preliminary investigation and left the issue to be decided by the emperor.'[2] So far Jones. In the

---

[1] Pliny, *Ep.* x. 81. 3–4.

[2] 'I appeal', 922, with citation of the basic evidence in the *Digest*, nn. 26–27, e.g. *D*. 49. 9. 1; 5. 2; 13. 1. Also 49. 4. 1. 5–15. See also Mommsen, *D. Pen. R.* ii. 154 ff., for the *appellatio* procedure and for the distinction from the earlier procedure, which he did not develop clearly, ibid. 160 n. 1. Strachan-Davidson, *Problems of the Roman Criminal Law* (Oxford, 1912), ii, ch. xx, confines himself to the later *appellatio*, fails to distinguish the procedure under the *lex Julia*, and has confused Cadbury, op. cit. 312–16. The confusion arises from the fact that the term *appellatio* was also used in con-

basic points the two systems are poles apart. It is apparent that the author of Acts has no knowledge of the later system, which was establishing itself during the second half of the second century. The earliest texts date from the time of Marcus Aurelius, though the complete system belongs to the period after the *constitutio Antoniniana*, which made all free men Romans.

This change goes hand in hand with another great social-political change which also came about during the second century. As the Roman citizenship became ever more widely spread, the privileged class of the Empire ceased to be the Roman citizens, as such. Their place was taken by the *honestiores*; that is, the families of moderate substance from whom the municipal magistrates and the municipal council-lors were chosen. In the final system the *honestiores* retained in a sharpened form the privilege that had once been the right of all Roman citizens—that only the Roman courts could sentence them on a capital charge. This right, which was at first limited to town councillors, decurions, became in time the special privilege of the whole class. This system, which first begins to emerge in the time of Hadrian, is unknown to the author of Acts.[1]

The study of *provocatio* in Acts thus provides a useful chro-nological countercheck in more ways than one. It is worth observing the difference between Acts and the account of the Aurelian persecution at Lyons in the well-known letter preserved by Eusebius.[2] The governor of Lugdunensis did not send the Roman citizens who had been arrested to

nexion with *provocatio* in the Republican procedure—the latter being used of the basic 'appeal to the people' and the former of the request for the intervention of a magistrate.

[1] G. Cardascia, 'L'Apparition dans le droit des classes d'*honestiores* et d'*humiliores*', *Rev. hist. droit. fr.* (1950), 305 ff., 461 ff., is the basic discussion. Cf. Jones, loc. cit. The earlier texts are in *D*. 28. 3. 6. 7; 48. 8. 16; 19. 27. 1–2.

[2] *HE*, v. i. 202, 207.

Rome, but wrote to the emperor about them. Aurelius confirmed the death sentence, which was then carried out in the mild form of execution by the sword. This is half-way towards the later *appellatio* procedure, but differs in that the reference to Aurelius was not due to an appeal by the condemned prisoners, and was based—as was the grading of their punishment—on the status of the prisoners as Roman citizens and not as *honestiores*. The Lyons procedure differs from the earliest procedure similarly in that the prisoners had not actively exercised the right of appeal: in this it is like the procedure followed by Pliny, but differs in that the emperor simply authorizes the trial and execution by the provincial governor on the spot.[1] In Acts we thus have a procedure that fits neatly into an early place in a developing historical series that advances from the Augustan phase through examples in Pliny and Eusebius, drawn from the second century, towards the system of the Late Empire.

[1] The trial and arrest of the first citizen Christian Attalus, before consultation with the emperor, was due to the governor's ignorance of his status. When this was discovered, the legate stopped the impending execution. The main group of citizen martyrs was arrested and tried only after the authorization had arrived from Rome.

Paul and the Cities

MINOR PUNISHMENTS

IN Acts the Roman citizen is still a prominent person. But over one detail of the Roman's privileges there is some confusion—the matter of beating and binding. Paul remarked to the centurion at Jerusalem who was preparing to have him lashed: 'Are you allowed to beat a Roman who has not even been sentenced?' The centurion in turn was alarmed because he had put Paul, a Roman, in chains. So, too, at Philippi the municipal magistrates became alarmed because, in the words of Acts, 'they gave us a public beating though we are Roman citizens, and though we had not been condemned by a court, and cast us into prison'.[1] According to the text of the *lex Iulia*, discussed above, the Roman citizen might not be beaten or bound by a magistrate *adversus provocationem* or by any other person in any circumstances.[2] This should be substantially correct, because the meaning of these texts is so different from the general doctrine of the classical lawyers, for whom immunity from flogging was limited to the class of the *honestiores*.[3] The narrative of Acts agrees with the *lex Iulia* except that it adds the qualification 'uncondemned'. This implies that the provincial authority might administer a flogging

[1] Acts xxii. 25. καὶ ἀκατάκριτον, Acts xvi. 37–39.

[2] Above, pp. 59 f., combining *D.* 48. 6. 8, with the second edict from Cyrene.

[3] Jones, 'I appeal', 922; e.g. *D.* 48. 2. 6; 19. 10. 2, &c., cited ibid., n. 30.

after sentence, presumably in a case in which a Roman citizen had not exercised his right of appeal, or alternately in a special category of cases at present unknown in which the *lex Iulia* did not apply. This second possibility fits one of the exemptions that the author of the *Sententiae Pauli* makes to the absolute rule of the *lex Iulia*. His first exception, discussed earlier, concerned actors. The second was, quite briefly, *iudicati*[1]. This exception does not make sense in the later system of *appellatio*, when appeal could only be made after judgment was given.[2] It therefore belongs, as it should, to the *provocatio* system, and is an exception made to accommodate the working of *provocatio* with practical government, like the other exceptions noted in this section of the *Sententiae*. A magistrate might condemn, and bind and beat, but not execute, for minor offences. This could tie in with the transfer to governors of jurisdiction over selected capital crimes according to the theory of Jones which has already been discussed.[3]

The *Sententiae* gives another exception in the words: 'quod ius dicenti non obtemperaverint quidve contra disciplinam publicam fecerint'. This provided for what the Romans called *contumacia*, flagrant disobedience towards a magistrate giving a legitimate order. There is an example of this in the story of the Sardinians and the proconsul.[4] These exceptions to the *lex Iulia* cannot be dated precisely, though it was argued earlier that the exception for actors was Neronian in its final form, and that the exception of the capital crimes in Jones's theory may also be Neronian. The exception for *contumacia* may underlie the defence put up by certain provincial Romans who were accused of complicity in the

---

[1] *Sent. Pauli*, v. 26. 2: 'hac lege excipiuntur qui artem ludicram faciunt, iudicati etiam et confessi.' The third exception must be of late date, since the Christian confessors of Roman status were referred to Rome under Marcus, above p. 64. [2] Above, p. 68.
[3] Above, p. 61. [4] Above, p. 19.

malpractices of a proconsul in A.D. 100. They excused their actions on the ground of compulsion: 'for they were provincials, and bound by fear to obey every order of the proconsuls'.[1] The fear should be fear of the rods of the proconsul's lictors. He can administer a beating for the disobedience of a direct order.

The second edict of Augustus from Cyrene showed that there was a tendency from early in the Principate to create exceptions, for practical reasons, to the *lex Iulia*.[2] That edict formed a precedent for the chaining of Roman citizens arrested on capital charges which has left some traces in the sources outside Acts. There is the case of Claudius Demianus, sent in chains by a proconsul of Asia to the tribunal of Nero, on an unknown charge, and a parallel example from Pliny's governorship of Bithynia.[3] An extreme instance is the chaining of the consular Valerius Asiaticus when charged with adultery before the tribunal of Claudius.[4] But what had become permissive for a holder of *imperium* would be very questionable for a municipal magistrate.

There are circumstances, then, in which by the latter part of the first century A.D. a Roman might properly be chained or beaten at the orders of a Roman magistrate. The author of Acts in the references under discussion follows the rules of this middle period both against the absolute veto of the original *lex Iulia*, and against the different system of the Late Empire. The centurion was alarmed because he had bound a man against whom there was no formal charge,

---

[1] Pliny, *Ep.* iii. 9. 15.   [2] Above, p. 60.

[3] Tac. *Ann.* xvi. 10. 2. Pliny, *Ep.* x. 57. 2: 'vinctus mitti ad praefectos praetorii mei debet.' This case is difficult to understand unless the man was of citizen status, as Jones suggests (art. cit. 924 n. 37a). But Pliny gives no indication of this in the present state of the text.

[4] Tac. *Ann.* xi. 1. 3. This case was political. C. Silius and the Pisonian conspirators were also tried in chains, ibid. xi. 32. 3; xv. 56. 1, 66. See p. 82 n. 2 on the procedure of arrest *extra ordinem*.

and the magistrates of Philippi because they had summarily
chastised a Roman citizen involved in some kind of civil
disturbance. Both instances were quite out of order in the
original system, with or without trial, but equally permissive under the middle system, on the condition given in
Acts—that there had been a trial. At least, a Roman could,
by the middle period, be sentenced and punished by a provincial governor's court—though certainly not by an ordinary municipal court—either if there was no act of appeal,
or if the charge was under certain sections of the *ordo*.

A very particular question arises over the beating at
Philippi, and the parallel statement in Second Corinthians,
'thrice I was beaten with rods'. Mommsen reasonably
connected this with municipal jurisdiction.[1] Philippi was
a Roman citizen colony, and the magistrates of a Roman
colonia possessed special powers conferred, in the last resort,
by a law of the Roman people. The late Republican system
is well known from the extensive fragments of the charter of
a Roman colony founded at Urso in Spain by Julius Caesar.[2]
This is sound evidence for the system at Philippi, which also
was a foundation of Caesar, extended or re-established by
Augustus.[3] At Urso the sanctions for the rules and laws of
the colony are expressed in monetary fines, which are to be
exacted in the court of the local magistrate. The basic power
of enforcement is the fine and the threat of seizure of property in case of a forfeit. Such seizure is a part of *coercitio*.[4]
The question for Acts is whether the local magistrates of
colonies possessed anything more than this civil *coercitio*.
They were allowed two lictors apiece, and the lictors carried
rods, which presumably could be used in certain circumstances. The magistrates were also allowed the authority of

---

[1] 2 Cor. xi. 25. Mommsen, *GS*, 439.
[2] For the *lex Ursonensis* see A–J, n. 26, or *FIRA*, i, n. 21.
[3] Below, p. 92.　　　　　[4] Mommsen, *D. Pen. R.* i. 41 f.

a military tribune in the Roman army: 'idem ius eademque animadversio . . . uti tribuno militum . . . in exercitu populi Romani'. But this applied only to a military levy used in colonial warfare, not to the control of the ordinary citizenry. There is no other evidence at Urso of magisterial *coercitio*.[1] It is extremely unlikely that the municipal court even of a Roman colony, which was a privileged organization, had the power to inflict severe punishments.[2] A general rule given by Ulpian forbids municipal magistrates to put slaves to death, while permitting a *modica castigatio*; whether the latter refers to slaves or free men is not clear.[3] This seems to be the sum of evidence about *coloniae Romanae* apart from that of Acts itself.

It is probable that for the purpose of keeping the peace local magistrates of privileged communities such as *coloniae* were allowed a minor degree of police-court jurisdiction in the early empire. Certain peregrine communes possessed such power. This was certainly the case with the category of privileged non-Roman communities, known as 'free states' and 'federated states'.[4] Equally the Sanhedrin of Jerusalem had at least the power of inflicting the 'thirty-nine stripes', though this may be a special case.[5] A certain example of an ordinary provincial commune where the magistrates had the power of castigation is Caesarea itself, according to Josephus' account of the measures taken by the local authority

---

[1] *lex Urson.* 62, 103.

[2] In *lex Urson.* 102 the accusations before the municipal *quaestio* should concern offences against the rules of the local constitution (cf. ibid. 91, 123) in so far as these were not covered by the provisions for *actio petitio persecutio* before a *iudicium recuperatorium* (cf. ibid. 125–6, 129–31). Mommsen, *D. Pen. R.* i. 262, admits that the obscure municipal *iudicia publica*, if concerned with crimes, inflicted only fines by a recuperatorial procedure.

[3] *D.* 2. 1. 12.   [4] Below, p. 36.

[5] Above, p. 40. Juster, op. cit. ii. 161 with full citations. 2 Cor. xi. 25 might refer to the jurisdiction of local sanhedrins of the Diaspora, cf. Mommsen, *GS*, 439.

to quell a riot between Jewish and Greek inhabitants: 'the governors of the city were concerned to keep all quiet, and whenever they caught those who were most for fighting on either side they punished them with stripes and bonds'.[1] This may prove the case *a fortiori* for a Roman colony; Caesarea was an unprivileged city and under the immediate eye of the governor.

Any such police powers were strictly limited and did not extend to serious crimes. In a passage from Philostratus the sophist Polemo reminds the magistrates of Smyrna, an ordinary provincial city, that they should not concern themselves with crimes such as murder, sacrilege, and adultery, but only with those for which the penalty was a fine.[2] This passage also shows that the civic authorities were capable of disregarding the limits to their powers. It is notable that in the later second century quite minor criminal jurisdiction found its way to the governor's tribunal. The lawyers speak of informal jurisdiction *de plano* in matters of *levia crimina* which a proconsul might settle out of hand with a beating. These included such minor matters that it is difficult to believe that any real power of correction was left to local courts in the later period.[3] Hence Acts is certainly not reproducing the system of a later age in implying in several places that the local courts could inflict certain minor personal punishments. The narrative agrees with the evidence of the earlier period that a Roman citizen of any social class was protected against a casual beating (without trial), whereas the *humiliores* of the late empire had lost this protection.[4]

[1] *BJ*, ii. 13. 7.   [2] Phil. *VS*, i. 25. 2 (p. 532).

[3] *D*. 48. 2. 6. Serious charges included minor thefts, as of small objects from shipwrecks (Pius, 47. 9. 1. 5), accidental movement of boundary marks (ibid. 21. 2), street brawling (48. 19. 28. 3), impropriety of freedmen to patrons (37. 14. 1 : this not specifically *de plano*). Cf. Mommsen, *D. Pen. R.* i. 265, iii. 335; *GS*, 439.

[4] Cf. Jones, 'I appeal', 922 n. 30, with *Sent. Pauli*, v. 21. 1, and *D*. 50. 2. 2. 2

Power of expulsion

Mommsen objected to the suggestion in the account of
Paul's adventures at Philippi that the local magistrates, in
ordering the release of Paul and Silas, ordered their expulsion from the city.[1] This implies that they possessed something akin to the governor's power of *relegatio*, expulsion
from the province. The wording of Acts does not quite bear
out Mommsen's interpretation. 'Do they now secretly cast us
out? Let them come in person and escort us out of the city.'
The original message given by the gaoler was: 'The magistrates have ordered your release. Now come out and go in
peace.' Finally the magistrates came in person and begged
Paul and Silas to leave the city. Mommsen is too sharp with
the author here. Doubtless the local magistrates, far from
the eye of authority, were capable of exceeding their powers.
The Sardinian affair showed the difficulty with which governors enforced the respect for law on local authorities in other
provinces.[2] In Pliny's Letters to Trajan there are other
examples of the violation of municipal statutes and proconsular edicts by civic authorities.[3] But the only precise
parallel to the affair at Philippi comes from a late source,
the *Sententiae Pauli*, on the treatment of itinerant seers or
soothsayers, 'Primum fustibus caesi civitate pelluntur'. 'The
custom is to give them a beating and drive them out of the
city.' Only if they persist are they formally put on trial.[4]

as clear instances. Some of Jones's examples refer to condemned persons, but
Roman citizens were flogged without trial in the *Acta S. Perpetuae*, *c.* A.D.
203; Jones, art. cit. 928.

[1] Mommsen, *GS*, 440. Acts xvi. 35–39.

[2] Above, p. 19. [3] Pliny, *Ep.* x. 31. 114. 3.

[4] *Sent. Pauli*, v. 21. 1. This text distinguishes clearly between expulsion
from a city and relegation from a province. Mommsen hesitated to maintain that even an Italian municipality had the power of expulsion from its
own territory, in the Republican period. Cf. *D. Pen. R.* i. 264 n. 3, citing
obscure implications of *Tab. Her.* 118. 119.

But this usage cannot be brought down, in evidence, to an earlier age.

CIVIC INDICTMENTS AND CIVIC GOVERNMENTS

Next for consideration come the judicial adventures of Paul outside Judaea, that is, in chronological order, at Philippi and Thessalonica before municipal authorities, before the proconsul Gallio at Corinth, and before the municipal authorities at Ephesus.[1] These are the detailed narratives, but before the affair at Philippi Paul had already been involved in a clash with municipal authorities at Antioch-by-Pisidia and at Iconium.[2] On these occasions the details are too slight to permit a separate investigation. At Antioch the Jewish community secured the help of 'the first men of the city' in driving Paul and Barnabas away, but there is no suggestion that this was done by magisterial action. At Iconium there is mention of the 'rulers of the people', that is, of the non-Jewish element, co-operating in a demonstration against Paul and Barnabas. This is a somewhat non-technical term, but may mean the annual magistrates. The apostles depart voluntarily. The general atmosphere of the narrative recalls that of the riots between Jews and Hellenes at Alexandria, in which the gymnasiarchs of the city played a leading role.[3]

The affair at Philippi is more revealing.[4] It is the first clash between the apostles and non-Jewish interests involving the ordinary citizens of a commune, which was in fact a Roman colony. Hence it is natural that the clash takes the

---

[1] Acts xvi. 19–40, xvii. 6–10, xviii. 12–17, xix. 24–40.

[2] Acts xiii. 50, xiv. 5.

[3] Cf. H. I. Bell, *JRS* xxxi (1941), 1 ff., 'Antisemitism in Roman Alexandria', with Philo, *In Flaccum*, generally.

[4] Acts xvi. 19–40.

form, not of a riot, as at Iconium or Antioch, where the quarrel was within the Jewish community, but of a formal indictment before the municipal magistrates. The power of local magistrates to administer limited personal punishments has already been discussed.[1] There remains the question of the charge. This is given in the remarkable form: 'these men who are Jews disturb our city and introduce—καταγγέλλουσι—customs which it is not allowed to us Romans to adopt and practice'. There are two distinct, though connected, charges here—the causing of riots and the introduction of an alien religion. The second charge is remarkable for what one may call its archaic form. This is not the place for yet another discussion of the rather hackneyed theme of the relation between the Roman State and foreign cults.[2] All Roman historians are aware of the dualism that typifies Roman policy in this matter. Officially the Roman citizen may not practise any alien cult that has not received the public sanction of the State, but customarily he might do so as long as his cult did not otherwise offend against the laws and usages of Roman life, i.e. so long as it did not involve political or social crimes. The Julio-Claudian period was characterized by general laxity towards foreign cults, which spread freely in Italy and Rome. But this laxity is occasionally interrupted by a sharp reversal of policy when the extravagances of a particular sect call down a temporary and ill-enforced ban upon its activities. This is notable in connexion with Druids, Magians, and devotees of Isis. The grounds of such bans, however, are found, not in the general principle of excluding alien cults as such, but in the criminal by-products of the cults: the *scelera* or *flagitia cohaerentia nomini*, as Pliny puts the matter in his

[1] Above, pp. 74 f.
[2] *JTS*, n.s. iii. (1952), 194 ff., contains my own views, to which I have nothing to add.

letter about the Christians of Pontus.[1] This is the general picture of the age, with which no historian seriously disagrees.[2]

What is remarkable in the charges against Paul at Philippi is that the dormant principle of incompatibility is revived against an alien sect: 'they introduce customs which we being Romans may not adopt'. The latest known exposition of this principle was that of Livy in the speech which he attributes to the Roman consul in charge of the famous inquiry into the Bacchanalian scandal of the second century B.C.[3] This speech gives Augustan authority for the reassertion of the ancient principle, though the speech as a whole devotes much more attention to the theme of associated crimes as the grounds of objection to the cult. S. L. Guterman tried in his book on the theme to make out a case for the occasional revival of the original principle in the Julio-Claudian period.[4] The clearest example is the banning of Druidism to Roman citizens under Augustus and Tiberius, before it was generally suppressed because of its horrid practices by Claudius. But even in the sporadic examples from which Guterman argued, the principle hardly appears in isolation, or even as the main ground of intervention or suppression. That is the peculiarity of the text in Acts. It is not because of the depravity of the practices introduced by Paul, but because of their un-Roman character, that the magistrates are urged to intervene. The associated charge of 'causing disturbances' is not presented as a *cohaerens scelus*, as in nearly all the other instances.

[1] Pliny, *Ep.* x. 96. 2.

[2] Cf. art. cit. 200, 207, with H. M. Last, *JRS* xxvii (1937), 80 ff. 'The study of the persecutions', as a characteristic exposition.

[3] Livy, 39. 16. 8–9, esp. 'iudicabant . . . nihil aeque dissolvendae religionis esse quam ubi non patrio sed externo ritu sacrificaretur'.

[4] S. L. Guterman, *Religious Toleration and Persecution in Ancient Rome* (London, 1951), esp. 27–48.

There is also a strong hint that the accusers are aware of the recent efforts of the emperor Claudius to discourage the spread of Judaism, evinced by his expulsion of the Jewish community from Rome: 'these men, being Jews, introduce customs, &c.'. This is all the more surprising in that there was no *positive veto* on Jewish proselytism under Claudius, or ever, not even after the Jewish rebellion. Professor Momigliano, in his very judicious summary of the Jewish policy of the emperor Claudius—in his book about Claudius—assumes, as many others have done before and since, that the Roman policy of toleration towards the Jewish folk and cult was balanced by an objection to proselytism.[1] This is probably true in general terms. But whether there was any precise enactment against proselytism is less certain, in default of positive evidence. Momigliano himself merely cites Mommsen's famous article on the religious policy of Rome, which does not attempt to prove anything so positive. Considering the very large numbers of Jews who became Roman citizens, and of Roman citizens, including persons of high station, who became Jews or half-Jews—the class known as οἱ εὐσεβεῖς—it seems unlikely that there was any precise rule about proselytism.[2] The usual Roman practice was to punish persons who joined undesirable sects when they became

---

[1] A. Momigliano, *Claudius the Emperor and his Achievement* (Oxford, 1934), 29 ff.

[2] The existence of the supposed rule has been freely assumed, cf., e.g., Cadbury, op. cit., appendix xxv. S. L. Guterman, op. cit. 106. But the evidence commonly cited proves little. Only Dio, 57. 18. 5a—which is merely a citation from John of Antioch—mentions proselytism: 'as many Jews were settling in Rome and converting many of the natives to their customs, he [Tiberius] expelled most of them'. Nothing in Tacitus' version (*Ann.* ii. 85) or in Suetonius' (*Tib.* 36. *Claud.* 25. 4) suggests a legal bar of this sort. Dio, 60. 6. 6, describing Claudius' veto on public assemblage, says nothing about proselytism. There is no sign of such a rule even after the first Jewish rebellion. The charges against Roman citizen converts under Domitian were on the older principle of incompatibility. Dio, 67. 14. 2; 68. 1. 2. The text in Suet. *Dom.* 12. 2,

objectionable for one reason or another. The only sect known to have been punished for giving instruction, as it were, was that of the fortune-telling Magi. But their case was different. In their consultations they did not turn their clients into Magi, but practised the black arts on behalf of their clients.[1]

The formulation of the charge against Paul at Philippi, then, so far from being anachronistic is positively archaic. But though it is unusual, it is not entirely unparalleled in Julio-Claudian usage. It is perhaps characteristic that it is in an isolated Roman community in the Greek half of the Roman empire that the basic principle of Roman 'otherness' should be affirmed, whereas in Italy the usual custom prevailed of treating alien cults on their merits.

The procedure followed at Philippi is in good order. Private accusers make the charge. The magistrates arrest the accused,[2] and had the case not been abandoned, the next step would have been the dispatch and arraignment of

refers only to those who tried to dodge the poll tax by failing to register as Jews and were prosecuted for that; *CAH*, xi. 42, n. 2. The classical lawyers, as represented by *D*. 48. 8. 11 pr. (Modestinus) and the late *Sententiae Pauli*, v. 22. 3, know at most a rule against the circumcision of Romans, which was in intention not against proselytism but against its by-product. Characteristically the surgeon was liable to punishment for the offence against the person. In the fuller of the two texts Jews were liable to punishment only in the case of circumcision of slaves; the rule aimed at the protection of the person of the slave, who had no choice, unlike the free man, who was punished for his own act. This rule dates back to Pius, and possibly to Hadrian (*SHA Hadr.* 14), i.e. to the time of the second revolt. But the earliest trace of a rule against proselytism as such is only under Severus (*SHA Sept. Sev.* 17). See now E. M. Smallwood, *Cl. Phil.* (1956), 1 ff.

[1] Cf. Ulpian's discussion, *Coll.* xv. 1. Suet. *Tib.* 36 and Dio, 57. 15. 8, confirm.

[2] They treat him as a *peregrinus*. Arrest is typical of *cognitio extra ordinem*, but not essential. Men of substance give sureties for appearance, but the most exalted are not required to do even this. Vagrants and *humiliores* were kept in chains, or prison, or under military guard until trial. Ulpian, *D*. 48. 3. 1. This can be traced back through texts of Pius and Hadrian to Domitian (ibid. 2. 1; 3; 12), and may be derived from a law of the *ordo*

the prisoner before the proconsul, either at the capital of the province, or at the nearest assize city.[1]

It is convenient next to discuss the activities at Ephesus, where the circumstances and technicalities are similar.[2] The party hostile to Paul and his friends is again non-Jewish—the master silversmith Demetrius, who organizes what appears to be an unofficial meeting of the city assembly.[3] The object of Demetrius appears to be to put pressure on the civic authorities to take action against the apostolic group. The official known as the Clerk of the People, whom we may call Town Clerk for convenience and who was the elected head of the city executive, puts in an appearance. He duly refers the contestants either to the proconsular assizes, if they have a private judicial dispute—εἰ ἔχουσι πρός τινα λόγον—or to the regular assembly of the city, if they are after something more than a private lawsuit—εἰ . . . τι περαιτέρω ἐπιζητεῖτε.[4] The quarrel concerned a matter of property in the first place—alleged interference with the sale of silver models of the great temple of Diana.[5] According to the clerk, no specific charges of impiety had been made, but Demetrius was alleging that in some way the prestige of the city was being attacked.[6] This is the 'further matter' which might be brought up at what the clerk calls a 'regular assembly'.

The whole affair is very reminiscent of the description of

(ibid. 2. 1). For the gradual limitation of the Roman's immunity from arrest by the *imperium*-holder see p. 73 (nn. 3–4). Most of these procedures can be detected in Pliny's administration, *Ep.* x. 29, 57. 2; 74. 81, 96, 4–5.

[1] Cf. *D.* 48.3.6.1, from the standing provincial *mandata* of Hadrian and Pius.

[2] Acts xix. 24–40. For the older bibliography on Paul and Ephesus—largely derivative—see Jackson–Lake, op. cit. iv. 19, 23 n.

[3] Below, pp. 87 f.   [4] Acts xix. 38–39.

[5] Acts xix. 25–27. For an alternative opinion about the silver shrines see below, pp. 90 f.

[6] Cf. ibid. and 37.

popular agitation in the civic speeches of Dio of Prusa, delivered between *c.* A.D. 96 and 106. There is the same atmosphere of indignant defence of the city's privileges and reputation. 'We are in danger of being blamed for today's uproar, for which there is no excuse', says the town clerk, 'and we won't find it easy to explain the agitation.' Many parallels could be cited from Dio, but the following are characteristic. 'These riots will be reported to the proconsul. Nothing that goes on in the cities escapes the notice of the governors.' 'The proconsul has permitted the city assembly to renew its meetings, because he knows that we will not abuse the right . . . we must behave well and put off our petition. . . . The proconsul is leaving tomorrow but will return later. Then we shall have an opportunity to make our speeches and demands.' 'Our behaviour is ridiculed at Rome and regarded as the folly of Greeks.'[1] The themes may differ: Dio's most characteristic speeches are about inter-city rivalry and concord between the orders of society.[2] But the tone is unmistakable.

There is something rather ominous in this tone. This was the last age of civic autonomy in the ancient world. Civic politics in the old pattern of the city-state, with its assemblies and councils, expired in the course of the later second and early third centuries A.D. The city councils became closed hereditary oligarchies. The stages of this decay can be traced in the great books of Rostovtzeff—*The Social and Economic History of the Roman Empire*—and A. H. M. Jones, *The Greek City*. The scene enacted at Ephesus could not have taken place in the third or fourth century A.D. The reference to the 'regular assembly', ἔννομος ἐκκλησία, is

---

[1] Dio Chrys. *Or.* 46. 14, 48. 1–3 (summarized), 38. 38. The dates of the speeches are not precisely known, but they belong to the decade after the death of Domitian.

[2] *Or.* 38, 41, 48. Also his harangue to Paul's own Tarsus, *Or.* 34.

valuable. The city assemblies were on the way out. Roman policy aimed over a long period at the elimination of the democratic element, both in the assemblies and in the councils. Dio's reference to the suspension of the civic assembly at Prusa, noted earlier, is characteristic. No such fate has yet overtaken the civic assembly at Ephesus, but the town clerk has his fears. The scene belongs unmistakably to an era that did not survive the age of the Antonines. In most cities the centre of gravity had shifted from the assembly to the council long before that. For civic policy to have been seriously debated in open assembly, as suggested by the town clerk of Ephesus, must have been rare in the mid-second century, when, as Professor Jones has demonstrated, the 'vote of the people' was generally an automatic endorsement of the decree of the town council. In Dio's orations the council appears as the principal organ of Prusa. It is marked as a rare occasion by Dio, when a new town building-scheme is formally approved at a public meeting of the people, specially convened—be it noted—by the proconsul.[1]

The evidence of Acts not only agrees in general with the civic situation in Asia Minor in the first and early second centuries A.D., but falls into place in the earlier rather than the later phase of development. This is not a subject in which fixed dates can be assigned. But the evidence for the civic institutions of Ephesus suggests that in the second century the initiation of policy depended on the council. The city was controlled by the council, and the council was controlled largely by the annual *strategoi* and town clerk, who alone could put proposals to the vote. By the time of Hadrian, for example, the election of councillors by the

---

[1] Ibid. 45, 15. For the decline of the assemblies see Jones, *Greek City*, ch. xi, esp. 179, 181. A useful *terminus a quo* for this process in one region of Asia Minor is given by Strabo's account of the struggle between democratic and anti-democratic forces in the assembly of Tarsus itself, in which the latter prevailed, led by a protégé of Augustus. Strabo, xiv. 5. 14, pp. 674–5.

assembly had become a formality.[1] The title of 'magistrate, council and people' persists in the protocol of Ephesus, but the inscriptions of the first half of the second century show that the council had effective power, though its proposals still required formal ratification of the assembly as late as A.D. 160.[2]

The prominence accorded to the town clerk in Acts fits the fairly copious evidence about this office at Ephesus and other cities of Asia Minor.[3] In general the γραμματεὺς τοῦ δήμου or γ. τῆς βουλῆς was the chief administrative assistant, annually elected, of the magistrates; he had a staff of permanent clerks, responsible for the paper work of the city. In the decrees of Ephesus, where the civic administration is well documented, he appears in conjunction with the *strategoi* as a senior partner, acting as the director of affairs in council or assembly. The People's Clerk is given his name and titles in city decrees while the *strategoi*, whom he has effectively supplanted, are not distinguished by name. He appears on the city coinage from the time of Augustus as the chief magistrate. On one document he is even named along with the proconsul of the year as if he were the eponymous magistrate.[4] This superiority of the clerk over the *strategoi* was not appreciated in the Jackson–Lake *Commentary* on Acts.[5] All this is well documented in a long series of inscriptions of A.D. 103–4 about the benefactions of a Roman knight called Vibius Salutaris.[6] There was a second clerk at

[1] Jones, *Greek City*, 179 n. 44, 184 n. 54. A–J, n. 85 (Ditt. *Syll.*[3] 838). Earlier, E .L. Hicks, *Inscr. B.M.* iii. 2. 71 ff., who was among the *fortes ante Agamemnona*.

[2] A–J, n. 98 (A.D. 138–9), n. 71, ll. 360–3. Ditt. *Syll.*[3], ii, n. 867, l. 45 (A–J, n. 105), A.D. 160.

[3] Jones, op. cit. 238–9 nn. 52–53.

[4] See A–J, n. 78 100 (Ditt. *Syll.*[3] 833, 849). *OGIS*, 493.6. *Greek Coins, Ionia*, s.v. 'Ephesus', Augustan series, 197 f.

[5] Op. cit. iv. 19. 35 n.

[6] Hicks, op. cit. iii. 2 n. 481, for the full text.

Ephesus called Clerk of the Council, but he is less prominent. In the early third century the two offices were merged
in that of the Sole Clerk, ὁ μόνος γραμματεύς.[1]

Thus the Clerk of the People was the official whom the
silversmiths would naturally approach first with their complaint. It was right, too, that the silversmiths should march
with their supporters into the theatre, because the Great
Theatre of Ephesus was the regular meeting-place of the
assembly. It is named as such in one of the inscriptions of
Salutaris.[2] The author of Acts is very well informed about
the finer points of municipal institutions at Ephesus in the
first and second centuries A.D. He even uses the correct
technical term ἔννομος ἐκκλησία to distinguish the regularly
appointed meetings of the people from the present con-
course.[3] This term is known from two other Hellenistic
cities, and turns up at Ephesus in the inscriptions of Salutaris in the phrase κατὰ πᾶσαν νόμιμον ἐκκλησίαν.[4] According to the latest restoration of the main document (l. 54)
there was one special monthly meeting called ἱερὰ καὶ
νόμιμος ἐκκλησία. Chrysostom in his Commentary said that
there were three monthly meetings.[5] Presumably there was
one regular and two extra meetings a month. So, too, in
Athens there were in the fourth century B.C. one κυρία
ἐκκλησία, or stated general meeting, and three other

[1] Cf. Hicks, op. cit. iii. 2. 71–81, still the best account of the magistracies
of Ephesus. For the late single Clerk see *Forschungen in Ephesus* (Vienna,
1906–51), iii, n. 70; iv (3), n. 36.

[2] *OGIS*, 480. 9. Probably the civic offices were housed in or near the
theatre. The hall of Hestia Boulaia, some distance from the theatre, recently identified as the Prytaneum (F. Miltner, *Ephesus*, Vienna, 1958, 15)
or office of the executive committee of the council, seems too small for the
main council chamber, since the council of Ephesus numbered 450 members.
Jones, op. cit., ch. xi, n. 40. Hicks, op. cit. iii. 2. 73.   [3] Acts xix. 39.

[4] Early, at Demetrias, *c.* 100 B.C. Ditt. *Syll.*[3] 1157, 50. In A.D. 149 at
Thera, ibid. 852, 20. For Ephesus, Hicks, op. cit. iii. 2 n. 481, ll. 339–40.

[5] *Forschungen*, ii, nn. 27, 53. John Chrys. *Hom.* 42. 2. Cf. Jackson–Lake,
ad xix. 39.

assemblies in each period of five weeks. The proceedings at
Ephesus are not quite so disorderly as might at first sight
appear. The town clerk is in control, and his authority is
recognized. Hence the statement—'saying this he dismissed
the assembly'—can be seen to have a technical under-
current. The meeting is an assembly, but not a regular or
νόμιμος ἐκκλησία. The town clerk simply asks Demetrius to
put off the question for a few days. The very language in
which the clerk refers to the abiding fame of the great
temple and cult of Diana, as a thing not easily to be shaken,
can be illustrated by the wording of a decree of the year
A.D. 160, about the honours of Artemis: 'The divine Artemis, [is] patron of our city, which she has made more
glorious than all other cities through her own divinity, both
among Hellenes and barbarians, so that everywhere shrines
and holy places are dedicated to her, &c.'.[1] So, too, the clerk
of Ephesus in Acts: 'Who is there in the world that does not
know that the city of Ephesus is warden of the temple of the
great Artemis . . . since all this is without dispute it is proper
for us to be calm, &c.'[2]

The use of the term 'warden of Artemis' here—νεώκορος
Ἀρτέμιδος—has attracted attention. In the imperial inscriptions of the second century the term is frequently used in the
phrase ν. τῶν Σεβαστῶν, 'Warden of the Emperors', or δῆμος
(or πόλις) νεώκορος, to indicate that Ephesus, like other
great cities of Asia Minor, had charge of a temple of the
imperial cult, under the authority of the provincial council
of Asia.[3] Similarly the term appears on civic coins of Ephesus
from the time of Trajan, though a generation later than on

---

[1] Ditt. *Syll.*[3] 867, 29 f. The version in the text is a paraphrase.

[2] Acts xix. 35–36.

[3] Cf. originally, Hicks, op. cit. iii. 2, pp. 164–7. For the history of the
successive grants of the title 'twice warden', &c., see J. Keil, *Num. Zeitschr.*
xlviii. 125 ff. For the imperial neocorate generally, V. Chapot, *La Province
romaine d'Asie*, &c., ch. iii.

provincial coins.[1] The application of the term to the wardenship of the great temple of Diana is not attested outside
Acts in the first two centuries A.D., as Professor L. R. Taylor
rightly noted in her appendix to the *Acts Commentary*, though
the imperial neocorate is very frequent in inscriptions from
Trajan onwards.[2] The connexion with Artemis is now known
on a few third-century inscriptions in honour of the Severan
dynasty. But in these it is merely an extension of the phrase
v. τῶν Σεβαστῶν; for the title 'thrice warden' is carefully
explained as including the wardenship of Artemis in an
inscription of Caracalla.[3] Hence the late inscriptions do
not illustrate the usage in Acts. This harks back to the
much earlier usage, first documented in 333 B.C., of the
title Warden of Artemis for the actual civic temple-keepers
of Ephesus.[4]

Nothing has yet been said about the Asiarchs, who advised

[1] See below, n. 4.

[2] Jackson–Lake, op. cit. v. 255. For the normal usage cf. *OGIS*, 481 (*c.*
A.D. 105), 493. 2 (Pius), 496. 7 (Pius). Hicks, op. cit., nn. 499–500 (Trajanic). Keil, art. cit. 130, dates the first neocorate of Ephesus from Claudius;
but see n. 4.

[3] *S.E.G.* iv. 523 (A.D. 244). *CIG* 2972. Cf. the inscription cited in Ditt.
Syll.[3] 867 n. 4. Keil, art. cit.

[4] Ibid. i. 282. A wardenship of Artemis is attested at Magnesia in 143
and 139 B.C., ibid. 679. 30–31, 685. 2. It is notable that in the imperial
inscriptions of Ephesus the title *δῆμος νεώκορος* is used rather differently
from *πόλις νεώκορος τῶν Σεβαστῶν*. Often there is no immediate or obvious
reference to the imperial cult; the form *δῆμος νεώκορος τῶν Σεβαστῶν* never
appears. Cf. esp. *OGIS*, 481. Hicks, nn. 499, 500. *Forschungen*, ii, n. 27 (i.
viii–x), iii, n. 60, iv, n. 33. Possibly the title reflects an original popular usage
in connexion with Artemis alone, with whose cult that of *Augustus et Roma*
was later associated. But in imperial usage the term has been adapted and
commonly appears in the double phrase *ἡ φιλοσεβαστὸς βουλὴ καὶ ὁ νεώκορος
δῆμος*. The relative lack of city decrees of the pre-Trajanic period leaves the
development uncertain. But it is noteworthy that the title *νεώκορος* appears
on the civic coins of Ephesus only from Trajan onwards, though it appears
on provincial proconsular coinage first in A.D. 65–66. *Greek Coins,
Ionia*, 76 n. Thus the usage in Acts fits the chronology of the formal documents. At the dramatic date the title might still primarily refer to the
wardenship of Artemis.

Paul not to appear before the Assembly, because they have been frequently discussed, and because, though they were a characteristic feature of the political scene, the reference is not specific. Asiarchs would be found at Ephesus, the capital city of Asia, at any time in the first four centuries A.D. The title either designates the annual presidents, and perhaps the ex-presidents, of the provincial council of Asia, or it also covers the administrators of the various temples of the imperial cult, which were under the charge of high-priests appointed by the provincial council, or it may merely designate the city deputies to that council.[1] The brief mention adds little to the pattern, except to indicate that Paul had wealthy and powerful friends at Ephesus. The one detail of significance is the use of the plural. This agrees with a brief reference in Strabo to the Asiarchs of Tralles as a group; Strabo was writing only a generation before the dramatic date of this story.[2] If the author of Acts had not known the peculiarities of the organization of Asia, he might well have made an error. In some other eastern provinces the corresponding title went only with the office of President of the Council. There was only one Lyciarch, and only one Pontarch or Bithyniarch.[3]

Considering the accuracy of Acts about Ephesus, the old suggestion of E. L. Hicks about Demetrius and his temple models gains weight.[4] Demetrius is described as ἀργυρο-κόπος ποιῶν ναοὺς ἀργυροῦς Ἀρτέμιδος. Nothing is known archaeologically about such 'silver temples', though models in pottery of holy buildings and effigies are familiar.[5] Hence,

[1] Chapot, op. cit. 468 ff. Ross–Taylor in Jackson–Lake, op. cit. v. 256 ff. Brandis, *RE*, iii. 539, (S) iv. 932 n. 4, 933, prefers the last explanation.

[2] Strabo, xiv. 1. 42, p. 649.

[3] Ibid., pp. 664–5, is definitive for the Lyciarchs in our period. Brandis reduces all to deputies, against the evidence.

[4] Acts xix. 24. Hicks, *Expositor*, i (1890), 401 ff.

[5] John Chrysostom in his commentary was puzzled by the silver temples,

Hicks suggested that the original source used the term ὁ νεοποιός, and that the Acts text represents a misunderstanding of this term. This is the technical term used in the Roman period for the officials elected by the city tribes of Ephesus to supervise the fabric of the great temple.[1] In an inscription of the early Hellenistic period the νεωποῖαι, as they were then called, appear also as introducing temple business to the city council; the latter fact was missed by L. R. Taylor in her appendix to the *Acts Commentary*.[2] It adds an extra touch of plausibility to the suggestion of Hicks. The νεοποιός was precisely the right official to bring to the attention of the town clerk any irregularity touching the cult of Artemis. But all this rests on a conjecture. Ramsay disputed it, perhaps rightly.[3] The man who knew about the unusual functions of the clerk and the rules of the regular assembly at Ephesus should have known about the officer of works. Besides, it is not surprising that no models in precious metal have survived from antiquity. Demetrius may still be a maker of temple models.

Another part of Hicks's case is, however, somewhat stronger now than then. Hicks suggested with some temerity that the Demetrius of Acts might be identified with a particular Demetrius known from an Ephesian inscription, who was a νεοποιός.[4] Though the dating of undated inscriptions of the imperial age is not an exact science, Hicks dated this document to the first century A.D. on one sound argument, the lack of any personal Roman names in a long list of citizens of

Jackson–Lake, op. cit. *ad* 19. 24. The use of large silver images of Artemis is well attested, cf. *OGIS*, 480. 7. *Forschungen*, ii, n. 27 (ii).

[1] Hicks, *Inscr. B.M.* iii. 2. 80 f.

[2] Ditt. *Syll.*[3] 353–4. For their executive duties, *OGIS*, 9. 5, 10. 16. Jackson–Lake, op. cit. iv. 254–5.

[3] For this old controversy see the references collected in Jackson–Lake, op. cit. v. 255 n. 3.

[4] Hicks, op. cit. iii. 2, pp. 208–9, and n. 578.

Ephesus, but partly on stylistic grounds, which cannot give a close approximation. It was thought to be a serious objection to this date that one of the six subdivisions of the tribes of Ephesus, known as 'Thousands' or *Chiliastys*, is given the name *Pius* in this inscription. When later evidence produced the names *Neronieus* and *Claudieus* for other Thousands, it seemed certain that the *Chiliastys Pius* took its name from that emperor, too late for Hicks's theory. But the multiplication of evidence from Ephesus proves that his document must be at least pre-Flavian.[1] So there is still a possibility that Hicks was right in his guess about Demetrius.

Acts does not show such detailed knowledge of any other city as of Ephesus. Philippi, as is well known, was a Roman veteran colony of the early Augustan period, possibly, to judge by its double name, Julia Augusta, first founded by Caesar the dictator.[2] In the affair at Philippi the general atmosphere is that of a Roman municipality in the Greek-speaking part of the Empire.[3] But the magisterial title used in Acts is the somewhat colourless term οἱ στρατηγοί.[4] The senior magistrates of a Roman colony of the late Republican period or later were called *duoviri iuri dicundo*. This title appears on the local coins of Corinth, another colony of the same period.[5] Στρατηγός is commonly used as the Greek equivalent of *praetores* in Graeco-Roman historians. The term *praetor* had been used in certain Roman colonies in Italy of the late second and early first centuries B.C. But it was already going out of fashion and becoming an archaism by the year 63 B.C. This is indicated by a passage in Cicero's speech *de lege agraria*.[6] Hence Acts can claim no credit for

---

[1] *Forschungen*, i. 76 n. 5, iv, nn. 31–32. Cf. J. Keil, *Jahresh. d. öst. Inst.* xvi (1913), 246 n. 7.

[2] Dio, 51. 4. 6, for the Augustan colonization. For the Caesarean colony, see M. Grant, *From Imperium to Auctoritas*, 274–5.   [3] Above, pp. 74, 80.

[4] Acts xvi. 22.   [5] *Greek Coins, Corinth*, xxxiii f.

[6] Sherwin-White, *Roman Citizenship*, 83 f. Cicero, *de leg. ag.* ii. 92–93.

calling the magistrates of Philippi στρατηγοί. The suggestion, still maintained in the *Acts Commentary*, that Acts is
translating *praetores* will not do. The author is simply using
the commonest Hellenistic title to render the untranslatable
term *duoviri*.

If Acts gains no credit for the *strategoi* of Philippi, the
author ought to be allowed full marks for his description of
the city as πρώτη τῆς μερίδος Μακεδονίας πόλις κολωνία.[1]
The *Acts Commentary* has dealt adequately with the administrative technicality. The survival of the four regiones
into which Macedonia was divided by the Romans after its
final conquest, and the use of the term μέρις πρώτη, &c., for
these districts is proved by an inscription of the Flavian
period.[2] There is also evidence in Livy that Philippi was in
the first district.[3] The text of Acts ought then, as Cadbury
argues, to be asserting that the Roman colony Philippi was
a city of the first region of Macedonia. As it stands the text
does not make clear sense. The suggestion is not so much
that the text should be amended, as that the proper phrase
τῆς πρώτης μερίδος Μακεδονίας πόλις was misunderstood and
hence garbled at an early date into πρώτη τῆς μερίδος. Cadbury fails to clinch his argument because he did not observe
that the subdivision of a province into official regiones of this
sort was very rare outside Macedonia. The four regiones of
Macedonia were genuine sub-provinces with a separate
regional council or συνέδριον for each district. The mention
of the districts suggests the eye-witness. In other provinces
there was a grouping of the cities into judicial *conventus* or
assize districts; such cities used a particular centre for their

[1] Acts xvi. 12. Jackson–Lake, ad loc.
[2] The evidence for the regions and the κοινόν of Macedonia has recently
been reviewed by several hands. The basic inscription is now available in
SEG, xvi, n. 391, with bibliography. Cf. esp. Larsen, *Cl. Phil.* (1945), 67;
(1949), 88. Earlier *RE*, xiv (i), 763 f., 767 f.
[3] Livy, 45. 29. 5–6, 'between Strymon and Nessus'.

proconsular assizes. But these *conventus* were not organized
like the *regiones* of Macedonia. The nearest parallel in the
eastern empire would be the conjoining of Pontus and
Bithynia under a single proconsul; both districts had a
separate provincial council; but there was no technical term
to designate the two parts.[1] The numbered districts of Macedonia were unique, and hence the correct term, which even
in its garbled form has the ring of an official designation,
was not understood outside the province. The worst solution of the problem presented by this text is to bracket the
difficult term μερίδος as an intruder, as Westcott and Hort
did. Its difficulty guarantees its authenticity.

Westcott and Hort wished to reduce the phrase to the
colourless πρώτη τῆς Μακεδονίας πόλις, 'First City of Macedonia'. But Cadbury objected that the Roman colonies of
the East never took the title First City, a title which was the
cause of great rivalry and civic pride among the great
Greek cities of the eastern provinces. The reason is evident.
The Roman colonies were well aware of their superiority to
any provincial Greek city, however large. They did not
need to print the title First City on their coins and inscriptions. They *were* the First People of the province, and though
not technically what the Romans called *civitates liberae*, or
free cities, they were apt to regard themselves as being *in* but
not *of* the province where they lay. The Roman colony of
Apamea in A.D. 110 registered a protest when the imperial
legate proposed to interfere with their internal arrangements, and required the assurance that this was at the
express wish of the emperor.[2] Philippi might not technically

---

[1] Cf. *RE* (S), iv. 932 n. 4. Cilicia Pedias also, while part of the Syrian
province, apparently had a separate κοινόν, ibid. 933, without the μέρις
system. In the western Empire the Spanish *conventus* of Bracaraugusta and
Asturia had a parallel organization, *ILS*, 6923–4, 6931–2.

[2] Pliny, *Ep.* x. 47–48, cap. 48. 2: 'ut iam nunc sciant hoc quod inspecturus
es ex mea voluntate salvis quae habent privilegiis esse facturum.'

call itself First City. But the author of Acts, himself no
Roman, could very well use the familiar Greek term to
describe the pre-eminence of Philippi: 'First city of its
region.' But even with this concession to the textual tradition the reading is still unsatisfactory. What is required is
πρώτη τῆς πρώτης μερίδος Μακεδονίας πόλις, κολωνία. But
perhaps too much attention should not be given to that unnecessary and offending definite article in πρώτη τῆς μερίδος.
Much more interesting is the question—why did the author
go out of his way to introduce Philippi thus, when he never
formally describes the technical status of any other city?
The reasonable answer could be that it was because Paul
had an adventure at Philippi of which the significance
depended upon the special status of the place. The notice is
a warning. Paul enters a Roman community and encoun-
ters special difficulties, such as he had not met earlier at the
Roman colonies of Antioch-by-Pisidia and Lystra, where
the action taken against him was not formal and official.[1]

At Thessalonica the orthodox Jews who were trying to
silence Paul and Silas, unable to find and seize them, took
his host Jason and 'certain brethren' before the magistrates,
who took security from them: λαβόντες τὸ ἱκανόν.[2] The term
is the equivalent of the Latin *satis accipere*, correlate of *satis
dare*, in connexion with the offering and giving of security,
in civil and criminal procedures.[3] The term turns up as an
accepted Roman usage in Greek civic practice, at Pergamum in an imperial rescript, probably of Hadrianic date,
organizing civic finances.[4] What is happening to Jason is
clear enough: he is giving security for the good behaviour of
his guests, and hence hastens to dispatch Paul and Silas out

[1] Below, p. 97.
[2] Acts xvii. 5–9.
[3] Cf. above, p. 82 n. 2.
[4] *OGIS*, n. 484. 50–51. Cf. Gaius, on *satisdatio* in provincial edicts, *D.*
2. 8. 1.

of the way to Beroea, where the jurisdiction of the magistrates of Thessalonica was not valid. Acts is particular and well informed about Thessalonica. The author knows the correct and fairly unusual title of the city magistrates: they were πολιτάρχαι, as inscriptions reveal. This title was replaced in a later age by the more common First Ruler.[1] The city also possessed the technical privilege of *libertas*, 'municipal freedom', which conferred great independence on its internal administration.[2] Though Acts makes no reference to this, the energetic action of the Jews against Paul and Silas might have been inspired by the knowledge that the hands of the city authorities, unlike those of Ephesus, were not directly under Roman control. Two actions were attempted. The first was against the apostles before the 'people', which should mean the city assembly, and then, when Paul and Silas could not be found, action was taken against their host Jason before the city magistrates.[3] The court of a *civitas libera* or free city was the one seat of jurisdiction where severe punishment could be inflicted, at least on non-Romans, *peregrini*, without invoking the governor.[4] The accusation brought against the apostles at Thessalonica is somewhat obscure, and possibly garbled.[5] But it includes the charge of acting contrary to the decrees of Caesar. Whatever this means, it was not strictly relevant in the court of a free city which lay outside the Roman jurisdiction; hence the city magistrates were not compelled to take serious action.

Paul and Silas fled from their enemies at Thessalonica to

[1] Cf. Jackson–Lake, ad loc. For the evidence, which is not very accessible, see C. Schuler, *Cl. Phil.* (1960), 90 f. The 'First Ruler' appears in a third-century inscription, *SEG*, ii. 410. Cf. Schuler, art. cit., nos. 16–18.

[2] Jones, *Greek City*, 129 and n. 62. Pliny, *NH*, iv. 36. Cicero spent his exile there for that reason, *ad Att.* iii. 8 ff.

[3] Acts xvii. 5 and 6–9 respectively.

[4] On the privileges of *civitates liberae* in the Empire see Jones, op. cit. 118 f., 131.

[5] See below, p. 103.

Beroea. Similarly, Paul and Barnabas took evasive action at Antioch and at Iconium, when the local magistrates had been roused against them. The details here are obscure and untechnical.[1] οἱ πρῶτοι τῆς πόλεως, 'the first men of the city', fits nothing in the civic organization of Antioch, another of the Roman colonies of Asia Minor. At Iconium the term is yet more colourless, οἱ ἄρχοντες, 'the rulers of the peoples', and the Jews acting together. The action described at either city—as at Lystra—sounds more like a mob-movement than a judicial proceeding. There is mention of stoning at Iconium, and at Antioch of an expulsion from the city territory, which might have been an official act.[2]

But the underlying idea of the retreat of Paul is more than a running away from trouble. Paul exploits the fact that there was no inter-city jurisdiction or authority except that of the Roman governor. If the proconsul or legate is not apprised of a political affair, a trouble-maker can continue his career indefinitely by moving from city to city. The cities kept control over their inhabitants in the last resort through their property. The property-lacking vagrant was very difficult to handle. Hence the significance of the action taken at Thessalonica against Paul's guarantor, as it were. The municipal authorities in turn, made uneasy by the political charges aimed at Paul and his companions, are only too glad to dodge responsibility, as at Philippi and Antioch, by encouraging the preacher to move on. Reciprocally, when the hostile Jews at Thessalonica fail to bring Paul to book, they have to pursue him to Beroea and start all over again before a new local authority. Paul is again whisked out of the city by his friends to avoid this action.[3]

These manœuvres were assisted by the inadequacy and

[1] Acts xiii. 50, xiv. 4–6.
[2] Cf. above, pp. 77–78. For Lystra, Acts xiv. 19—an attempted lynching.
[3] Acts xvii. 10–14.

limited powers of the police system. Local officials, known most commonly as Guardians of the Peace, had forces of constables under their authority, but these were based on the Greek cities, which were widely separated and had very extensive territories in most of Asia Minor. There is no evidence that the police forces of different cities ever acted in concert. The firm local control exerted by the Roman military patrols in Jerusalem was exceptional. Only the governors of the frontier provinces had large military forces at their disposal. The proconsuls and legates of peaceful provinces had only small units, if any, which were stationed at the capital city.[1] Even in Judaea the procurators left the extermination of brigands in part to the local authorities.[2] In only two of these civic intrigues does the local authority apparently attempt the positive expulsion of the unwanted stranger, if one may interpret the evidence of Acts in that way. It may be no accident that the two municipalities, Antioch and Philippi, where a civic expulsion was at least envisaged, were both Roman colonies.[3] The superiority of their civic status has already been noted; it was analogous to that of the *civitates liberae*, which enjoyed full internal autonomy. A more positive authority was allowed to the colonial magistrates, akin to the Roman *coercitio*, and symbolized by the use of lictors.

[1] For civic police see Jones, *Greek City*, 212 f. G. Lopuszansky, *Ant. Class.* (1951), 46 f. Troops are rarely mentioned in proconsular provinces, and do not exceed a single cohort where known, as in Macedonia (Cheesman, *Auxilia of the Roman Imperial Army*, 159) and Baetica (cf. Pliny, *Ep.* iii. 9. 18). Bithynia-Pontus seems to have been without troops until the annexation of Pontus Polemoniacus *c.* A.D. 60 or even until its transference to the emperor in 111–12 (Tac. *Hist.* 3. 47 with Pliny *Ep.* x. 21). Asia lacked any regular formation, V. Chapot, *La Province romaine d'Asie* (Paris, 1904), 368–9.

[2] Jos. *B.J.* ii. 14. 1, cited Lecture Two, p. 43 n. 2. Cf. also ibid. 12. 2: 'Cumanus complained that the villagers had not chased and arrested the brigands.'

[3] For Philippi, above, p. 74.

Paul and the Proconsul Gallio, and Paul at Rome

PAUL AND THE PROCONSUL GALLIO

TWICE in Acts Paul is brought into connexion with proconsuls, Sergius Paulus in Cyprus and Annius Gallio at Corinth. Juster, in his book about the Jews in the Roman empire, made a great onslaught upon the latter incident.[1] He regarded it as an historical fiction, a doublet concocted from the account of the trials before Felix and Festus. The *Acts Commentary* of Jackson and Lake made no reply to this, though Juster had made some shrewd observations. His principal objection was that no specific charge was brought against Paul in the narrative, whereas in the later trials there was at least one specific allegation against Paul, concerning the introduction of strangers into the Temple. Juster might have done better to attack the charge that is in fact put forward before Gallio: 'this man persuades men to honour God contrary to the law'.[2] He might have argued that this charge could not have been put forward in that form and those circumstances, i.e. outside Judaea, where alone a Roman governor could be expected or invited to take cognizance of breaches of the Law in the Jewish sense. The narrative of Acts makes the absence of any specific malefaction the ground on which the proconsul refuses to take cognizance.[3] It is rather severe to make this recognized defect the grounds for objecting to the narrative itself. The narrative in fact agrees very well with the workings

---

[1] Acts xviii. 12–17. Juster, op. cit. ii. 154 n. 4.
[2] Acts xviii. 13.   [3] Acts xviii. 14–15.

of *cognitio extra ordinem*. It is within the competence of the judge to decide whether to accept a novel charge or not.[1] In the middle of the second century there were proconsuls of Asia who were ready to refuse to accept even the generally recognized charges against Christians, and to dismiss them out of hand.[2]

The question is whether Jewish residents at Corinth, who presumably were not citizens of Corinth, could expect the proconsul to enforce their domestic law within the territory of a community that was a Roman colony; the passage in Acts distinguishes amply the Jews from the Corinthians proper.[3] This in turn raises the question of the synhedria and synagogues of the Diaspora, and the privileges granted to them by the Roman government. All that is certain, from the numerous decrees quoted by Josephus, is that the Jewish communities were protected against any interference with their religious and social customs on the part of the local governments of the Hellenistic cities.[4] There is no clear evidence that the local Sanhedrins had any formally recognized right to force obedience upon their own adherents. Juster argued that the high-priest or Ethnarch at Jerusalem had a general control in matters of faith over the local communes of the Diaspora, derived originally from Caesar the Dictator's edict of toleration; which control might be delegated to the local Sanhedrins.[5] Certainly Saul's authority in the mysterious mission to Damascus derived from the high-priest and not from the local community of Jews.[6] Only at Alexandria in Egypt is there clear evidence that the Jewish colony possessed internal self-government, in

[1] Above, p. 14 ff.
[2] Tertullian, *Scap.* 3–5. Cf. Sherwin-White, *JTS* (1952), 209.
[3] Acts xviii. 4, 'Jews and Greeks'. 5, 'Jews'. 8, 'many of the Corinthians'.
[4] For the documents see Jos. *Ant.* xiv. 10, xix. 5. 2–3
[5] Loc. cit.
[6] Acts ix. 2, xxvi. 12. Juster, op. cit. 145 n. 5

matters of the Hebraic law, under the authority of the Ethnarch.[1] But it is not safe to generalize from the special conditions of Alexandria, itself a vast city by ancient standards, where the Jewish colony was very large indeed, to the small communes of the lesser cities in the eastern provinces.[2]

It is not certain that the charge made against Paul at Corinth was intended to refer primarily to the Hebraic law, though Gallio found it convenient to take it that way. The accusers do not say that Paul is persuading *Jews* to worship contrary to the law—but that he is persuading *men* to do so, τοὺς ἀνθρώπους.[3] It is the way of Acts to summarize and at times to garble the charges variously brought against Paul. The narrative, sufficiently clear about the charges before Felix, is very summary about them in the hearing before Festus.[4] At Philippi, when Paul is first brought before a Roman tribunal, Acts is remarkably precise: Paul is causing disturbance by preaching about an un-Roman cult. Then at Thessalonica there is a rather garbled version of a charge of causing disturbances and alleging, 'contrary to the decrees of Caesar', whatever that may mean, that there is 'another king'.[5] At Corinth in chapter 18 Paul is again before a Roman tribunal, that of the proconsul himself, and on Roman territory, that of a *colonia civium Romanorum*. The best charge for the Jews to bring was that Paul was preaching to *Romans*, not to Jews, contrary to the Roman law, not the Jewish law, just as at Philippi. And that may well be what the narrative is meant to convey, as Lake and Cadbury surmised in the

---

[1] Strabo, in Jos. *Ant.* xiv. 7. 2; cf. ibid. xix. 5. 2.

[2] Jones, *Cities*, 305 n. 10. The suggestion of Mommsen, *GS*, iii. 439, that in 2 Cor. xi. 24 the 'thirty-nine stripes' were inflicted by Jewish courts of the Diaspora is insecure, as is the correlated suggestion (ibid. 435–6) that Paul's activity before his conversion was outside Palestine. Gal. i. 13–14, 22–23 should be taken with Acts xxvi. 11. Cf. Juster, op. cit. 155 n. 1.

[3] Acts xviii. 13.

[4] Above, p. 50. [5] Acts xvi. 20–21, xvii. 6–7.

Commentary on xviii. 13. Probably some at least of the persons covered by τοὺς ἀνθρώπους were Roman citizens of Corinth, either Jewish converts or sympathizers. Paul's host Titius Justus ὁ σεβόμενος was such a one. Acts speaks of 'many of the Corinthians' being baptized.[1] But the Jews, being Jews, could only make their accusation in terms of the Judaic law. By dragging in 'the Law' in the scriptural sense they provided Gallio with his way out by interpreting ὁ νόμος of s. 13 as ὁ νόμος ὁ καθ' ὑμᾶς of s. 15.

There was no compulsion on the proconsul to enforce the principle of conformity and exclusiveness of cult within the Roman community.[2] His final words, κριτὴς ἐγὼ τούτων οὐ βούλομαι εἶναι, are the precise answer of a Roman magistrate refusing to exercise his *arbitrium iudicantis* within a matter *extra ordinem*. Compare the formula of the edict from Nazareth: τοῦτον κεφαλῆς κατάκριτον θέλω γένεσθαι.[3]

An alternative explanation is that the Jews were invoking against Paul the edicts of Claudius which guaranteed them the quiet enjoyment of their native customs throughout the Diaspora. This is the uncontroversial part of the texts quoted by Josephus in the *Antiquities*, however much he may have fudged on behalf of the Jewish claim to citizenship at Alexandria.[4] The decisive words in the edict concerning the Diaspora are: 'It is proper that the Jews through the world under Roman rule should keep their native customs without let or hindrance.' The genuine character of the wording of most of these edicts cannot be called in question. They contain the various quirks and oddities of expression that characterize the several genuine decrees and edicts of Claudius.[5] The Jews of Corinth may

---

[1] Acts xviii. 7–8.
[2] Above, pp. 79 f.
[3] *FIRA*, i, no. 69.
[4] *Ant.* xix. 5. 2. 3, xx. 1. 2.
[5] Cf. the references to the odd behaviour of Caligula, *ILS*, 205, 206, and the warning to the Jews against disturbances in *P. Lond.* 1912.

not themselves have had the power of enforcement,[1] but they might hope to invoke the proconsul's authority against a fellow Jew who interfered, as Paul certainly was interfering, with the quiet practice of their customs. But the intention of the edict of Claudius was merely to reaffirm the Jewish privilege of toleration, granted in the Triumviral period and confirmed by Augustus, that they should not be prevented by the Greek city governments from assembling for the purposes of their cult. This is made abundantly clear by the long series of documents quoted by Josephus in *Antiquities*, xiv. 10. Cities of Asia, such as Pergamum, Sardes, and Ephesus, had been interfering with Jewish assemblies. When the Claudian edict in Josephus adds: 'I think it right that no Hellenic city should be without these privileges' the reference is clear.

It is relevant that the 'decrees of Caesar' had been invoked at Thessalonica against Paul by the Jewish commune.[2] This is the most confused of the various descriptions of charges in Acts, though the *Acts Commentary* does not notice the difficulty. There are three items: 'these men disturb the world, and act against the decrees of Caesar, and say that there is another king.' The decrees of Claudius Caesar were very much concerned, as we have seen, with preventing 'disturbances of the world'.[3] But at Corinth the Jews were exceeding the intentions of Claudius. If the civic magistrates of Corinth had prevented the Jews from celebrating the Sabbath, Gallio must have defended the Jews or risked imperial displeasure. Nothing compelled him to interfere with the internal quarrels of the Jews. The curious incident following Gallio's dismissal of the case perhaps confirms this interpretation. The Jews, bidden by Gallio to see to the matter themselves, seized Sosthenes, one of the

---

[1] Above, p. 96. [2] Acts xvii. 7.
[3] Above, pp. 51 f. and 100 n. 4.

Elders of the Synagogue, and beat him before the tribunal.[1] This makes sense if one may assume that Sosthenes was a Christian sympathizer of sorts, and that the beating was that of the formal 'thirty-nine blows', administered by the authority of the local Sanhedrin, which had taken Gallio at his word. The *Acts Commentary* makes nothing of this incident.

Either of these alternative explanations of the accusation before Gallio provides an adequate historical context, and a context different from that of the trials before Felix and Festus. The doublet theory of Juster can hardly be sustained against both of them. Juster was somewhat bothered at the necessity of explaining away the name of an actual proconsul, for whose government of Achaea in the year 52 or 53 there is independent evidence.[2] He asserts rather airily that the author of Acts could easily have found the name of a chronologically appropriate proconsul. This is by no means certain. The same question arises concerning Sergius Paulus, proconsul of Cyprus. For these two one cannot invoke Josephus, as a hostile critic may do for the names of the procurators of Judaea and the legateship of Quirinius. These men, Gallio and Paulus, were senators and proconsuls of the second grade, ex-pretors, *praetorii*, who had not yet reached the fame of the consulship and the posts associated with it. Their proconsular offices are not mentioned in the *Annals* of Tacitus, and are not likely to have decorated the lost pages of his predecessors. Gallio appears in Tacitus as a consular in the story of the great conspiracy against Nero, and in two anecdotes of Dio Cassius, with no reference to his

[1] Acts xviii. 17. The ἀρχισυνάγωγοι are Elders, not annual presidents. Two are named at Corinth, Crispus s. 8 and Sosthenes s. 17. Cf. Jackson–Lake, ad loc. A new inscription from Cyrene confirms this—*SEG*, xvii 823, A.D. 56—naming ten ἄρχοντες.

[2] Juster, ii. 154 n. 4. For the inscription of Junius Gallio as proconsul of Achaea, discussed at length in Jackson–Lake, v. 460 ff., see Ditt. *Syll.*³ 801 D.

provincial career.[1] Even the reference to his departure from Achaea in Seneca's Letters makes no mention of his official position.[2] Diligent search in the archives of the Senate might have produced the annual decree which authorized the regular choice of the proconsuls of the year. But the archives of the Senate were available only to persons of high rank and at Rome. It has been suggested, in connexion with the *Acts of the Pagan Martyrs*, that Roman archives were tapped with the help of corrupt clerks, by the gentry of Alexandria, in whose circles those documents were produced. But that is a mere possibility supported only by parallels from the third and fourth centuries.[3] The probability in the case of the author of Acts is a good deal lower.

There remains the possible use of municipal or provincial calendars or *fasti*. Many Italian municipalities kept and published on stone the consolidated list of their annual magistrates and of the Roman consuls, sometimes with reference to notable events of the year. The *Fasti* of Ostia are the most complete example of this.[4] But no comparable document has been discovered in the eastern provinces.[5] The Roman colonies of the east, such as Corinth, Pisidian Antioch, and Beirut, might well have copied the Italian custom.[6] But whether they would have included the list of proconsuls or legates in addition to the Roman consuls is

[1] Tac. *Ann.* xv. 73. 4. Dio, 61 (60). 35. 2–4; 62. 20. 1.

[2] Sen. *Ep.* 104. 1.

[3] Musurillo, *Acts of the Pagan Martyrs*, 252 n. 1. Prudentius and Augustine indicate that copies of trial records could be secured from the public archives by bribery.

[4] Collected now with other municipal *fasti* in *Fasti Italici*.

[5] The sole document which names a series of governors is the list of public games in honour of *Augustus et Roma* found at Ancyra, from the time of Tiberius, *OGIS*, 533. Oddly, this uses only *cognomina*, in the formula ἐπὶ Φρόντωνος, &c.

[6] It is remarkable that no municipal calendars have been discovered in Africa, epigraphically and archaeologically the best documented of the Latin provinces.

very doubtful. The consuls were eponymous, they dated the year. But the legates held office for irregular terms, and even the proconsuls occasionally held office for more than a single year.

Yet greater uncertainty attends the question of provincial archives. These sections of Acts are concerned only with proconsular provinces, Cyprus and Achaea. There were organized archives in the imperial provinces, governed by legates. The *tabularium principis* and the *officium legati* had a permanent establishment of clerks, consisting of imperial slaves, freedmen, and soldiers.[1] Equally, municipalities seem to have kept civic records in a registry. But to judge by the best-documented example, Bithynia-Pontus, the proconsular provinces were different in this respect. Most in the first century A.D. had no regular archives or permanent personnel. The clerical assistants of the proconsuls and provincial quaestors consisted still of the Republican *scribae* and their assistants, provided by the *Aerarium Saturni* at Rome. These came out with the proconsul and quaestor from Italy on an annual basis, and returned in like manner.[2] In the numerous judicial and administrative disputes described in Pliny's Letters to the emperor Trajan, the formal documents of an official nature are produced not from a public archive, but by the petitioners and defendants themselves.[3] Only once does Pliny himself refer to a document which did not originate with one of the parties. Once, also, he asks the emperor to check a document quoted by the contestants

[1] The *lex provinciae* and the edicts of Augustus quoted in Pliny, *Ep.* x. 79. 112–15, were referred to Pliny by the municipal officers for his elucidation. For the *tabularium principis* in provinces, which was primarily a financial bureau, see *RE*, (2) iv. A 2, 1966, and for municipal archives, ibid. 1968 f. For the *officia*, staffed by soldiers, see *RE*, xvii. 2. 2045 f.

[2] For *scribae*, Mommsen, *DPR*, i. 397 ff. Pliny, *Ep.* iv. 12, gives an example in A.D. 104. The proconsul of Africa, however, had an *officium* because he had troops, *RE*, loc. cit.

[3] Pliny, *Ep.* x. 31. 4, 56. 2, 59. 3, 65, 72. 1.

from the archives at Rome, because its genuine character was in doubt.[1] Pliny evidently could not check it in the province. All this takes place in a province that had been governed by independent proconsuls since 27 B.C., and which had only passed under imperial control with the arrival of Pliny himself as legate. It is reasonable to assume that this was the usual condition of the proconsular provinces.[2] If this was so in the time of Trajan, when the emperors were beginning to cast an eye upon the administration of the proconsular provinces, it must have been much worse in the earlier period. Hence it is rash to presuppose in these provinces the existence of a central archive where the calendar of proconsuls might be found, and rash to invoke proconsular archives in the solution of any problem connected with the activities of Paul in western Asia Minor and Achaea.

There remains the possibility of coins as the source of proconsular names. In some provinces there were local coinages which bore the names of proconsuls as well as the 'image and superscription of Caesar'. But this was not so in Achaea.[3] The local coinage at Corinth was municipal, and bore the names and titles not of the proconsuls but of the municipal magistrates, the *duoviri*. In Cyprus the names of proconsuls appeared on coins of the Julio-Claudian period, and those who like may believe that the author of Acts found the name of Sergius Paulus in a handful of small change.[4] But Juster's suggestion that the author could easily have found the chronologically correct proconsul for Paul's adventure at Corinth, turns out to be surprisingly improbable.

[1] Ibid. x. 72 *ad fin.* 65. 3.
[2] Cf. p. 106 n. 2.
[3] For the coinage of Corinth see Lecture Four, p. 92, n. 5. The proconsular coins from Achaea are a few issues of Augustan date: R. Munsterberg, *Num. Zeit.* xlvii. 69 and 71.
[4] *Cat. Greek Coins*, 'Cyprus', cxix–cxxi.

PAUL AT ROME

One last judicial puzzle concerns the trial of Paul at Rome. Before what tribunal would he be tried, and what happened to him? Those are the questions. The only clues in Acts are two statements. First, the reading in the western tradition of the text in xxviii. 16, that 'when we came to Rome, the centurion handed over the prisoners to the commandant of the camp—τῷ στρατοπεδάρχῳ—and Paul was ordered to remain by himself with the soldiers who were guarding him'. Second, the statement in xxviii. 30, 'he remained for two whole years in a private lodging'. The first of these statements might suggest that the centurion handed over his shipment of prisoners to the custody of the Prefect of the Pretorian Guard. From this it might be inferred, conceivably, that the trial would take place before the Pretorian Prefect as the deputy of the emperor, as in the late empire. But this is not probable. At this period there is no evidence that the Prefects had any judicial functions at all.[1] Their jurisdiction developed in the late second and third centuries.

That the Pretorian Guard took charge of prisoners sent

[1] Very little is known of the jurisdiction of the pretorian prefects before the Severan period. Only three texts of the classical lawyers refer to their criminal jurisdiction, of which the last is manifestly interpolated; Ulpian in *Collatio*, xiv. 3. 2. *D.* 32. 1. 4, 49. 3. 1. The last-named is the only reference in the books of the criminal law in the *Digest*. Cf. Mommsen, *DPR*, v. 256 n. 2. 258 ff. A single instance of their jurisdiction is known, and that under Commodus, *SHA Sev.* 4. The subsequent development is another matter. The *praefectus urbi* is more likely to be the judge in question, since in the later Principate he was the only authority other than the emperor with the power to sentence Romans and *honestiores* to death. The limitation of their authority to a hundred miles around Rome refers to their primary jurisdiction. *D.* 1. 12. 4. In the only text that touches on the delegation of appellate jurisdiction by the emperor in the earlier period, Trajan refers the investigation to consulars, below, p. 111 n. 4. In the earlier period the pretorian prefects were concerned with jurisdiction simply as advisers to the emperor at judicial sessions of the *consilium principis*. Crook, op. cit. 70, and, at length, *RE* xxii. 2. 2412 ff. Dio, 52, 24, 3 limits their jurisdiction to their troops.

from provinces to the jurisdiction of the emperor is not seriously in doubt. This was the obvious authority; the *praefectus urbi* and his urban cohorts were busy with the policing of the capital and the custody of lesser criminals. Similar procedure was followed in the time of Trajan when in a specific case he ordered that a provincial offender should be sent in chains 'to the prefects of my *Praetorium*'.[1] More contemporary with Acts is a political case under Claudius in which a distinguished prisoner is in the hands of the Pretorian Prefect.[2] But the στρατοπέδαρχος of Acts is not likely to be the great Afranius Burrus himself, sole Prefect from A.D. 51 till his death in 62. T. S. R. Broughton, following Mommsen, suggested that Acts meant another officer, the commandant of the *castra peregrina*, known as the *princeps peregrinorum*.[3] This term is actually used by the Latin manuscript *Gigas* to render στρατοπέδαρχος. The *castra peregrina* were in the late Empire the home of the secret police called *frumentarii*, a corps of centurions on special duty. But though the office of *princeps peregrinorum* is known in the time of Trajan, nothing suggests that the *frumentarii* assumed their later functions before the second century.[4] Their original duty was to organize the supply of corn, as their name implies, and their police duties arose as a by-product of their peregrinations around the Empire. In the first century there is nothing to connect them with police functions, still less with the organization of appellate jurisdiction. The soldiery that function in the way of the later *frumentarii* in the pages of Tacitus are the *speculatores*, a special body of imperial guards who tend to appear in moments of military intrigue.

---

[1] Pliny, *Ep.* x. 57. 2. Cf. *RE*, loc. cit., on this point.

[2] Tac. *Ann.* xi. 1, above, p. 73. The trial was heard by the emperor in person. [3] T. S. R. Broughton, in Jackson–Lake, v. 444.

[4] *AE*, 1923, n. 28. Cf. Ditt. *Syll.*[3] 830. For the later *frumentarii* see *RE*, vii. 1. 122 f. Aurelius Victor, *de Caes.* xiii. 5–6, seems to attribute the system to Trajan.

The Latin term is used appropriately by Mark for the Herodian soldier who executed John the Baptist.[1]

The most likely identification of the στρατοπέδαρχος is not with the *princeps peregrinorum*, but with the officer known as *princeps castrorum*, the head administrator of the *officium* of the Pretorian Guard. This post happens to be known at Rome only from the Trajanic period onward,[2] but it corresponded in duties and standing to the like-named officer in the legionary army, the *princeps praetorii legionis*, the head of the organizational command of a legion.[3] This necessary post is testified, in the legions, from the time of Claudius onwards, and there is no reason to suppose that the *princeps castrorum* of the Pretorian Guard was a later creation.[4] This official is the personage most likely to be in executive control of prisoners awaiting trial at Rome in the Julio-Claudian period. He was the subordinate of the Prefect of the Pretorians. But this does not mean that Paul's case would come before the Pretorian Prefect.[5] Down to the time of Nero the emperors themselves heard the cases that fell under their *cognitio*. Claudius had been particularly zealous in this respect, and there is no suggestion in his reign of any delegation of jurisdiction.[6] With the youthful Nero things were different. Tacitus implies that down to the eighth year—A.D. 62—Nero avoided personal jurisdiction, and then only accepted a case for special reasons, because a member of his entourage had abused his personal influence. In 65 Nero presided, in personal *cognitio*, over the trial of the

---

[1] Tac. *Hist.* i. 24–25, ii. 73. Mark vi. 27.

[2] Cf. *ILS*, 9189.

[3] Vegetius, *De re mil.* 2, 8 f. Mommsen, *Eph. Epigr.* iv. 241. The form στρατοπεδάρχης is used in *CIL*, 3. 13648 for the camp-commandant of a legion, *praefectus castrorum*, who is a different officer.

[4] *ILS*, 2283, 2648.   [5] Above, p. 108 n. 1

[6] Cf. Suet. *Claud.* 15. Tac. *Ann.* xiii. 4. 2. In the *Acta Isidori* he presides in person, Musurillo, op. cit., no. iv.

conspirators associated with Piso.[1] But these were great political affairs. The silence of Suetonius, who was interested in routine administration, indicates that normally Nero took little part in jurisdiction. In an obscure passage Suetonius says that Nero disliked signing warrants of execution, which was evidently a routine duty of the Princeps.[2]

It would seem that under Nero the necessary personal jurisdiction of the emperor, such as the trial of capital cases on appeal, was delegated to other persons, and the sentences confirmed by him afterwards. There is a passage in Tacitus which obscurely indicates that the court of the *praefectus urbi* was beginning to attract cases that might have gone before the tribunals of the *ordo*, but this is not connected by Tacitus with the jurisdiction of the Princeps.[3] One may surmise that the procedure followed on occasion by Trajan was employed earlier. Though he was active in personal jurisdiction with the help of his court of assessors, the so-called *consilium principis*, Trajan twice referred a complicated judicial problem, affecting a person of no exalted station, to the judgment of a leading consular senator, chosen from the inner circle of his advisers.[4] In the affair of the Great Fire of Rome and the trial of the Christians it is impossible to make out the exact part played by Nero. Tacitus' language is non-technical in the crucial sentence: 'Nero subdidit reos et quaesitissimis poenis adfecit.'[5] Lower down, the term

[1] Tac. *Ann.* xiv. 50. 2, xv. 69. 1, 71. 6, 72. 1–2.

[2] Suet. *Nero*, 16. 2–17, listing the legislative and administrative reforms of Nero, has nothing to say about jurisdiction. Ibid. 17. 2 refers to the 'ordinary' civil jurisdiction of the *praetor urbanus*, which is not relevant here. Ibid. 10. 2 for the warrants.

[3] Tac. *Ann.* xiv. 41. 2, with Furneaux, ad loc.

[4] Pliny, *Ep.* vii. 6. 8–10. The case is complex, and some details are obscure, but the main point is clear: 'mater . . . reos detulerat ad principem iudicemque impetraverat Iulium Servianum.' Servianus was a *bis consul* of the period. [5] Tac. *Ann.* xv. 44. 3.

convicti sunt indicates *cognitio extra ordinem*, but does not reveal the judge.[1] But if Nero conducted the trial after the Fire in person, that was because, as in the trial of the Pisonian conspirators, he had a particular interest in the matter. If Paul came to trial some time after the period of two years mentioned in Acts xxviii. 30, it is probable that his case was heard by someone other than the Princeps.

The suggestion has been made by Cadbury and others that Paul was never tried on the charges forwarded by Festus.[2] This suggestion is perhaps partly motivated by the desire to connect the execution of Paul with the affair of the Great Fire in the tenth year of Nero. The starting-point is the statement in Acts that Paul remained awaiting trial for two years.[3] Cadbury tried to prove the existence of a rule by which accused persons were released after a lapse of time if their accusers failed to appear and proceed with their charges. He suggested that Paul benefited from this rule. Was there such a rule? It was necessary for a deputation from Jerusalem to follow up their accusations at Rome, producing witnesses and other evidence. This is common ground. But Cadbury has misunderstood the evidence with which he supports the rest of his theory. The emperor Claudius, who took great interest in the administration of justice, proposed measures to discourage accusers who failed to follow up their charges. There is a fragment of his speech to the Senate on this theme in a well-known papyrus.[4] But nothing in it suggests that the accused should be released after a legal interval. Claudius was there discussing, not his personal jurisdiction, but the system of the *ordo*. So far as can be made out, accusers were pressed to complete their cases as soon as the time allowed for investigation was ful-

---

[1] For the use of this term for sentence by *cognitio* cf. Tac. *Ann.* xv. 71. 6.
[2] Op. cit. 326–37.   [3] Acts xxviii. 30.
[4] Above, p. 25. *BGU*, 611.

filled. In default they were to be charged with *calumnia*, or
vexatious prosecution. Claudius' proposals were eventually
codified and completed by the *SC. Turpilianum* of A.D. 61,
which defined the offence of *destitutio*, as it came to be called,
and enacted penalties for defaulting accusers. But the *SC.*
did nothing for the accused persons. Its intention was to
enforce prosecution.[1]

A passage of Cassius Dio, cited in support of Cadbury's
suggestion, summarizes an edict of Claudius concerning
accused persons, not accusers, who, having a bad case,
failed to appear at their trial.[2] This edict concerned the
personal jurisdiction of Claudius, and not the *ordo*. In it the
emperor announced that he would give sentence for the
prosecutor or plaintiff by a given day in the absence of the
accused or the defendant. Suetonius confirms Dio, but does
not mention a specific enactment. If these texts are read
without close attention they might give the impression that
Claudius' rule applied to both sides, prosecution and defence alike.[3] But Dio, in defining the persons affected, uses
the term ἀπαντᾶν ἐπὶ δίκην, 'appearance before the court'.
This is the regular Greek term for the accused who faces,
or in the negative, fails to face, the charge in court.[4]

It is, from the general consideration of Roman criminal
procedure, extremely unlikely that there was such a rule as
Cadbury supposes in classical Roman law, or down to the
end of the Severan dynasty. The amplification of the *SC.*

[1] Above, p. 52.

[2] Dio, 60. 28. 6. 'Since there was an innumerable mass of cases and those
who thought that they would be worsted did not appear in court [ἀπήντων],
he declared by an edict [διὰ προγράμματος] that he would himself give
sentence even against absentees within a fixed period.' Suet. *Claud.* 15. 2:
'absentibus secundum praesentes facillime dabat nullo dilectu culpane an
quis aliqua necessitate cessasset.'

[3] So Mommsen, who thought the edict referred to cases on appeal,
D. Pen. R. ii. 159 n. 1.

[4] Cf. L–S, s.v. citing, e.g., Plato, *Laws*, 936 e. Demosthenes, 21. 90.

Turpilianum by the classical lawyers in the *Digest* shows that every effort was made to compel accusers to carry through their charges.[1] To deal with special cases rules were made which allowed accusers acting in good faith to withdraw charges. This was called *abolitio criminum*. What was not tolerated was failure to maintain a serious charge. This attitude is illustrated, at the beginning of the second century, as so often, by a passage in Pliny.[2] At a judicial session in 107 the emperor Trajan was greatly enraged at certain accusers who tried to withdraw a charge made against an imperial freedman. Trajan would only let them do so if they could produce good reasons: 'aut agerent aut singuli approbarent causas non agendi'. The Roman tradition in this matter is thus firmly established from the time of Claudius and Nero to that of Ulpian. Its keynote is the insistence that the prosecutor must prosecute. The protection of the accused person lay not in any provision for automatic release if his accuser were absent, but in the severity of the sanctions against defaulting prosecutors. The frivolous charge rebounded against the accuser in the procedure known as *calumnia*, which was fairly and regularly enforced.

The proposal of Claudius in the edict cited by Dio was out of line with normal usage in a different way. The citations in the *Digest* title called *de absentibus damnandis*, supported by a ruling from a governor of the Flavian period, shows that the idea of condemnation in absence was contrary to the usage of Roman law, at any rate from the time of Domitian onwards.[3] That is why the Claudian edict was cited by Dio. It is an example of the absurdity of Claudius, as Suetonius makes clear in his comment: 'Claudius did not

---

[1] D. 48. 16.   [2] *Ep.* vi. 31. 7–12.
[3] D. 48. 17. 1 and 5. 3. Cf. *FIRA*, iii, no. 169, dated to A.D. 89 and 93, where, however, the governor is impatient with the absent *rei*.

even bother to find out whether the absentees had a legitimate excuse.' As such, it is no evidence for the procedure of
the Neronian period. The object of Roman criminal procedure was to insist not only that prosecutors should prosecute, but that prisoners should be tried.[1]

The edict in Dio does not support Cadbury's suggestion
that Paul was released by a prescription of time. But Cadbury mainly relied on an edict of an unnamed emperor,
known from a Latin papyrus.[2] This deals with cases, both
civil and criminal, sent on appeal to the emperor. It lays
down a time allowance of eighteen months for provincial
appeals in criminal cases; after that period the case goes by
default in the absence of either party. This appears to fulfil
Cadbury's requirement. But it is a curious aberration of
judgment by distinguished Roman lawyers that ever attributed this document to the first century A.D. To Mommsen
it was quite apparent that this was a post-classical document, and so it must be to any historian.[3] Riccobono has
duly restored it to its proper date in the Italian *Fontes Iuris
Romani*. A lengthy discussion is not necessary here. The basic
fact is that this document is dealing with the late-empire
system of *appellatio* after sentence and not the early-empire
system of *provocatio* before sentence.[4] The appeals concern

[1] Above, p. 52. Cf. the passage from Papinian cited below, p. 117,
n. 3.

[2] Op. cit. v. 332 f. *BGU*, ii. 628. *FIRA*, i, no. 91, with bibliography.

[3] *D. Pen. R.* ii. 154 n. 2, 158 n. 5.

[4] Cf. ibid., col. i *ad fin.*, &c.: 'qui nisi adfuerint vel defensi fuerint . . .
scient fore *ut* stetur sententiae [*sic*] et accu*s*atores ad petendam poenam
iure cogantur', i.e. the previous sentence is to stand in such circumstances.

The rule that Cadbury requires does not make its appearance until A.D.
529. In texts dated to A.D. 385 and 409 Theodosius enacts that if an accuser
fails to proceed with his case within a fixed period, finally defined as two
years, he shall be punished. But that the accused should be acquitted is
only laid down in a rule of Justinian dated A.D. 529. The previous two
enactments specify only the punishment of the absent accuser. *Cod. Iust.*
ix. 44. 1–3.

criminal cases in which judgment has already been given, and the appeal is against the sentence, whereas in the original system *provocatio* prevented the holding of any trial of first instance at all.[1] The later system of appeal did not become established at any rate in the period before Hadrian. This edict belongs to a period when the methods of the *SC. Turpilianum* had become ineffective, as it does not fit or make any reference to the body of rules that had gathered round the *SC. Turpilianum*.

If this document were Julio-Claudian it would belong to either Tiberius or Nero, since the author refers to 'my divine father'. But the style and phraseology do not fit such a date. The term *ordo cognitionum officii nostri* is used in the edict to mean the list of cases in the emperor's court. It is difficult to believe that such a phrase could be used in the best period of Roman Law: *ordo* and *cognitiones* are self-contradictory.[2] So too the strange phrase 'causae quae ad principalem notionem provocatae essent', where one expects 'ad cognitionem principis' (or 'imperatoris'), or simply 'ad principem'. Something is known of the strong and forceful style of the emperor Tiberius and of the peculiar personal style of the emperor Claudius, if not of Nero.[3] But the language of this edict is quite unlike either, and recalls the style of the late third and fourth centuries. So this document is irrelevant to the judicial adventures of Paul at Rome.

Still less convincing was an attempt of Lake, quoted by Cadbury in the *Commentary*, to prove the existence of a rule of the required sort from a passage in Philo concerning the trial of the Alexandrine Lampon.[4] He is said to have been

---

[1] Above, p. 68.   [2] Above, pp. 13 f.

[3] For Tiberius see R. Syme, *Tacitus*, appendix 39, and E–J, no. 102, where the keynote is simplicity. For Claudius see the well-known documents collected in Charlesworth, C. nos. 2–3, 11, 49, or A–J, 49–51. *SEG*, iv. 516. The style of Nero's Greek chancellery can be judged from A J, nos. 54, 56.

[4] Op. cit. 330. Philo, *In Flaccum*, 128–9.

brought to trial after deliberate judicial delays amounting to two years, described as μήκιστον χρόνον, a very long time. Lake rendered this 'the longest time allowed', and thence inferred the existence of a rule limiting detention without trial. But that simply is not the meaning of the Greek. Even ὡς μήκιστον would not quite carry the meaning required by Lake. Besides it was not the accuser but the governor himself who caused the delay. Hence there is no parallel.

Cadbury and Lake missed a passage about the *lex Iulia de vi* which is relevant to their purposes. There was a provision, apparently in the original law, that in the event of an accuser's death, or of a 'just cause' which prevented the action, the accused person might request the cancellation of the charge.[1] But later enactments—before the time of Trajan—limited even this privilege, by allowing another party to renew the accusation.[2] The reluctance of the judicial administration to permit the abandonment of charges except in most extreme circumstances is apparent.[3] An observation of Macer might give pause to those who strive to maintain the *biennium* theory. He remarks that an accuser who has been unable to proceed with his charge for a year after the formal act of delation (*inscriptio nominis*) because of public engagements and duties, is not liable under the *SC. Turpilianum* to a charge of dereliction.[4]

---

[1] *D.* 48. 2. 3. 4 and 16. 10 pr. (*ex lege*). This applied both to the *lex de vi* and to the *lex de adulteriis*.

[2] Ibid., cf. 48. 16. 10. 2.

[3] Papinian, *D.* 48. 1. 10, insists that once issue has been joined in a criminal case *excusatio pro absente* should be allowed to either party for just cause. He particularly objects to a procedure whereby after three citations on three successive days either an absent *reus* is condemned or an absent prosecutor is declared guilty of *calumnia*, automatically. This procedure possibly connects with the innovation of Claudius noted above, p. 113 n. 2. There is no suggestion here of any prescription of time, in Cadbury's sense.

[4] *D.* 48. 16. 15. 5. In this passage the addition *vel biennio* is suspect as an obvious interpolation.

The administration was prepared to allow the prosecution a very ample allowance of time. It is also worth observing that, except for the fourth-century edict, none of the evidence under discussion is related directly, in the sources, to the imperial court of appeal, whether by *provocatio* or *appellatio*. It all concerns courts of first instance. Any time allowances in cases taken to Rome are likely to have been longer, because of the distances of travel involved and other practical complications.

The plain fact remains that Paul was not brought to trial for two years. This may well be connected, as Cadbury supposed, with the failure of his accusers to continue their accusation at Rome. But it may also be due to the congestion of the court list, which moved Claudius earlier to take unorthodox methods of cutting it down.[1] When a man became emperor who lacked Claudius' interest in jurisdiction, or indeed in administration of any sort, it is likely that delays would increase. The young Nero's principal advisers, Seneca and Burrus, were serious men who would do their best to grease the wheels of justice. But the imperial cabinet had plenty of preoccupations in the first part of Nero's reign. When in his seventh or eighth year—if Paul's advent is put so late—Nero began to assert himself as the effective head of the government, it is likely that the routine judicial business of the cabinet suffered first and most. Even if there was some unknown device by which an accused person could draw attention to the neglect of his case, it remains an open question whether Paul's interest required that he should use it. Just as in Palestine, it may have suited him to be left to continue his evangelism in the capital of the Empire, rather than provoke a sentence which even if not capital could severely limit his mission.

A more probable technical solution than that of Cadbury

[1] Above, p. 113.

lies, as so often, in the nature of *imperium*. Claudius in his edict about absent prosecutors did not establish a law. For that he would have used a decree of the Senate, as was his custom. He simply stated what he himself was going to do. So, at a lower level the procurator of Palestine, Lucceius Albinus, at the end of his term coolly emptied his prison of untried and unexecuted prisoners, dismissing them from his jurisdiction.[1] Rather similarly, the proconsuls of Bithynia were given to cancelling their own or their predecessors' sentences of relegation, a practice which the emperor Trajan tried to stop.[2] These judicial measures were simply acts of *imperium*. Nothing prevented the successor of Claudius from taking a similar line if he chose—if, for example, a show of clemency were thought desirable at some moment, or simply to shorten the court list by dropping the arrears. In the first five years of Nero there are several analogous actions or proposals—notably the cancellation of long-standing debts to the treasury, and Nero's own proposal for the abolition of indirect taxation.[3] There is also a certain show of *clementia* in some judicial incidents, and in dealing with the lower social classes of Italy.[4] It was this quality which Nero's tutor Seneca particularly tried to instil, in a famous essay, into his unpleasant pupil. Perhaps Paul benefited from the clemency of Nero, and secured a merely casual release. But there is no necessity to construe Acts to mean that he was released at all.

[1] Above, p. 53.   [2] Pliny, *Ep.* x. 56. 2–3.

[3] Tac. *Ann.* xiii. 23, 50.

[4] Ibid. xiii. 11. 2, 27. 6, 43. 7, xiv. 45. 4. Cf. Suet. *Nero*, 10. 2 (above, p. 111 n. 2).

LECTURE SIX

The Galilean Narrative and the Graeco-Roman World

IN Acts or in that part of Acts which is concerned with the adventures of Paul in Asia Minor and Greece, one is aware all the time of the Hellenistic and Roman setting. The historical framework is exact. In terms of time and place the details are precise and correct. One walks the streets and market-places, the theatres and assemblies of first-century Ephesus or Thessalonica, Corinth or Philippi, with the author of Acts. The great men of the cities, the magistrates, the mob, and the mob-leaders, are all there. The feel and tone of city life is the same as in the descriptions of Strabo and Dio of Prusa. The difference lies only in the Jewish shading. The scene is observed through the eyes, not of a citizen, but of a resident foreigner, a πάροικος, to use a Pauline term, from the synagogue.[1] The Jewish colonies and their Greek sympathizers and adherents—the εὐσεβεῖς or σεβόμενοι—occupy the foreground, in a setting of Hellenes, but looming larger than they are likely to have done in the daily life of most Hellenistic cities of the east.[2] The obvious analogy is with Josephus, in those passages where he stresses the privileges and importance of the Jewish settlements of the Diaspora, or conversely, where he tries to give a respectable Hellenistic colouring to the more advanced city-settlements of Jewish Palestine.[3] But, whatever the differences

[1] Eph. ii. 19.
[2] Acts xiii. 50, xiv. 1, xvi. 2, xvii. 4, 12, xviii. 7, xix. 10, 17, xx. 21.
[3] Jos. *Ant.* xiv. 10. 8–24, xviii. 2. 1. *Vita*, 9. *BJ*, i. 12. 4, iii. 3, 4–5.

of degree, Acts and the *Antiquities* describe unmistakably the same world as Strabo and Dio. The four form a continuous cultural series.

It is similar with the narrative of Paul's judicial experiences before the tribunals of Gallio, Felix, and Festus. As documents these narratives belong to the same historical series as the record of provincial and imperial trials in epigraphical and literary sources of the first and early second centuries A.D. They stand closest of all perhaps to the well-known *Acts of the Pagan Martyrs*, but are markedly superior to these in clarity and accuracy of detail. The trials in Acts belong unmistakably, as has been shown at extreme length above, to a particular phase in the history of Roman provincial jurisdiction.

These lectures have not been concerned with the actual journeying of Paul by sea and land, his use of particular Roman highways and sea-routes, and the specific technique of travel. The subject has been well examined by diverse hands, but the material lacks the chronological precision which is largely the aim of these lectures. Paul might have journeyed by those roads and through those ports and in those ships, through the most peaceful provinces of the Roman empire, at any time after the completion of the *Pax Augusta*, the Roman peace, in Asia Minor. That means, in effect, after the final pacification of the wild Isaurian and Pisidian highlanders in the last decade B.C.[1] Until then a traveller would not have found his journey safe and easy between Iconium and Antioch. It is a commonplace to refer to the safety of travel in Acts as an unconscious tribute to the Roman peace. There are no longer brigands in the traditional land of brigands. This condition did not last many centuries, but it lasted long enough to make the record of travel in Acts of no special value for the kind of

[1] *CAH*, x. 270 f. with bibliography.

phase-dating that these lectures are attempting. So too with
the material technique of travel. Conditions remain similar
for too long a period. So far as is known, none of Paul's
ports or highways or sea-routes silted up, was destroyed by
earthquakes, or fell into disuse in the following two centuries. The journey in Italy from Puteoli or Brundisium to
Rome, past Three Taverns, is familiar from Cicero and
Horace, but equally from the Map of Peutinger in the late
Empire.[1] But save for this point of chronological precision,
the journeys of Paul have the same historiographical value
as the account of the Greek cities and of Roman jurisdiction. We ride and sail with Paul as we may with Horace and
Cicero, or better still, with the younger Pliny, travelling
fifty years later, like Paul, partly by ship and partly by
land, and touching at Ephesus and Pergamum on his long
journey from Rome to Prusa in Bithynia.[2]

In all these ways Acts takes us on a conducted tour of the
Graeco-Roman world. The detail is so interwoven with the
narrative of the mission as to be inseparable. But when one
turns from Acts to the Gospels the impression is totally different. The narrative of the three synoptic gospels is set in
a world which reflects hardly a touch of Greek or Roman
influence until the arrival of Christ in Jerusalem. What is
true of the setting is equally true of the content, and particularly of the pattern of life revealed to a social and economic
historian by the parables. This will be discussed at greater
length below. But briefly, hardly anything in the parables
would suggest at first sight that Alexander and Pompey
the Great had brought Hellenistic civilization and Roman
organization into the kingdoms of the east.

The material of the Gospels is not capable of the sort of

[1] Horace, *Serm.* i. 5. 1 ff. Cicero, *Ad Att.* iv. i. 4–5. K. Miller, *Die P. Tafel*
(Stuttgart, 1929).

[2] Pliny, *Ep.* x. 15–17 A.

treatment that historians since Ramsay have given to the Acts. From the Graeco-Roman point of view this poses a problem. The specific historical references in the three Gospels are extremely few, and with one exception are concentrated at the beginning or the end. The narrative is given a rough chronological fix by the reference to Herod the King and Archelaus at the beginning and to Pilate the Roman governor at the end. But the reference to Herod and Archelaus keeps bad company in Matthew, is absent from Mark, and even in Luke is involved with the difficult question of Quirinius and his census.[1] Between these two terminals, inside the narrative, there are the references to Herod the Tetrarch of Galilee, neatly identified in Mark and Matthew as the brother of Philip. In Mark and Matthew he occurs only once, in the isolated and awkwardly inserted story of the death of the Baptist.[2] In Luke he plays a more curious role, appearing no less than four times within the Galilean narrative, in addition to his use as a marker in the chronological exordium, and in the final trial scene.[3] There is also a very strange reference to Pilate peculiar to Luke, within the Galilean narrative.[4] Apart from the two Herods there are no chronological markers in the narrative of the mission in Mark and Matthew, and practically none in Luke, until one comes to Pilate and Caiaphas. Not only are there no other precise historical cross-references inside the narrative, but the narrative of all three Gospels is largely devoid of other material references that might tie the story to the Roman period.

There is the centurion with the palsied servant at Capernaum.[5] The text uses the Greek form ἑκατοντάρχης and not

---

[1] Matt. ii. 1–17, 22; Luke i. 5, ii. 2.
[2] Matt. xiv. 1–12; Mark vi. 17.
[3] Luke iii. 1, xxiii. 6–12. Cf. below, p. 138.
[4] Luke xiii. 1; below, p. 138.
[5] Matt. viii. 5–13; Luke vii. 1–10.

the graecized Latin κεντυρίων as in the crucifixion narrative
of Mark.[1] This centurion cannot be a Roman soldier,
though the story implies that he is not a Jew. Capernaum
was in the heart of the tetrarchy of Herod. Galilee was never
part of a Roman province until the death of Agrippa I in
A.D. 44. The centurion must be a soldier of Herod, who
certainly affected Roman terminology. In the story of the
execution of John the Baptist Herod's officers include χιλίαρ-
χοι and a *speculator*.[2] The terms χιλίαρχος and ἑκατοντάρχης
are the usual equivalent of *tribunus militum* and *centurio*,
though they are also in common usage as early as Herodotus
in their literal sense.[3] But there is no mistaking the *speculator*
whose title is given in the Latin form. The *speculatores* were
a well-known division of the Imperial Guard at Rome.[4] It
would seem probable that the other terms are due to Roman
influence, but the only certain case is the *speculator*; and he
appears in a story that is outside the main narrative of the
mission in Galilee.

There are references to coins in various incidents and
parables. The coins of the Gospels are a curiously mixed
collection, as was noted long ago in the basic work of
F. W. Madden. In Mark we have Roman *denarii*—bread to
the value of 200 *denarii*—and the Roman *quadrans*, which is
a gloss on δυὸ λεπτά in the story of the widow's mite.[5] In
Matthew there is the Roman *as*—two sparrows for an *as*—

---

[1] Mark xv. 39.   [2] Mark vi. 21, 27.   [3] L–S, s.v.
[4] Above, pp. 109 f.

[5] Mark vi. 37, xii. 42, xiv. 5. See still F. W. Madden, *Coins of the Jews* (London, 1881), 289 f., and E. Rogers, *Handy Guide to Jewish Coins*, &c. (London, 1914), 67 ff., for a full discussion. A. Reifenberg, *Ancient Jewish Coins*[2] (Jerusalem, 1947), does not discuss denominations, and with other modern numismatists prefers to classify the local bronze coins only by weight and size. Cf. L. Kadman, *Corp. Num. Pal.* ii. 39. The identification of biblical *asses* and *lepta* has long puzzled numismatists, but the latter may well be the Jewish *prutah*: Rogers, op. cit. Cf. Kadman, *Num. Stud.* ii (Jerusalem, 1958), 100–1.

and the Greek *didrachma* and *stater* in the story of the tax at Capernaum.[1] There are Greek talents and Roman denarii in the parable of the king and his debtors.[2] Luke has denarii in the story of the two debtors and of the Good Samaritan, and *asses* in the phrase about the sparrows, Greek *drachmae* in the tale of the woman who loses one out of ten drachmas.[3] The *mina* occurs in the parable of the king and the three servants, and *lepta*, as in Mark, but unglossed, for the widow's mite.[4] Asses, lepta, drachmas, denarii, staters. As the auctioneers say, they are a mixed lot. No wonder there were money-changers at Jerusalem. Such coins could have been found in the markets of Syria at any time from the wars of Pompey onward. Setting aside the minas and talents, which are not coins but weights or money of account, there is a certain preponderance of Roman and Roman provincial units, though the exact identification of the smaller bronzes is unsure. Such a mixture is perhaps unlikely after the first century A.D. Coin hoards of a somewhat later date are confined to Roman denarii and Syrian tetradrachms— i.e. staters—so far as silver is concerned.[5] But the coins as whole are like the centurion at Capernaum. They do little to sharpen the focus of the scene.

The references to tax-gatherers, publicans, and the Roman census might be thought more helpful. For the former the Gospels use the ordinary Greek terms τελώνης and ἀρχι-τελώνης.[6] No latinized term appears, not even the word δημοσιώνης, which was the usual rendering of the Latin *publicanus*. The *publican* of the Authorized Version contains a *suggestio falsi*. Except at Jerusalem and perhaps Jericho the tax-farmers must be collecting either for the Tetrarch

[1] Matt. x. 29, xvii. 24–27. [2] Matt. xviii. 24–28.
[3] Luke vii. 41, x. 35, xii. 6, xv. 8. [4] Luke xix. 12–20, xxi. 2.
[5] H. Hamburger, 'Hoard of Syrian Tetradrachms from Gush Halav', *IEJ*, iv (1954), 201 ff.
[6] Luke v. 27, 30, xix. 2; Mark ii. 15–16.

or for the municipality. But it is very questionable whether there were any municipal taxes in Jewish lands except at the very few cities which had been given Hellenistic city organization by the Herods. Capernaum, where the 'receipt of custom' is specially mentioned, was not one of these. Josephus gives no indication of local taxation in Jewish communes.[2] The only specific indication is in Matthew's version of the tax-gatherers at Capernaum.[3] They ask Peter, 'Does your master pay the didrachma?' Peter answers 'yes', and then at Christ's bidding he catches the fish with the stater in its mouth to pay for both. Christ's question suggests that this is a royal tax: 'From whom do the kings of the earth collect tax?' The text here uses the term *censum*, in Greek form $\kappa\hat{\eta}\nu\sigma o\nu$. The sum is likely to be the Jewish notion of a reasonable poll-tax. It is commonly taken, with Madden, to refer to the subscription of a half-shekel or didrachma made by Jews throughout the world to the Temple funds, perhaps rightly.[4] But it is surprising if this was farmed, and the term *censum* is against the notion. This story fits the Galilean background, but the use of the word *censum* reflects the impact made by the introduction of the Roman taxation into the Judaean province in A.D. 6. The use of the term stater in its late Hellenistic sense of a four-drachma piece is also of interest; four drachmas were required to pay the tax of Peter and Christ. The tetradrachm is the silver coin most commonly found in Palestine hoards of the period.[5]

The story of Christ and the tribute of Caesar is equally appropriate in its location at Jerusalem within the Roman province. In the most precise version Christ asks not just for a coin, but for 'the coin of the taxing', $\tau\grave{o}$ $\nu\acute{o}\mu\iota\sigma\mu a$ $\tau o\hat{v}$

---

[1]   Mark ii. 14. For Jericho, within the province, see Luke xix. 2. Zacharias the 'chief publican' may be local, but no $\tau\epsilon\lambda\acute{\omega}\nu\iota o\nu$ is mentioned.

[2]   Josephus, *Ant.* xiv, 7. 2, asserts roundly that 'we have no public money'.

[3]   Matt. xvii. 24–27.   [4]   Madden, op. cit., p. 290.

[5]   Above, p. 125 n. 5.

κήνσου.[1] The underlying suggestion is that the Roman tax could only be paid in Roman coin, which is probable enough, and that the *denarius* was by no means the only currency available, which is certainly the case. Witness— apart from actual coin-finds—the diverse coin types mentioned in the Gospels, and the presence of money-changers in the Temple, where only Jewish coins were accepted.

The indications of types and patterns of human settlement and of local administration in the Galilean narrative— in which the parables of all periods may be included—are worth investigation. A. H. M. Jones's great book on the Greek city in the eastern provinces brought the local study of the settlements in Palestine into line with the study of civic life throughout the eastern empire. It placed the Galilean and Judaean scene to a certain extent in a new light, or a new perspective.[2] Judaea and the tetrarchies were administered under the house of Herod and the procurators alike by the Ptolemaic system of villages grouped into districts known as toparchies.[3] The village clerk, or κωμογραμματεύς, administered the village as an official of the central government, and the commandant or στρατηγός controlled the toparchy. A large village acted as the administrative centre of the toparchy. The number of genuinely self-governing cities, πόλεις, with the Hellenistic civic machinery, was very small, and these controlled only their urban area; mostly they had no authority over the adjacent territory, which was part of the toparchy.[4] In Galilee there was only Tiberias and possibly Sepphoris, both very new creations. But Caesarea Philippi or Paneas across the Iturean border controlled its own territory and points the contrast.[5]

---

[1] Matt. xxii. 18. [2] Jones, *Cities*, ch. x.

[3] Ibid. 274 f. For the village clerks, not well documented in Judaea, see ibid., n. 62. Jos. *Ant.* 16. 7. 3.

[4] Jones, *Cities*, 276.

[5] Ibid. 277 n. 67, 283 n. 76.

The village clerks and the commandants of toparchies were concerned only with the interests of the central government. It is not surprising that they are never mentioned directly in the Gospels; at most they appear indirectly behind the tax-collectors. What mattered to the Jew in his village was the authority of the village congregation, the rulers of the synagogue. That appears explicitly in the story of Jaeiros.[1] There is a characteristic reference to the essentials of city life in the phrase about 'those who expect the first seats in the synagogue and greetings in the market-place'.[2] When Christ was involved in what might be called a municipal row at Gadara, which was the capital of a toparchy, there is a remarkable difference from the pattern of activity which attended on Paul's troubles in Asia Minor. No municipal magistrates or assemblies or officials intervene. Simply, the whole population—$\pi\hat{a}\sigma a$ $\dot{\eta}$ $\pi\acute{o}\lambda\iota s$—comes out to ask him to go away.[3] There are certain references to what appear to be local councils of Elders on the model of the Sanhedrin. The offending brother is bidden to tell his tale of wrong to the 'assembly' in the presence of three witnesses, and the angry brother is said to be 'in danger of the council—$\sigma\upsilon\nu\acute{e}\delta\rho\iota o\nu$'. That is as far as municipal life extends in the Gospels, and there is nothing in Josephus to contradict the impression that outside the Herodian city foundations there was any developed system.[4]

---

[1] Luke viii. 41 f.; Matt. ix. 18 f.; Mark v. 22 f.

[2] Luke xi. 43, xx. 46.

[3] Matt. viii. 34; Mark v. 14; Luke viii. 26–30. The strange variant *Gerasa* for *Gadara*, and the supposed difficulties of topography even with Gadara, do not affect the point under discussion. The administrative situation supplies a possible solution of the difficulty, which may have arisen through a confusion between the place and the toparchy. The incident may have taken place at a suitable locality within the territory of the toparchy but remote from the town, so that the name of the toparchic capital replaced that of the particular village concerned.

[4] Matt. v. 22, xviii. 16; also Mark xiii. 9; Matt. x. 17, 'They will deliver

The use of the terms 'village' and 'city', κώμη and πόλις, in the Gospels repays investigation. Luke uses such terms as 'by city and by village' of the journeying of Christ. The first mission of the Twelve is 'by villages', and the mission of the Seventy goes to 'every city and place', κατὰ πᾶσαν πόλιν καὶ τόπον.[1] Similarly, Matthew speaks of cities and villages. He contrasts the word 'city' with household οἰκία in his account of the missions.[2] In Matthew and Luke Capernaum, Gadara, and Bethsaida are 'cities'.[3] Mark is a little more precise. In the story of the swine at Gadara or Gerasa he has the contrast, which is also in Luke, of 'city' and 'fields' where Matthew has only 'city'.[4] Once Mark substitutes the term κωμόπολις. Christ visits the κωμοπόλεις of Galilee, which are contrasted with Capernaum as 'city'. Somewhat later his mission is through 'villages' or 'villages and fields'.[5] In the mission of the Twelve 'place', τόπος, is used instead of 'city', which is in the other two Gospels.[6] In viii. 23–27 Christ travels from Bethsaida, which Mark calls a village, to the 'villages of Caesarea Philippi'. This recalls the phrase used in vi. 56: 'whenever he visited their villages, cities, and fields.'

The two terms are evidently sadly confused, especially in Luke and Matthew. But the term 'city' does not deceive. Josephus in his description of Galilee clarifies this terminology of cities which are villages and villages which are cities.

---

you up to councils, etc.' One might expect the democratic system known from Transjordan and the Hauran (Jones, *Greek City*, 271 f.) to flourish also in Galilee, as Mr. P. A. Brunt suggested to me privately. But the hierarchy seems to have stunted any such growth. Josephus refers generally to the local sanhedrins as the 'councils of every city'. *BJ*, ii. 14. 1. Schürer, *Jewish People*, &c. ii. 1. 149 f. Cf. also Jones, *Cities*, 284 f.

[1] Luke viii. 1, ix. 6, x. 1.
[2] Matt. ix. 35, x. 8–15. Cf. Luke ix. 4–5.
[3] Matt. viii. 34, ix. 1, xi. 20–23; Luke iv. 31, ix. 10.
[4] Mark v. 14; Luke viii. 34; Matt. viii. 33–34.
[5] Mark i. 38, vi. 7, 36.   [6] Mark vi. 11.

He observes in the *Jewish War* that Galilee was a land of great villages: 'The cities lie very thick and the very many villages that are here are everywhere so full of people, by the richness of their soil, that the very least of them contained above fifteen thousand inhabitants.'[1] This to modern ears is somewhat startling; we are not accustomed to thinking of agricultural villages of 15,000 souls. A. H. M. Jones noted that Strabo called Jamnia, which was the capital of a toparchy, a village, despite its great size.[2] The clue may be found in two other passages of Josephus, where, in a more technical moment, he speaks of four cities with their toparchies, which Nero made over to Agrippa II, and of one of them, Julias, as a 'city and its fourteen surrounding villages'.[3] Of the four named places only one, Tiberias, was certainly a 'city' in the technical Hellenistic sense.[4] Evidently Josephus often uses 'cities' to denote merely the capitals of toparchies, though in a very few instances such as Tiberias the toparchic capitals happen also to be cities in the technical sense.

This solution might work for the cities of the Gospels, or for some of them. Gadara was almost certainly a toparchic capital.[5] Strabo, the Hellenistic Greek from Pontus, was more exact when he called Jamnia a village. Mark's use of κωμόπολις for the villages of Galilee is precise. These large Galilean settlements had the size of a city, as Josephus revealed, but the nature of a village. Strabo used the same word for a great native town in the fastnesses of Cappadocia,

---

[1] Jos. *BJ*, iii. 3. 2. D. H. K. Amiran, 'Settlements in . . . Lower Galilee', *IEJ*, vi (1956), 69 f., discusses the pattern but not the scale of village settlement.

[2] Strabo, xvi. 2. 28, p. 759. Jones, *Cities*, 275 n. 63.

[3] *BJ*, ii. 13. 2. *Ant.* xx. 8. 4.

[4] Jones, op. cit. 275–7.

[5] Jones, loc. cit. For a similar view of the 'cities', not pushed so far, see Schürer, op. cit. ii. 1. 154 ff.

in a passage where it is equated with the phrase 'having the establishment of a city'.[1] Josephus concedes this by the observation that Philip the Tetrarch advanced the village of Bethsaida to the dignity of a city, both by the number of its inhabitants and its other grandeur. But despite its new title of Julias Bethsaida remained a mere toparchic capital—of Gaulanitis—down to the late empire.[2] Mark scores heavily when, unlike Matthew, he calls Bethsaida a village, and distinguishes it from 'the villages of Caesarea Philippi'; for the latter was a genuine city which controlled an extensive territory and even possessed the privilege of coining money.[3] Mark may be using a phrase meant to designate the capital of a toparchy and its subordinate villages. Josephus in his *Life* describes Sepphoris, which was a city without a territory, and at the same time a toparchic capital, as having many villages round about it.[4] This is parallel to his description of Bethsaida and Mark's description of Caesarea. But whichever solution is preferred, Mark comes closer than any other Gospel to denoting the technical difference between a village and a true city.

The elucidation of the terms under discussion belongs to the field of human geography. The late Professor John Myres in his *Frazer Lecture* took the Mediterranean κώμη in Greece and Anatolia as his theme.[5] He established a thesis which can be demonstrated from most parts of the Mediterranean world, and in particular from the social history of Roman Tunisia (*Africa proconsularis*), and equally from

[1] Strabo, xii. 2. 5, p. 537. Cf. xiii. 1. 27, p. 594, used of second-century Ilium at a time of civic and material depression.

[2] Jos. *Ant.* xviii. 2. 1. Jones, *Cities*, 283. Cf. Betherampha-Julias, in Peraea, a 'city' only in name despite Jos. *Ant.* loc. cit.; Jones, op. cit. 277, and n. 64.

[3] Mark viii. 26–27. Jones, op. cit. 283–4 n. 76. [4] Jos. *Vita*, 65.

[5] Sir J. L. Myres, *Frazer Lecture 1943*, 'Mediterranean culture' (Cambridge, 1943). Cf. Sherwin-White, *JRS* (1944), 8 f.

ancient and modern Sicily. In the Mediterranean environment the natural pattern of human settlement is what the
French geographers call the *gros bourg*. The primary value
and scarcity of agricultural land, the rarity of permanent
water, the necessities until modern times of local defence,
are factors which combined to congregate the peasant culti-
vating population into large communities, the κῶμαι, and
the κώμη was the nucleus of the πόλις. In classical Hellas and
in the Hellenistic world the complicated and highly evolved
structure of the city-state or territory-owning and governing
municipality developed out of the κώμη. A Greek πόλις may
be a single κώμη or a combination of several κῶμαι. Myres
showed how after the decay of civic government, the basic
element, the κώμη, survived because it was the product of
elementary natural forces. It needed piped water, a national
police force, and industrialization to break up the big-village
system of the Mediterranean. Josephus' villages of 15,000
souls are precisely the kind of thing that Myres had in mind.
In classical Athens, the 3,000 fighting men of Acharnae, a
figure which implies a local population of the same scale as
in Josephus, is a famous example.[1] On a modern distribution
map of Sicily one may count seventy-six inhabited centres
containing from 10,000 to 50,000 persons and about fifty
with from 5,000 to 10,000.[2] These are κῶμαι.

The classical Greek city developed because the people of
the κῶμαι ran their own affairs and administered their own
territory. In Palestine a very different evolution took place.
It became a land of rulers and princes. The villages remained villages, however big. Even when the Herods introduced in a few localities the foreign pattern of Hellenistic

---

[1] Thucydides, ii. 19. 2, 20. 4. 'The greatest locality [χωρίον] of the so-
called demes.' This passage should be taken with the description of Athens
as a land of small 'cities' in the archaic period, ii. 15. 1-2.

[2] Cf. *Admiralty Geographical Handbook Series*, 'Italy', vol. ii, fig. 32.

city government, as at Tiberias and Samaria, the cities did not control the territory outside the walls. A κώμη became a πόλις, but there was no combination of κῶμαι and the surrounding land remained under the toparchic officials. The exception which tests the rule, Caesarea Philippi, was outside the predominantly Jewish zone. All this is implied in the terminology of the Gospels. A πόλις is just a grander κώμη. It is not a community in which men are found governing themselves. In so far as there is an element of self-government it is in terms of the synagogue and the sacred law, and the largely ecclesiastical *synhedria*. It is not by chance that τόπος and πόλις are equated in alternative versions. When in the parable of the talents the faithful servant is given the rule over five or ten cities, we know just what is meant.[1] In more prosaic terms he was appointed commandant of a toparchy—a group of τόποι.

Another administrative figure in the Gospels which is fundamentally un-Roman and un-Hellenistic is that of the judge, ὁ κριτής. The Gospels speak of 'judges' where the Acts speaks of city magistrates, ἄρχοντες, πολιτάρχαι, στρατη-γοί, the annually elected presidents of the Hellenistic and Roman municipality. 'Agree with your adversary while you are coming along with him, or he may hand you over to the judge, and the judge give you to his servant, and you will be put in a prison, and you will not escape thence until you have paid the last farthing.' This scene has a very un-Roman and un-Greek ring to it. The judge does what he likes, he is a permanency.[2] So too in the tale of the importunate widow. 'There was a judge in a certain city.' The judge does as he likes, and no one can control him.[3] The word κριτής corresponds to nothing in Roman usage or in the magisterial hierarchy. The Roman single *iudex* of the civil law was

---

[1] Luke xix. 17–20.   [2] Matt. v. 25; Luke xii. 58.
[3] Luke xviii. 2.

an arbitrator appointed separately by the proconsul or pretor for each particular case. Judging is only one aspect of the *imperium* of the Roman magistrate, as we have seen. But in the Gospels it is the whole matter, or a function in its own right. Josephus, referring to the Roman annexation of Judaea, says that Quirinius came at this time into Syria, being sent by Caesar to be the judge of that nation[1]— κριτής. It is the Gospel usage.

The notion of government, above the level of the κώμη and its synagogue, is otherwise represented in the parables and the Galilean narrative as a matter of kings and princes. The king's servants or ministers are slaves in the parable of the king and his debtors. Yet these slaves and fellow-slaves own property on a big scale, like the ministers of the Great King of Persia in Herodotus.[2] Matthew has the same picture of the king and his slaves in his version, much clearer and more intelligible than that of Luke and Mark, of the tale of the wedding feast for the king's son.[3] Here is a little kingdom, in which one village—πόλις is the word—defies the king's authority, who sends his 'hosts' of armed men to destroy it. The same view of the small kingdom, its ruler and his slaves reappears in Luke's version of the parable of the talents.[4] A 'man of noble birth', ἄνθρωπός τις εὐγενής, who has inherited a kingdom, instructs his slaves to manage his affairs during his absence, while he goes off to be installed in his new kingdom. In due course he rewards them with the government of toparchies in this new kingdom. The general mass of his subjects, however, are not slaves; they are called, oddly, πολῖται, citizens. These rebel against him and are ferociously punished. The rebellion took the form of sending an embassy 'after him', ὀπίσω αὐτοῦ, which

---

[1] *Ant.* xviii. 1. 1. Cf. also Philo, *Leg.* 180, and Jos. *BJ*, ii. 20. 5, with Schürer, op. cit. ii. 1. 153.   [2] Matt. xviii. 23–34.
[3] Matt. xxii. 2–14.   [4] Luke xix. 12–27.

declared that they wanted a different king. The story is somewhat obscure, but the underlying notion is that of a client king and a suzerain. Commentators have observed the parallel with the embassy to Augustus that objected to the succession of Archelaus to Herod the Great.[1] Somewhere there is a Great King, a king of kings, who will replace the unpopular king or satrap by another. The story is slightly garbled in Luke, and reads as if an older version, in which the subject was an oriental monarch in the Persian style, has been refurbished in Hellenistic dress to fit one of the more limited monarchies of the Roman period, in which the subjects objected to the old totalitarian methods.[2]

This world of little kings is late Hellenistic and early Roman Syria, with its complicated pattern of minor principalities, extending from the kingdom of Petra and the Nabatean Arabs in the far south to the princedom of Commagene in the far north. Of these kings, Herod and the tetrarchs are merely the most familiar to modern ears. The protégés of Pompey the Great form another group—Samsiceramus of Emesa, Tarcondimotus of the Cilician mountains, Ptolemy of the Iturean kingdom in Lebanon and Anti-Lebanon.[3] There were yet smaller units, such as the principality of Theodore, son of Zeno, around Philadelphia, which included three other cities, and that of the Iturean Ptolemy, who ruled Arca in the northern Lebanon. Similar was the dominion of that obscure Lysanias who ruled in Abilene, between Anti-Lebanon and Damascus, and is known to Luke and to Josephus.[4] These provide another sort of illustration for the story of the king and his servants.[5]

[1] Jos. *Ant.* xvii. 11. 1.
[2] In Matthew's version the process has gone further. There is no king, no kingdom, no rule over cities. Matt. xxv. 14–30.
[3] Jones, *Cities*, 256, 260.
[4] Luke iii. 1. Jos. *Ant.* xx. 7. 1. *BJ*, ii. 12. 8.
[5] Jones, op. cit. 257, 260 nn. 40, 45.

A. H. M. Jones's account of southern Syria in the *Cities of the Eastern Roman Provinces* brings out the diversity of the little kingdoms in the period after the breakdown of the Seleucid and Maccabean powers. The pattern persisted into the early Roman empire as long as the Herodian tetrarchies and the Nabatean monarchy survived. But it is past its prime by the time of Claudius, and the second half of the first century A.D. saw the disappearance of the last kingdoms and their incorporation into Roman provinces. The principality of Commagene lasted until Vespasian's reign. Agrippa II and a certain Aristobulus survived in the Iturean area until about A.D. 93, and the last kingdom vanished with the annexation of the Nabatean realm in A.D. 105.[1]

This little world forms the historical reality behind the 'kingdom' parables. It belongs to a definable historic period, beginning at the end of the second century B.C. and continuing into the early Roman period. But from the time of Trajan until the Arab conquest such a situation did not exist. In the age of the Antonines the little kingdoms must have been a dim memory. In Graeco-Roman literature their last impact appears faintly in the discourse delivered in the time of Vespasian by the philosopher Musonius Rufus, on the subject of kingly rule, to a personage described as a 'Syrian king', some last scion of the Iturean or Herodian line, or else an Antiochus of Commagene.[2] He remarks: 'at that time there were kings in Syria'.

The style of these princelets is neatly displayed in Mark's brief sketch—peculiar to him—of the Galilean court of Herod Antipas.[3] 'On his birthday Herod gave a feast to his great men, his commanders of battalions, and the first persons of Galilee.' Two terms are of special interest: τοῖς μεγιστᾶσι καὶ τοῖς χιλιάρχοις. The first word, which appears

---

[1] For Agrippa and Aristobulus see Jones, *Cities*, 273 n. 60.
[2] Musonius, *Rel.* viii.   [3] Mark vi. 21.

only here in the Gospels, is current in the Septuagint. Its usage is appropriate to an oriental environment. Tacitus uses it to describe the barons of Armenia who resist the Roman predominance, and the Septuagint used it in Daniel's apostrophe to Belshazzar: 'thou and thy lords, thy wives and thy concubines' in a not dissimilar context.[1] Here and in Mark the *megistanes* appear to be not just the men of substance, who must be identified with Mark's 'first men of Galilee', but the inner circle of the king's government. The term *chiliarch*, with its Roman overtone, has been discussed already.[2] They are the commanders of those hosts—στρατεύ-ματα—which the king in the parable sent against his rebellious subjects.[3] But they are only 'commanders of a thousand'. The term fits the scale of Herod's kingdom. His hosts are only at battalion strength. Since the Roman term *speculator* appears in the continuation of this account of Herod's administration, everything in this sketch is in focus. It shows the court and establishment of a petty Jewish prince under strong Roman influence.

Luke touches again on the late Hellenistic monarchy in his version of Christ's sarcasm about the rulers of the peoples who lord it over them, adding to Matthew's simpler phrase the term 'benefactors'. 'They that hold authority are called benefactors.' This neatly identifies the kings as Hellenistic kings, who of course used this term εὐεργέτης as a stock title.[4] An ingenious scholar might argue that the verb κατ-εξουσιάζουσιν, common to Luke and Matthew, reflects the contemporary title of the Roman emperor, as the holder of ἐξουσία δημαρχική. But this is less convincing.

The explicit historical allusion of the Herod story is an exception in the Galilean narrative of Mark and Matthew. It is the only place where the contemporary historical setting

---

[1] Tac. *Ann.* xv. 27. Dan. v. 23 (Sept.).   [2] Above, p. 124.
[3] Matt. xxii. 7.   [4] Luke xxii. 25; Matt. xx. 25.

emerges clearly. Mark and Matthew contrast with Luke in this respect. In the two former the Galilean narrative is anchored firmly in time only by the story of Herod and the Baptist.[1] Luke ties his narrative down in time by his careful distribution of the four interventions of Herod. At the beginning of Christ's mission Herod arrests John.[2] In the first phase there is a seemingly casual reference to the convert Joanna, wife of Chuza, the procurator of Herod.[3] At the time of the mission of the Twelve Herod is informed of the new preaching and takes alarm.[4] Towards the end of the mission in Galilee there is the strange story of the warning given to Christ that Herod means to kill him, and of Christ's message to the Fox.[5] Luke has attached yet another historical marker by bringing the name of Pilate into the Galilean narrative. This is in the report to Christ—if that is what is meant—of the massacre of the Galileans 'whose blood Pilate mingled with their sacrifices'.[6] The story is peculiar to Luke, and the incident itself cannot be satisfactorily identified. Thus Luke gives his Galilean narrative five anchors in chronology, where Mark and Matthew have but one. But apart from these cross-references the story floats loosely in time and space, and contains very slight indications to anchor it more firmly. The place-names help a little—Tiberias, Caesarea Philippi, the Decapolis—but place-names live long, and these in particular give only a *terminus post quem*.

When one lays aside the Graeco-Roman spy-glass, and looks at the narrative in another manner, it coheres beautifully. The pattern of life, both social and economic, civil and religious, is precisely what is to be expected in the isolated district of Galilee, a land which retained its Jewish characteristics long after the christianization of Judaea. The absence

<hr />

[1] Mark vi. 14–29; Matt. xiv. 1–12.   [2] Luke iii. 19–20.
[3] Luke viii. 3.   [4] Luke ix. 7–9.
[5] Luke xiii. 31–32.   [6] Luke xiii. 1.

of Graeco-Roman colouring is a convincing feature of the Galilean narrative and parables. Rightly, it is only when the scene changes to Jerusalem that the Roman administrative machine manifests itself, in all three accounts, with the procurator and his troops and tribunal, and the machinery of taxation.

The social and economic pattern in the Galilean narrative differs markedly from that of the Hellenistic world of Acts in a major respect. Something will be said later of the great part played in the municipal life of the eastern provinces by the men of moderate wealth, who formed the magisterial class of the cities—the *honestiores* and *curiales* of the late Empire, but present from the beginning under other guises.[1] These were a numerous and solid section of the population. The city councils were large, with 500 or 600 members apiece. The topmost stratum of this class contained a few families of immense wealth, which were gradually incorporated into the international hierarchy of the Roman State as Roman citizens, knights, and finally senators. This is a familiar pattern, much studied in recent years, which holds good for most of the Roman empire. It is the world as reflected, for example, in the civic orations of Dio of Prusa, and it is the world that appears in Acts. But the world of the Galilean narrative seems different. It is difficult to be precise, but one has the impression that the numerous and solid third estate of the magisterial class is absent, or much weaker in numbers and solidity. The narrative presents a world of two classes, the very rich and the poor. There is the Rich Man, or Prince, with his steward, and the peasantry who owe debts of a hundred measures of oil or wheat.[2] If the steward is dismissed his only alternative is to dig or to beg. There is the rich man wearing purple and fine linen, and the beggar Lazarus at his gate—admittedly an extreme

[1] Below, pp. 173 ff.   [2] Luke xvi. 1–6.

contrast, but it recalls a phrase of Christ about the Baptist:
'What went ye out for to see? . . . those that are clothed in
fine raiment live in kings' palaces.'[1] At Antioch or Ephesus
one would not need to look so far. There is the prince setting
off for his kingdom who entrusts to his two servants in Luke's
version a mere hundred silver coins.[2] There is a nice contrast
in the parable of the king and the two debtors in Matthew.
The king's debtor owes the king himself the enormous sum
of 10,000 talents, while his own debtor owes him a mere
hundred *denarii*. In the Lucan parable of the money-lender
there are two debtors of 50 and 500 *denarii*.[3]

In another type of parable the small scale of property is
equally apparent. The story of the Prodigal Son reflects
a small peasant economy—a few hired servants and a single
beast kept for a special feast. So, too, the hired servants of
the fisherman Zebedee.[4] There is the owner of a vineyard
which contained a special fig-tree, watched for three years.[5]
There is the owner of another vineyard, in the parable of
the hired labourers, who went down to the village square
five times on his own feet to hire his harvesters, though he
had a bailiff in his service.[6] The vineyard owner is a favourite
figure. There is yet again Matthew's graphic account of the
walled vineyard and its strong barn or tower. This seems to
be a man of some substance for once, with a staff of slaves,
though he does not work his land by slave labour, but lets
it on lease.[7] Land predominates, even more than in other
accounts of the working economy of the ancient world.[8]
There is but a single merchant in all the material of the
three Galilean narratives—the pearl buyer who sells his all
to secure one, and only one, costly pearl.[9]

---

[1] Luke xvi. 19–20, vii. 25.   [2] Luke xix. 13.
[3] Matt. xviii. 23–34; Luke vii. 41.   [4] Luke xv. 11 f.; Mark i. 20.
[5] Luke xiii. 6–8.   [6] Matt. xx. 1–8.   [7] Matt. xxi. 33–41.
[8] Strabo, for example, has a good deal to say about the industrial and
commercial activities of the cities of the east.   [9] Matt. xiii. 45–46.

It is a principle of modern literary criticism to consider the poet or author in relation to his audience. Christ primarily addresses the crowds, οἱ ὄχλοι, and his illustrations must have been chosen with their preoccupations in mind. Hence the stress on the worker, the proletarian, the sower, or the hired man, or the woman with her treasure of ten *denarii*, ten silver shillings, with a value comparable to such a sum in the eighteenth century. But the proletarian has his counterpart in the Rich Man, ὁ πλούσιος ἄνθρωπος in simple terms. The contrast of poor and rich is a standard type in the parables. If the scale of wealth and the proportion seems different in the Galilean scene from the pattern of organized wealth in the more developed areas of the Hellenistic world, that is as likely to reflect the actual situation in Galilee as the bias of the writer or speaker. It would agree with the general indications of Josephus' account of Galilee, and with the failure of the Hellenistic city system to catch hold, that Galilee should have been less dominated by a landowning class or a middle class of moderately wealthy *bourgeoisie*.

Another negative aspect of the Galilean material tends to the same conclusion. Though the tax-gatherer is a persistent feature of the scene, the urban money-lender, the δανείστης, or the *negotiator*, bane so often of a peasant class in more modern as in Roman times, seems a rarity. There is no counterpart in the Gospels of the many Italian money-lenders who harried Asia in the age of Sulla and Mithridates, and who repeated their performance in the lifetime of Christ, in Gaul, and later in Britain.[2] The moneylender in Luke remits his due, and in the parable of the talents the

---

[1] Appian, *Mithridatica*, 22–23. Cf. also Sallust, *BJ*, 26. 3, for businessmen in Numidia earlier. Tac. *Ann.* iii. 40; *gravitas faenoris* is among the causes of the rebellions in north Gaul under Tiberius; cf. Dio, 62. 2. 1, on usury in Britain in A.D. 61.

third man is told that he might at least have invested his lord's money with a banker, ἐπὶ τράπεζαν.[1] The debtors and creditors in the parables are of a different sort, and reflect a more patriarchal society. The peasant borrows from the baron or prince, from the great landowner.[2] The fault of Zacchaeus was not that he exacted usury, but that he exacted taxation beyond his precise due as a tax-farmer.[3] This is the very thing that is picked out in Luke's summary of the preaching of John the Baptist. He bids the tax-farmers 'take no more than your due', and the soldiers not to extort money under pressure, but has not a word to say about usury. At Jerusalem, outside Galilee, the money-makers in the Temple are money-changers, κολλυβίσται not δανεῖσται.[4]

It would seem that Jews observed the rules of the Law about usury.[5] It is clerics, not usurers, who devour the estates of widows. The lack of prominence given to the professional banking class, like the scarcity of references to traders, is yet another distinction between the world of the Hellenistic provinces and the remote district of Galilee.

Nothing can be made precise, but the sense of difference is marked. There are certain references to political and worldly power and influence, which though equally vague, underline this difference. The dominant class in the Galilean narrative, far more than the court of the tetrarch or the landowners, is that of the clergy, if one may so term them, the priests and scribes, the exponents of the Law. These are the persons who expect to be pointed out in the 'assemblies and synagogues and market-places'. They and their san-hedrin control local society.[6] Otherwise there seems to be

---

[1] Luke vii. 41–42, xix. 23; Matt. xxv. 27. Cf. also Luke vi. 34 f.
[2] Matt. xviii. 23–34; Luke xvi. 1–8, xix. 12–23.   [3] Luke xix. 8.
[4] Luke iii. 12–14, xix. 45; Matt. xxi. 12; Mark xi. 15.   [5] Luke xx. 47.
[6] Luke xi. 43, xx. 46. Cf. p. 128 n. 4 above.

a certain republican spirit about Galilean life. The remark of Christ to the sons of Zebedee, who wanted to sit on thrones, is in this vein. 'You know that the rulers of foreign peoples have lordship over them, and their great ones exercise power over them.' The notion is treated as un-Jewish.[1] That sort of thing may go on among the alien peoples, or at the court of the tetrarch. The picture of power in general terms is either clerical or regal. It is never in terms of the στρατηγός or ἄρχων, the annually elected magistrate, and the civic council. And only once, in the Galilean narrative, is there a reference to the existence of the Roman government, and that is uncertain: 'They will deliver you up to councils, and bring you before kings and governors.'[2] The term is ἡγέμονες. It is the usual term for the procurator in the latter part of the Gospels.

[1] Matt. xx. 25; Luke xxii. 25.

[2] In Matt. x. 17 the context is the mission of the Twelve, but in Mark xiii. 9 and Luke xxi. 12 the scene is Jerusalem. In Matt. v. 25 only the judge appears.

LECTURE SEVEN

The Roman Citizenship and Acts

I HAVE discussed at some length the technical privileges of Roman citizens in the criminal procedure. There remains the citizenship itself, the social and civic status of provincials who acquired it and the attitude of provincials towards it. Professor Cadbury, in his short essay on the Roman background of Acts, asked some eleven questions about the citizenship of provincials, and complained that he could not find the answers in the books of Roman historians.[1] Not all his questions were necessary for the full understanding of the passages in Acts, and the answers are not so hard to find when one realizes that the privileges of a Roman citizen depended upon his grading, his *ordo* in the social sense. The proper place to investigate the function of a Roman is not in a book about the citizenship, but in the numerous treatises about the Senate, the Equestrian Order, the municipalities, the army, and the order of freedmen. Each *ordo* had duties and privileges of its own. These may be summed up in the two legal terms *munera* and *honores*— the civic obligation of the wealthy, and the local magistracies which they held. The most vital question of all is missing from Cadbury's list: to what *ordo* did Paul belong? Adapting his list, the following would seem to be the most relevant themes, apart from the question of jurisdiction: the means and conditions of acquiring citizenship, and the proof of possession; the effect of citizenship on a man's other loyalties, notably to his local community and to his cult. This

[1] K. S. Cadbury, *The Book of Acts in History*, ch. iii, 68.

last theme becomes in reverse the interesting question about the attitude of oriental provincials to Roman citizenship and to Roman supremacy. We not only want to know the answers to these questions, but to know the answers for the first century A.D. Then one must consider whether the allusions and hints in Acts and Epistles fits that period.

There is no mystery about the granting of Roman status to men of free birth in the late Republic and early Principate. This had come to be one of the powers conferred by the Roman people through a *lex de imperio* on the great military commanders of the late Republic, such as Pompey, Caesar, and the members of the Second Triumvirate.[1] As such it was undoubtedly included in the bundle of rights and privileges conferred upon Augustus and his successors by the analogous *lex de imperio*, which gave them their powers, though the direct evidence for this particular clause is lacking after the Triumvirate. Special enactments of the Senate or the legislative assembly were not required for particular grants to individuals of citizenship.[2] The procedure is well documented in the case of men serving in the auxiliary units of the Roman army and the fleets from the time of Claudius onwards. There are enough examples of particular grants by earlier emperors to individuals and communities to leave the matter beyond doubt.[3] The enfranchised person

[1] The practice antedates the creation of the great commands on the model of the *lex Gabinia*, cf. *ILS*, 8888, 89 B.C.; Cic. *pro Balbo*, 8. 19, for the *lex Gellia Cornelia* of 72 B.C. Direct evidence is lacking for this clause of the later commands of Pompey, in which he broadcast the Roman citizenship among the gentry of the east. For the *lex Vatinia* see Suet. *Caes*. 28. 3 with Strabo, v. 1. 6, and the discussion of the related passages in T. Rice-Holmes, *Roman Republic*, ii. 317. For the Second Triumvirate the clause of the *lex Munatia Aemilia* is cited in the letter of Octavian about Seleucus of Rhosus, E–J, no. 301, l. 10 (*FIRA*, i, no. 55); cf. also the contemporary edict *de privilegiis veteranorum*, *FIRA*, i, no. 56.

[2] *Pace* Cadbury, op. cit. 76.

[3] *ILS*, 1986–7, A.D. 52 and 60, are still the earliest regular military *diplomata*, giving citizenship to *classiarii* and auxiliaries. Cf. Sherwin-White,

commonly takes the first two names—*praenomen* and *nomen*—of his benefactor, and retains his own original single name as a *cognomen*. No other ethnic units apart from the Romans in the ancient world used more than one personal name. The enfranchised person is also formally listed as a member of one of the thirty-five Roman tribes.[1] Thus the British chieftain known from the inscription on the town-hall of Chichester when enfranchised by the emperor Claudius became Ti. Claudius Cogidubnus. One can infer from the imperial *nomen* of the new citizen—Claudius here—the name of the emperor by whom the grant was made, though when, as in the early Empire, there was more than one imperial Iulius or Claudius the indication is not very exact. Claudius serves Claudius and Nero, but Iulius may mean the dictator Caesar, Augustus, Tiberius, and Caligula.

When auxiliary soldiers were enfranchised, a special document, known as *diploma civitatis Romanae* or *instrumentum*, was issued containing a copy of a man's certificate of citizenship, which could be used as a card of identity.[2] In grants to private persons there is no evidence that such documents were normally issued, though in a famous example Octavian as Triumvir sent a copy of his edict to the man's municipality, and Nero distributed such certificates paradoxically to a troop of dancers.[3] It is likely that, as with other grants

RC, 191–2. For private persons and communities, cf. *ILS*, 1977, with formula 'civitate ab imperatore donatus', for Augustus; and the reference to him of questions affecting newly enfranchised persons in Cyrenaica, E–J, no. 311, iii. For Claudius see the well-known Volubilis inscription, *ILA*, 634 (Charlesworth, *Documents*, &c., C. n. 36) and *ILS*, 206 *ad fin*. See generally Sherwin-White, *RC*, chs. vi–vii, where, however, the technicalities of enabling laws are not discussed.

[1] For the formalities of enrolment see *FIRA*, i, no. 55, ii. 1–2, no. 56, ll. 8–15.

[2] These are discussed in the introduction to *CIL*, xvi, which contains a large collection of them.

[3] Above, p. 145 n. 1. Suet. *Nero*, 12. 1, evidently mentioned because it was exceptional.

of privilege, it became customary for the emperor to send the man concerned a *libellus* recording the grant, which must also have been noted not only in the tribal list at Rome, but in the municipal registers. The lists of Roman citizens were checked locally every five years in the municipal census, which was taken throughout the boroughs of Italy and those communities in the provinces which possessed the citizenship as communities. New citizens from outside such territory were also registered on the tribal lists at Rome. This is known from an edict of Octavian in which provision is made for the registration at Rome of veterans resident in Egypt, in their absence.[1] Only new citizens could produce documents of the sort described.

Provincial Roman citizens, not living in Roman communities, of the second generation or later, were registered in the taxation tables drawn up for each commune at a provincial census, which was taken at irregular intervals. This provincial census was the basis of Roman direct taxation, the land and poll tax. Provincial Romans paid the land tax, unless they had a special grant of immunity, but not the poll tax. They were also liable for local municipal taxes, again unless they had a grant of immunity.[2] The issue of immunity from municipal taxation was squarely raised in Cyrenaica under Augustus, who confirmed the right of the municipality to tax enfranchised provincials of Cyrenaica unless they had special exemption.[3] Hence it was in the interest both of the communes and of their members that registrations should be properly kept. The Greek cities of the Empire commonly classified their local citizens by a tribal system, like the Roman State. Hence it is to the lists

---

[1] *FIRA*, i, no. 56, ll. 13–15.

[2] For grants of immunity along with citizenship see citation in n. 1 and Volubilis, p. 145 n. 3.

[3] E–J, no. 311, iii. Sherwin-White, *RC*, 213.

of the commune that a provincial would most conveniently refer for proof of his status. Cadbury rightly notes the implication in the first Cyrene edict of 9–8 B.C. that there existed a list of all the Roman citizens in Cyrenaica, but he did not observe that this was a regular census list drawn up in terms of property value: ἔχοντα τίμημα καὶ οὐσίαν.[1] In the edict of Octavian granting citizenship to Seleucus of Rhosus it is particularly laid down that the document should be registered at his native city and at certain other great cities of Asia Minor, including Tarsus.[2] This was to ensure certification of the various privileges including immunity from all taxation that were granted to him.

Failing the census archives, a Roman who was a citizen by birth could produce a copy of the original *professio* or registration of his birth recording his Roman status and made before a magistrate. Many examples are known among Egyptian documents. The system was established by Augustus in his social legislation of A.D. 4 and 9. Various difficulties and technicalities in the evidence, which has been much discussed, were resolved by F. Schulz in a definitive article in the *JRS* of 1942–3, unknown apparently to Professor Cadbury.[3] Schulz could have answered one of his questions for him: what was there to prevent the forging of a certificate, or of an actual registration for that matter? The answer is, nothing. But the law was 'agin it'. It is stated in the documents that the registrations were accepted *citra causarum cognitionem*. But the criminal law of forgery applied specifically to falsifications of this kind.[4] Whether or not Romans carried such certificates about with them, as Schulz

---

[1] Cadbury, op. cit. 72. E–J, 311, i, ll. 15–20.

[2] *FIRA*, i. 55 (i).

[3] F. Schulz, 'Roman registers and birth certificates (i)', *JRS* (1942), 78 f.; (ii) (1943), 55 f. The basic fact about the origin of the system had been established in 1938 by M. Guérard.

[4] Schulz, art. cit. i. 87 n. 67, quoting *D*. 48. 10. 13 pr.; cf. ibid. 10. 1. 4.

and Cadbury suppose, we simply do not know.[1] They were
convenient in shape and size, being small wooden diptychs.
But it is more likely that they were normally kept in the
family archives. The itinerant is the exception in the ancient
world. The general mass of the population stay in one place
from one generation to another, except for merchants and
soldiers; hence the latter were given metal certificates of
citizenship, the *diplomata* mentioned above. It is known
that Suetonius had occasion to check the actual registration
of the birth of the emperor Gaius in the Roman register.[2]
These documents, like the military *diplomata*, were guaranteed by the signatures of the seven witnesses required by
Roman law in the certification of all documents. If your
certificate is challenged, you produce your witnesses if you
can. That was easy enough at home, but there may have
been a certain awkwardness in asserting one's Roman status
on alien territory. Hence perhaps the rarity of the occasions
on which Paul asserted his rights as a Roman.

When Paul made his claim to Roman citizenship before
the captain, Claudius Lysias, the latter appears to have
expressed surprise in the emphatic remark: 'Why, I paid
a great price for this citizenship.'[3] There was no external
mark of the Roman citizen unless he wore the toga. But
this was improbable, on the ordinary occasions of daily life
in the eastern provinces. Even at Rome itself the cumbrous
garb was unpopular, especially with the mass of the population, and imperial measures were sometimes necessary to

[1] Schulz, art. cit. ii. 64. Cadbury in Jackson–Lake, op. cit. v. 316.

[2] Schulz, art. cit. ii. 56. Suet. *Gaius*, 8. 2, 'ego in actis Anti editum invenio'.
But Schulz's assumption that *in actis* refers to the register of the *Aerarium
Saturni*, because Suetonius calls it an *instrumentum publicum*, rather than to the
publication or gazette known as the *diurna urbis acta*, is not quite convincing.
In literary usage *acta* or *publica acta* in such contexts refers to the *diurna*.
Cf. Pliny, *Ep.* v. 13. 8, vii. 33. 3; Pan. 75. 1–3; Tac. *Ann.* 12. 24, 13. 31, 16.
22; elder Pliny, *NH*, vii. 60.

[3] Acts xxii. 27–28.

compel the citizens to dress properly.[1] Nobody but a Roman was supposed to wear a toga, and in the Greek provinces the popular *pallium* must have been universal.[2] It is certainly most unlikely that Paul would have worn a toga in Palestine, where, as Mommsen observed, he preferred in Jewish company to keep his Roman status obscure.

Professor Cadbury did not ask what clothes Paul wore, though he might well have done so. Even the cloak left at Troas, a citizen colony, might be relevant. It was a φενολή, that is, the Latin *paenula*, but there is nothing prescriptive about that.[3] However, Cadbury raised the question of Paul's Latin, and suggested that he possibly conversed in Latin with Claudius Lysias.[4] This was an unlucky suggestion, because only a few paragraphs earlier Lysias asked Paul in surprise the question, Ἑλληνιστὶ γινώσκεις;[5] The suggestion of Cadbury was legitimate, because Roman citizens were supposed to have an adequate knowledge of their official language, which was the service tongue of the Roman army everywhere. But Greek was more than the lingua franca of the eastern provinces. It rated with Latin as *uterque sermo noster*—'our two languages'.[6] Though the emperor Claudius deprived a man of Roman citizenship because he could not speak Latin, there were no proficiency tests, and in the nature of things there could not be any, because the grant of citizenship passed on in law to a man's descendants.[7] The problem only arose practically in the eastern provinces, because in the western Empire for a variety of reasons the

---

[1] Suet. *Aug.* 40. 5. Cf. Pliny, *Ep.* iv. 11. 3.

[2] Cf. the later criticism of the Christians for not wearing their togas, in Tertullian, *de pallio*. Macer, in *D.* 49. 14. 32: 'si accepto usu togae Romanae ut cives Romani semper egerint.' Pliny, *Ep.* iv. 11. 3: 'carent enim iure togae quibus aqua et igni interdictum est.'

[3] See s.v. φαιλόνης, *Arndt-Gingrich.*

[4] *Book of Acts*, 68.   [5] 'Do you know Greek?', Acts xxi. 37.

[6] Suet. *Claud.* 42. 1. Cf. *Aug.* 89. 2; Horace, *Odes*, iii. 8. 5.

[7] Dio, 60. 17. 4. Cf. Sherwin-White, *RC*, 189–90.

use of Latin spread at a faster rate than the extension of the citizenship.[1] The very paucity of the Latin vocabulary in the New Testament, limited to a few technical terms, mostly military, bears out what is amply demonstrated in Egypt: Greek was an official language of the public administration in Syria and Palestine, Latin being normally confined to the internal organization of the army, and to documents affecting Roman citizens.

There has been some speculation as to how Paul or his family acquired the Roman citizenship. His reply to Lysias was ἐγὼ δὲ καὶ γεγέννημαι.[2] This has been taken in two senses: 'born' and 'become'. Mommsen thought the words meant that Paul's father became a citizen when Paul was a child, and that Paul became a Roman as his father's legitimate son, which was the custom.[3] This is less probable than the more obvious rendering: 'I was born a citizen', which is an apt answer to Lysias' remark: 'I got it by paying.'[4] When in a similar passage Paul says that he was γεγεννημένος ἐν Τάρσῳ, he can only mean that he was born in Tarsus.[5]

To speculate how and when the family of Paul acquired the citizenship is a fruitless task, though lack of evidence has not deterred the ingenious. One suggestion has been that Pompey the Great, in his settlement of the eastern provinces in the sixties B.C., transferred a group of Jewish prisoners to Tarsus and set them free.[6] This is based on a misunderstanding of Roman customs. Prisoners of war and defeated troops did not automatically become slaves. They were in the category of *dediticii*, which meant that they had no civic status at all. In some instances they were sold into slavery,

---

[1] Cf., e.g., *ILS*, 206. Strabo, iii, p. 151, iv, p. 186.
[2] Acts xxii. 28.   [3] Mommsen, *GS*, iii. 435.
[4] Cf. Cadbury, op. cit. 68 ff. Schulz, art. cit. ii. 63 n. 93.
[5] Acts xxii. 3, not noted by others.
[6] Cf., e.g., Cadbury, op. cit. 73–74.

but usually they were restored to the liberty of their native communities, and resumed the ordinary condition of *per-egrini*.[1] Pompeius certainly resettled the defeated Cilician pirates in Cilician cities. But this did not make them Roman citizens. The notion of a Roman transference of Jews from Judaea to Tarsus is a useless fiction, derived from the misunderstanding of a tradition preserved in Jerome and of a passage in Acts. Jerome merely says that the family of Paul left Judaea after a war had devastated the region of Giscala.[2] The passage in Acts refers to 'certain of those from the synagogue known as that of the freedmen and of the Cyreneans and of the Alexandrines, and certain of those from Cilicia and Asia'.[3] This passage, so far from connecting freedmen and Cilicians, as has been suggested, carefully distinguishes them.[4] Besides, the descendants of persons freed in about 60 B.C. would no longer be, or be known as, freedmen one hundred years later. So the connexion with Pompeius will not do.

Mommsen suggested his odd version of ἐγὼ γεγέννημαι to help explain Paul's retention of the Jewish name Saul, and the particular phrase used in the Cyprian narrative, Σαῦλος δὲ ὁ καὶ Παῦλος.[5] This is more natural in a first-generation citizen than in a member of a long established family. The formula of the type *qui et Paulus* is paralleled in various Latin inscriptions of newly enfranchised persons.[6] But a similar formula occurs equally commonly in an oriental setting. The Greek citizens of Doura on Euphrates, the river-port of Palmyra, frequently have an Aramaic name in addition to their Greek name, which they give with the formula

---

[1] Cf. Sherwin-White, op. cit., index, p. 307.

[2] Cf. Cadbury, *Commentary*, ad loc., Jerome, *in Philemonem*, 7, p. 672 (Vall.); *De v. illustr.* 5, cited ibid.   [3] Acts vi. 9.

[4] Cf. also Mommsen, *GS*, 432 n. 5, on these various contradictions.

[5] Acts xiii. 9.

[6] Mommsen, art. cit. 435 n. 1; e.g. *ILS*, 2839.

ὁ ἐπικαλούμενος.[1] This phrase is used twice at least in Acts without reference to Roman citizens: Σίμων ὁ ἐπικαλούμενος Πέτρος and Συμεὼν ὁ καλούμενος Νίγερ. Hence Paul's double name is not proof that his family was enfranchised in his own lifetime.[2] It is just a matter of local usage.

There is another and simpler explanation. It is surprising that in the Cyprian narrative of Acts xiii. 9 the formula is not ὁ ἐπικαλούμενος or ὁ λεγόμενος but ὁ καὶ Παῦλος. Perhaps the author was only trying to distinguish *his* Paul, the apostle, from the proconsul Sergius Paulus in the same passage. This may explain the surprising change from Saul to Paul at this moment.

In the Julio-Claudian period every Roman citizen normally had the *tria nomina*. *Paulus* should be the *cognomen*, according to the usage of the time. It does not greatly help the recovery of the man's full name, because, though an enfranchised person ordinarily took the *praenomen* and *nomen* of his patron, he commonly retained his original personal name as a *cognomen*, or third name, either unchanged, if it was Greek, or, if it was barbarian, either latinized in form or translated. The latter is not uncommon with Semitic names in North Africa. The frequent *cognomen* Saturninus replaces compounds of *Baal*. The theme is discussed at length in Toutain's excellent old book on the Roman cities of Tunisia. Despite the adoption of the Roman pattern of names the *cognomen* continues to be the real personal name.[3] The most likely explanation of the *cognomen* Paulus is that it was chosen as the most similar Latin name to the Hebraic name of Saul. Among Roman families the *cognomen* Paulus is rather unusual. It is used only by three well-testified

---

[1] F. Cumont, *Les Fouilles de Doure*, inscr. nos. 2, 122. *Yale Report of Excavations at Doura-Europus*, vii–viii, Parchment no. 40—three examples, A.D. 86-87.

[2] Acts x. 18, xiii. 1.

[3] J. Toutain, *Les Cités romaines de la Tunisie* (Paris, 1896), pt. ii, ch. 1.

senatorial families of the first century A.D., the Aemilii Pauli, the Vettenii Pauli, and the Sergii Pauli.[1] There is also its odd use as a *prenomen* among the Fabii. There are also two Italian municipal families of Acilii and Salvieni who use the *cognomen*.[2] It is of interest that this fairly rare *cognomen* is used by two Asiatic Roman families, one of which hails from Pisidian Antioch.[3] There can be no proof but there is a strong probability that Paul did not derive his *cognomen* from a Roman patron.

After Paul, the origin of the citizenship of Claudius Lysias, the military tribune, who acquired it for a great price, is easy, though some have managed to muddle the matter. From the gentile name Claudius and the dramatic date of the incident, it is not in dispute that this man secured the citizenship from the emperor Claudius. But there can be no question of his being an imperial freedman, as Cadbury in one place surmises.[4] He holds an equestrian commission in the Roman auxiliary army, stationed in Palestine and Syria. Equestrian status could be acquired by freedmen only in the most exceptional circumstances. Only for the personal favourites of an emperor were the numerous barriers sometimes set aside, which prevented the ex-slave from securing the coveted status of a Roman knight. There was a noted scandal in Roman society when the great Pallas, manager of the imperial accounts under Claudius, secured equestrian status and a series of equestrian appointments for his brother Felix, including the procuratorship of Judaea.[5]

The 'great sum' which Lysias paid was not the price of freedom. It was the bribe given to the intermediaries in the

---

[1] Cf. *ILS*, iii. 1, index ii.   [2] *ILS*, 163, 6253.

[3] Ibid. 7200, 7687.   [4] Cadbury, *Book of Acts*, 78 f.

[5] Cf. Sherwin-White, *BSR*, xv. 24 n. 89; Suet. *Claud.* 25. 1, 28; Pliny, *Ep.* viii. 6. 4.

imperial secretariat or the provincial administration who put his name on the list of candidates for enfranchisement. The well-known passage in Cassius Dio about the sale of citizenship under Claudius is not to be taken too literally. Agents of the government made what they could, on the side, out of the growing demand for Roman privileges. A Roman senator and courtier was still trafficking in honours and appointments in the time of Nero, who was extremely angry at the discovery.[1]

It is possible that Claudius Lysias was by origin a promoted common soldier. The Principate of Claudius is precisely the time when the organization of the officer system in the auxiliary army was being standardized. Previously the prefects and tribunes commanding auxiliary regiments of the provincial armies had been either promoted centurions, not holding equestrian status, or men of equestrian standing who had not served in the ranks.[2] From Claudius onwards the promoted centurions ceased to become auxiliary officers in the ordinary course, but were commissioned henceforth in the various corps—Pretorian Guard, urban cohorts, &c.—that served at Rome. The recent investigations of Dr. Birley into the history of equestrian officers have shown that most of them, in the final system, were not young men recruited in their early twenties. Commonly they were men of substance who had held political office in their municipalities, and entered the Roman army as officers in their middle thirties.[3] But from the date of Lysias' career it is possible that he had worked his way up through the ranks

[1] Tac. *Ann.* xiv. 50. 1.

[2] Cf. G. L. Cheeseman, *Auxilia of the Roman Imperial Army* (Oxford, 1914), 90 ff. From his title of tribune ($\chi\iota\lambda\acute{\iota}\alpha\rho\chi$os), instead of the commoner *praefectus* ($\check{\epsilon}\pi\alpha\rho\chi$os), Lysias was probably commander of a *cohors Italica* (as in Acts x. 1) whose officers were tribunes.

[3] E. Birley, *Roman Britain and the Roman Imperial Army* (Kendal, 1953), 133 f.

and the centurionate of the auxiliary army of Syria, and
bought his way into the citizenship—and equestrian status
and a military tribunate too—with his personal savings.

The status of centurion itself in the auxiliary army varies.
Some were drawn from the ranks, and hence were of peregrine or provincial status. Others were transferred from
service in the legions, and hence were Roman citizens.
There can be no certainty that any of the centurions in the
stories of Acts or Gospels was a Roman. Even Cornelius at
Caesarea seems to be a provincial, living with his kinsmen.[1]
In the interchange between Lysias and Paul the tribune
regards Paul as his social equal. This suggests that Lysias
was a promoted man of the older style rather than one of the
gentry-officer class. In the story as told there is no suggestion
that Lysias was of equestrian status. But the possibility must
remain. Josephus indicates that there were natives of Judaea
who held the standing of Roman knights at this period.[2]
One thing is clear: the historical atmosphere of the Lysias
incident is exactly right for the time of Claudius. For a writer
of the second century the commander of an auxiliary cohort
could not be written down, as he is in Acts, as a man of no
great social standing. The reference to the difficulty of acquiring Roman citizenship would be much less appropriate
in a later age, even if the venality of the Claudian administration in this respect were not so well documented. It is
characteristic that the abuse goes unchecked under Claudius,
is punished when detected under Nero, and in later reigns
is not mentioned as among the defects of the times.

Attempts to distinguish other Roman citizens in Acts, in
addition to Lysias, Paul, and the governors, are rather uncertain. The use of single Latin names does not prove much,
particularly when they are personal in type, prenominal,
or cognominal. In the procedures of epigraphical prosopo-

---

[1] Acts x. 24.   [2] *BJ*, ii. 14. 9.

graphy it is reckoned that there can be no certainty about the status of a person with Latin names unless he has at least two, including a recognizable gentile name, and mentions either his tribe or a post in the Roman public or municipal service.[1] The difficulty is that Acts follows the Greek usage common to all folks except the Romans, that a man is known, as was said earlier, by a single official name and a patronymic. Acts xx. 4 gives the provincial style: 'Sopater the son of Pyrrhus, from Beroea.' The Latin names in Acts and Epistles may cover some genuine Roman citizens, but equally they may be names assumed for purposes of prestige. In many parts of the Roman empire Latin names were adopted voluntarily by provincial *peregrini* in a spirit of imitation. Though less frequent in areas where the Greek spirit was strong, it yet occurs even in the old Greek provinces at a surprisingly early date.[2] But there were a fair number of individual Roman families, often of humble status, scattered about Asia Minor. This is shown by the remarkable diversity of proper Roman names among soldiers enlisted in Bithynia in a legionary levy held under Trajan.[3] Of sixty persons only three had an imperial gentile name characteristic of recently enfranchised citizens. Most likely these persons were the descendants of the freedmen of Roman and Italian business men of the Republican period. Or else there may well have been an anomalous population formed by the illegitimate children of soldiers, officials, and business men, persons of uncertain status, who might adopt Latin rather than Greek names. Some of these might secure the envied status of Romans. The inevitable Pliny records just such a request in the time of Trajan, from an auxiliary

---

[1] Cf. Birley, op. cit. 154 ff., for a formal study of prosopographical method.

[2] Cf. W. Schulze, *Zur Geschichte d. lateinischen Eigennamen*, 506 f.

[3] *CIL*, viii. 18084, containing three Flavii and some ten Iulii and Claudii out of about sixty complete names.

centurion for the legitimization of his daughter's status, which the emperor duly granted.[1]

The proportion of Latin names that occurs in the entourage of Paul is, at first sight, surprisingly high for the period. Even in the upper stratum of the Greek cities the Roman citizens are not remarkably numerous in the middle of the first century A.D., though there is nothing statistical about this impression. There is always the possibility that these Latin-named persons in Acts and Epistles are freedmen and not full citizens. A Roman freed slave is a half- or a quarter-citizen, according to the precise formality of his manumission.[2] He had some or all of the civil rights, but not the political rights, of a full Roman. The Romans were generous with grants of manumission, especially to their personal servants, though statute laws controlled the numbers that an individual might set free.[3] But as far as names go it is not easy to distinguish the free-born enfranchised person from the freed slaves, especially in the east, where both may have a Greek *cognomen*.

Of all the persons with Latin names only one has two convincing Roman names, Titius Justus in Acts xviii. 7. Even here Titius has been explained away on textual grounds as a dittography, but unjustly. The scene takes place in Roman Corinth. Titius is not a Jew but a σεβόμενος, a sympathizer. Paul's visit to his house fulfils the threat of the previous verse: 'henceforth I will go to the gentiles'. Even the refugees from Rome, Priscilla and Aquila, must remain

---

[1] Pliny, *Ep.* x. 106–7.

[2] The freedman is not given membership of a tribe, and hence lacks the political rights of the *suffragium*. He may either have the *ius Quiritium*, or civil law status as a Roman, or be of 'Latin' status as a *Latinus Iunianus*, under the *lex Junia*, which secured him most of the privileges of civil law enjoyed by full freedmen, but only for his lifetime, without the power to transmit property rights after death. See A. M. Duff, *Freedmen in the Early Roman Empire* (Oxford, 1928), chs. ii, iv, v.   [3] *CAH*, x. 432 f.

under suspicion. Though the conjunction of names is strik-
ing, and there were many Jewish freedmen-citizens at Rome,
Aquiia originated from Pontus, not Italy. There is special
interest in the name of Gaius, the Macedonian from the
remote district of the Doberi.[1] It is possible that Gaius is
a proper *nomen*, or family name, and hence that the man was
a Roman. The *nomen* exists, though rare, and was borne by
the family of the famous Roman lawyer, as has been recently reaffirmed. It persisted as a family, or gentile, name
in parts of central Italy.[2] The Umbrian L. Gaius L. f.
Nerva is characteristic.[3] But the name Gaius is equally well
attested as a *cognomen* in provincial usage in the second and
third centuries, including several examples from the Balkan
area.[4] A cognominal Gaius from Thessalonica is at least *bien
trouvé*. The usage of it as a Greek name, or a name in
Greece, can be traced back to examples at Delos in 115–114
B.C. and at Athens in 52–51 B.C.[5] Yet a Macedonian from
a remote district might well have acquired citizenship and
Latin names by military service in this period. If the Gaius
of Acts is not demonstrably a Roman, there is no case
for regarding the other commoners with single names as
Romans.

The test cases for usage of names are given by the Roman
officials. Acts uses either the *cognomen* alone, as Felix, Gallio,
Festus,[6] or *nomen* with *cognomen*, as Sergius Paulus, Claudius
Lysias, and Porcius Festus.[7] Pilate is Pilatus in Acts and

[1] Acts xix. 29, xx. 4. Cf. Pliny, *NH*, 4, 35, the only source for Doberi. No
Macedonian Derbe is known to the geographers Strabo and Pliny, or to
modern scholars, hence the reading Δοβραιος must be preferred to ΔΕΡΒΑΙΟΣ
—unless his companion Τιμόθεος can be shown to be from Asia. Then there
would be two Gaii, the Macedonian and the man of Derbe.

[2] Cf. Kunkel, *Herkunft . . . der R. Juristen*, 198 n. 371, quoting *CIL*, x.
6233–5, &c.   [3] *CIL*, xi. 6610.   [4] Kunkel, op. cit. 199 n. 373.

[5] Ditt. *Syll.*³ 1133, 756. 3.

[6] Acts xxiii. 27, xxiv. 22, 27, xxv. 1, 4, &c.

[7] Acts xiii. 7, xxiii. 27, xxiv. 27.

Pontius Pilatus in 1 Timothy.[1] This is in line with the prevalent Latin usage in the first century A.D. Pliny, in the Letters, at the turn of the century, regularly uses these two forms of reference for contemporaries.[2] So too, in the time of Claudius and Nero, does Seneca in his Letters.[3] So, too, emperors and legates in the substance of their decrees and edicts in this same period.[4] But the two subordinate officers in Acts, the centurions, are called by their gentile *nomina* only: Cornelius and Julius.[5] They are the only persons certainly so designated in Acts, and the designation is curious, because the gentile name is undistinctive. These men by their status as centurions in the auxiliary forces—for there were no legionary forces in Judaea—were not necessarily Roman citizens. The bulk of the auxiliary troopers were *peregrini*, and only became Roman citizens after twenty-five years' service.[6] But about Cornelius there is less serious doubt. His troop, one of the *cohortes Italicae*, belonged to a special group recruited originally in Italy, though it is true that auxiliary units were kept up to strength after their formation by local recruitment, which Josephus specifically mentions in Judaea.[7] However, in the Roman army the old

---

[1] Acts xiii. 28; 1 Tim. vi. 13. Cf. Matt. xxvii. 2, 13, &c.: Pilatus, of a living person.

[2] *Passim.* Very rarely he used the *praenomen–nomen* form, e.g. i. 14. 6, ii. 9. 4, with a touch of formality, and less rarely the *nomen*, when of an uncommon type, e.g. Marius in preference to the common *cognomen* Priscus for Marius Priscus, ibid. in ii. 11.

[3] e.g. *Ep.* 30. 1, Bassus Aufidius, with *Bassus noster*, ibid. 3. 5. *Ep.* xxix. 1, 4, Marcellinus, ibid. 6, Iulius Graecinus. In the text of the will of Dasumius, the *praenomen–nomen* is used as the current legal designation in A.D. 108. *FIRA*, iii, no. 48.

[4] e.g. *ILS*, 206, Pinarius Apollinaris (Claudian), Camurus Statutus. A–J, no. 68, legates of Moesia under Claudius and Nero: Flavius Sabinus, Pomponius Pius, Aemilianus. Cf. also *P. Lond.* 1912, where single and double names are used in the informal citations—double for the prefects and *cognomen* only for 'my friend Barbillus'.   [5] Acts x. 1, &c., xxvii. 1.

[6] Cheeseman, op. cit. 38 f.   [7] Jos. *BJ*, ii. 13. 7.

Republican style of name composed of *prenomen* and *nomen* without *cognomen* persisted into the early Julio-Claudian period, when it had gone out of fashion elsewhere. Many legionary tombstones of the early first century show names of the type 'M. Caelius Titi filius,', a centurion who perished in the Germanic disaster of A.D. 9.[1] The latest that can be easily dated concerns a legionary of the African legion, recruited not before A.D. 33 and killed on active service not before the year 54. He is still called 'L. Flaminius D. f.'.[2] Centurions were frequently elderly men, and Cornelius and Julius of Acts may well have followed the earlier fashion. There was a good reason why an enfranchised man should prefer to be known by his *nomen* alone. It indicated and to a certain extent guaranteed his citizen status, whereas a Latin *praenomen* or *cognomen* might be used by anybody. There is a certain formality in the use of the *nomen*. Seneca uses it in the letter-headings of his letters to Lucilius, though he uses the other style inside the letters.[3]

In Acts and Epistles, then, there are three types of nomenclature that correspond very exactly to the classes of persons concerned and to the usage of the first century. The private folk, of peregrine status, have and are addressed formally by a single personal name which may happen to be Latin, and, if Latin, is of a *cognomen* or *praenomen* type—Paulus, Secundus, Pudens, Lucius, Titus. The upper administrative officers are named in the contemporary informal style, either by *cognomen* or *nomen* with *cognomen*. Roman citizens of lower degree are indicated in a way appropriate to each class—the significant *nomen* for the auxiliary centurion, and the double name for the private citizen of Philippi. In

---

[1] *ILS*, 2244.
[2] *ILS*, 2305. He was recruited *c.* A.D. 33–35, and killed twenty-one years later, nn. ibid.   [3] Cf. Pliny's usage, p. 160 n. 2 above.

no case is a Roman citizen certainly indicated by use of *praenomen* alone.

When one turns from the public atmosphere of the Acts to the private atmosphere of the Epistles it is not surprising that the Hellenistic and oriental style of the single name reigns supreme. It is profitless to speculate about the status of those baldly indicated as Clemens, Ampliatus, Tertius, Quartus, or Pudens.[1] It is significant that Titus is designated as Ἕλλην ὤν in Gal. ii. 4. Perhaps after considering Cornelius and Julius the centurions it is tempting to linger over the ladies Junia, Julia, and Claudia, because the rules for ladies' names are different.[2] The feminine gentile *nomen* is the proper and formal way of indicating the daughter of a Roman citizen. Most Roman girls had no real names at all unless they took their father's *cognomen*, sometimes in the diminutive form, e.g. Julia Priscilla for the daughter of a M. Julius Priscus. Usually the daughters of a Julius are simply called Julia Prima, Julia Secunda, &c. It seems unlikely that a provincial would pick on these common gentile names for his daughters, and just possible that these ladies are the daughters of enfranchised provincials. But the most characteristic thing about the names in the Epistles is that only one person is properly designated by Roman names in citizen style, and that is the procurator Pontius Pilatus.[3] The names then are such as one might expect, and appropriate to the different classes of men to whom they are applied.

QUIRINIUS: A NOTE

There is one name that has caused more controversy than any other of the Roman phenomena in the New Testament, that of Quirinius, the governor of Syria. A few remarks

---

[1] Rom. xvi. 3–16, 22; 2 Tim. iv. 10, 18–21; 2 Cor. i. 19; 1 Cor. xvi. 17; 2 Thess. i. 1; Philipp. iv. 3; Philem. 23.

[2] Rom. xvi. 15; 2 Tim. iv. 21.   [3] 1 Tim. vi. 13.

may here be added by way of a footnote to the Quirinius question, which appears to have reached a condition of agnostic stalemate.[1] The point at issue is familiar. Luke dates the birth of Christ by connecting it with the census of Judaea taken, as is made abundantly clear in Josephus, when Sulpicius Quirinius was governor of Judaea after the annexation of the province in A.D. 6.[2] This date conflicts with that of Matthew, who connects the nativity with the last years of Herod and the accession of Archelaus, ten years earlier. Luke's date also conflicts with his own setting of the nativity of John in the 'days of Herod the king of Judaea'.[3] From Mommsen onward those who would save the credit of Luke have tried to maintain that Sulpicius Quirinius was twice governor of Syria, first about 4–2 B.C. and then again ten years later, as in Josephus, assuming a confusion in Luke's information and thereby reconciling the dates in Luke and Matthew.[4]

This rearguard action rests on the attempt to identify Quirinius with an anonymous consular personality whose career is given in an incomplete inscription of early date. This inscription could, but need not, mean that the nameless person was twice legate of Syria.[5] Great ingenuity

---

[1] The general bibliography of the Quirinius question may be found in D. Lazzarato, *Chronologia Christi seu discordantium fontium concordia*, &c. (Naples, 1952), 44 f., or in F. X. Steinmetzler, *Realencyclop. ant. Christ.* ii. 971 f. But the points of any substance in articles of the last twenty years are summarized in the well-balanced article of H. Braunert, 'Der römische Provinzialcensus, &c.', *Historia* (1957), 192 ff.

[2] Luke ii. 1–2. Jos. *Ant.* 18. 1. 1 and 2. 1 with 17. 13. 2 fixes the date of Quirinius' census-taking to the tenth year of Archelaus' government and the thirty-seventh year after Actium, strictly A.D. autumn 6 to autumn 7.

[3] Matt. ii. 1, 19–22; Luke i. 5.

[4] This solution still leaves the question of the census unsolved. For a provincial census in Judaea in the time of the kingdom is an impossibility. Cf. Braunert, art. cit. 210. In Tac. *Ann.* vi. 41 it is a matter of a client king introducing the Roman census of his own initiative.

[5] *ILS*, 918. The inscription comes from Tivoli, source of numerous

has been devoted to this cause. But the career of Sulpicius Quirinius is relatively well known from various documents, including a summary of his achievements in Tacitus, and nothing in them supports the conjecture of a double legateship of Syria.[1] It is difficult to convince oneself of its truth,

inscriptions of Julio-Claudian consulars. It is dated by mention of *Augustus* and *divus Augustus* to a period after A.D. 14. After summarizing certain martial exploits, including the conquest of a kingdom or tribe and the restoration or conquest of a king, for which the consular received triumphal decorations, it continues: 'proconsul Asiam provinciam op[tinuit. legatus pr. pr.] divi Augusti iterum Syriam et Ph[oenicem optinuit].' It is commonly held, following Groag (*Jahresh. Oest. A. Inst.* xxi–xxii. 473 f.), that *iterum* qualifies *legatus* rather than *Syriam*, and hence that a second legateship of Syria does not arise. But Groag, loc. cit., did not establish a rule from a collection of examples. He made a suggestion, quoting only one other instance, *ILS* 932, where Varius Geminus is described as 'leg. Aug II' without mention of specific provinces. Careful examination of the use of *iterum* in Augustan and Julio-Claudian inscriptions of careers shows that when the office or magistracy is given in full with *iterum*, it is always the repetition of precisely the same post or provincial command. Cf. *ILS* 915, twice proconsul of Cyprus (Augustan). *ILS* 942, twice *curator locorum publicorum* (Tiberian), ibid. 2721 twice tribune of the XXI Rapax legion (Claudian or Neronian). *AE* 1925, n. 85, twice assistant legate of Asia (Neronian; but the reading is partly a restoration). Without naming a province, *iterum* or *bis* occurs after *legatus Augusti* in *ILS* 932, and after *legatus pr. pr. ex sc.* ibid. 942; *ter* occurs (ibid. 943) after *legatus pr. pr.* (all Augustan or Tiberian). Otherwise, when a series of legateships and other appointments is written out with full indications, *iterum* is not used, even where a man lists two quaestorian provinces (ibid. 967). Cf. for legateships ibid. 971, 972, 975—all Claudian or Neronian; the paucity of the material provides no earlier examples of 'full' records of several legateships. Cf. also ibid. 984, 'praefecto urbi [iterum]' (A.D. 70), 6286, with *IIvir*, Tiberian.

Hence the evidence does not support Groag's supposed rule. In *ILS* 918, *iterum* should mean that the anonymous consular was twice legate of Syria. Alternatively, if usage in brief personal inscriptions is thought irrelevant to an *elogium* such as this, then *iterum* ought to qualify the verb, with the same result. But it remains true that rules and usages in the epigraphy of the pre-Flavian period were far from stabilized.

[1] Tac. *Ann.* 3. 48, lists, in his obituary of Quirinius, his consulship (12 B.C.), his war against the Homonadenses, and his mission as *rector* to Gaius Caesar in Syria and Armenia between A.D. 1 and 4 (Dio, 55. 10 a 4–5, with Veleius, ii. 102, *pace CAH*, x. 275 n. 3, 276 n. 3. Syme, *Roman Revolution*, 430; both date it from A.D. 2, but the epitomator of Dio clearly distinguishes the

though the case is not as improbable as many assume. That, without delving into details, is the consensus of cautious opinion today. Three comments may be added. First, that a headless inscription is at best a dangerous ally who may change sides at any moment.[1] Second, that Quirinius was in

consular years here). Tacitus omits specific reference to his earlier war in Cyrenaica (Florus, ii. 31), but indicates it by the phrase 'impiger militiae et acribus ministeriis'. Jos. *Ant.* 18. 1. 1, mentions specifically only his consulship; his silence about a double legateship of Syria (*pace* Braunert, art. cit. 210 f.) is not decisive, since his primary interest was in Judaea. Two inscriptions, *ILS*, 9502 and 2683, give but partial aid chronologically. The former mentions Quirinius by name only, as holding an honorary municipal office at Antioch-by-Pisidia; this might belong to the period of the Homonadensian war or to that of the mission with Gaius Caesar. The second confirms the legateship of Syria and the census, but provides no clue as to date (below, p. 169 n. 1).

The basic difficulty in identifying Quirinius with the consular of the inscription is that the military achievements described do not properly fit the circumstances of the Homonadensian war, since the conquest or restoration of a king, *regem*, is mentioned as well as the subjection of a tribe (and there was no king of the Homonadenses). At most this might fit the activities of Quirinius with Gaius, who recovered a kingdom (Armenia) and set up a king there. *Pace* A. G. Roos, 'Die Inschrift von Quirinius' *Mnemosyne* (1941), 306 ff., the identification remains improbable. It is also not known that Quirinius was ever proconsul of Asia.

The notion that Quirinius conquered the Homonadenses as legate of Syria has been shown by R. Syme to be improbable for geographical reasons; Galatia is the obvious base for a Homonadensian war (*Klio*, xxvii (1934), 133 f.). So the best evidence for an earlier legateship in Syria collapses. Cf. Braunert, art. cit. 211. The date of this war remains uncertain. Strabo (xii, p. 569) describes it without giving any date. Dio, who mentions the subjection of the Isaurians, neighbours of the Homonadenses, unfortunately puts it in A.D. 6. But this cannot be Quirinius' war, which Tacitus puts before the mission of Gaius; evidence connected with the military colonies of Pisidia also suggests that it was much earlier; cf., e.g., *ILS*, 5828 (road-building in the region by a legate of Augustus in 6–5 B.C.). Dio, 55. 28. 3.

[1] Other and more convincing candidates have been suggested by R. Syme (*Roman. Rev.* 398–9) and others (e.g. Groag, art. cit., L. R. Taylor, *JRS*, 1936, 161), notably L. Calpurnius Piso, who dealt with kings and tribes in Thrace and received the rewards mentioned in the inscription (Dio, 54. 34. 5–7), but for whom a Syrian legateship is uncertainly testified (Syme, op. cit. 398 n. 8).

the Syrian area before his legateship, as one of the advisory staff of Gaius Caesar from 1 B.C. to A.D. 3 or 4. In A.D. 1 he replaced the dead Lollius as the young prince's chief adviser, and returned to Syria as legate in A.D. 6.[1] Hence Quirinius was a prominent name in the Syrian zone for most of the period in which the birth of Christ should fall. Third, that uncertainty still prevails about the legate of Syria in the very last years of Herod's reign, to which the alternative versions assign the nativity.[2] Quintilius Varus took office in 6 B.C., and held it until at least 4 B.C. If his tenure then ended, his successor down to the arrival of Gaius is unknown.[3]

The attempt to defend Luke in Mommsen's fashion was misconceived. It was noted in an earlier lecture that Luke alone among the Gospel writers is imbued with the notion of chronology, and he alone tried not only to date the beginning and end of the life and the mission of Christ, but to fix in time the otherwise timeless narrative of the mission in Galilee by the fourfold introduction of cross-references to Herod the Tetrarch.[4] The chronology of Luke is deliberate. The internal coherence of the lengthy formula by which Luke dates the beginning of the mission in iii. 1 cannot be challenged for accuracy: 'in the fifteenth year of Tiberius

---

[1] Above, p. 164 n. 1; Gaius visited Egypt in 1 B.C., *CAH*, x. 274. Since Volusius Saturninus is testified as legate of Syria in A.D. 4–5 (*PIR*[1], V. 660) Josephus, loc. cit., must be correct in implying that Quirinius was sent out from Rome after the deposition of Archelaus; otherwise his 'at that time' might be taken elastically, and the suggestion made that Quirinius stopped on after the death of Gaius Caesar as legate of Syria.

[2] Matt. ii. 1–18 gives no precise indication of the year, but in 19–22 he implies that the death of Herod followed fairly soon. Luke iii. 1–3 and 23 can be taken to imply a nativity in *c*. 2 B.C. But a careful reader might observe that Luke in iii. 1–3 dates the beginning of the mission of John, not that of Christ, to 'the fifteenth year of Tiberius Caesar, &c.', and hence only gives a *terminus post quem* for the baptism of Christ.

[3] For the arrival of Varus see Jos. *Ant.* xvii. 5. 2. He was still legate at the death of Herod, ibid. x. 1, 9–10.   [4] Above, p. 138.

Caesar, when Pontius Pilate was governor of Judaea, &c.'
The details are not in dispute.[1] Why then should one
challenge the equally coherent dating of the nativity in ii.
1–2? It is a false procedure to attempt to explain it away as
a confusion with earlier events. The taking of the Roman census in Judaea made a tremendous impact in Jewish history.
It was a most notorious event, as Josephus makes clear.[2]
The author of Luke cannot have been under any doubt
or confusion when he selected that date. But its selection
was a deliberate rejection of the tradition of Matthew,
which connects the nativity with Herod and Archelaus. This
notion is confirmed by Luke's acceptance of the visit of the
Holy Family to Jerusalem, soon after the birth, 'when the
days of purification were accomplished'. This visit excludes
the connexion with the angry Herod of Matthew.

So far Luke seems to be systematically contradicting the
Matthew version. All would be straightforward if Luke had
not unfortunately managed to include, or failed to exclude,
from his long version of the nativity of John, the setting of
the story 'in the days of Herod the king'. It is not within the
competence of a Roman historian to judge the compilation
of these chapters. But one may well suspect that the root of
the chronological difficulty is that Luke, though determined
to date the birth of Christ to the year of the census, has
accepted the incompatible synchronism of the two nativi-
ties, of John and Christ.[3] The dating of John's birth being

[1] Even the obscure Lysanias of Abilene can be identified; Jos. *Ant.* 18. 6.
10, 19. 5. 1, 20. 7. 1. Cf. Jones, *Cities*, 272 n. 59. On the different persons
called Lysanias see A. R. C. Leaney, *Gospel according to S. Luke* (London,
1958), 47; *OGIS*, no. 606.
[2] Cf. Jos. *Ant.* xviii. 1. 1; Acts v. 37. The fact of the census in Judaea
cannot be questioned. It is a necessary consequence of the establishment of
direct provincial government. Cf. Braunert, art. cit. 198 f., who disproves
conclusively the notion of a Roman census before the creation of the province. Ibid. 210 ff.
[3] His reasons may have been akin to those urged in the theory of Braunert

too firmly established as in the days of Herod to be set aside, this date slips in as part of the accepted story.

One phrase in Luke that has commonly been regarded as an error may bear a very different interpretation: 'An edict went out from Caesar Augustus that all the world was to be taxed, and this first happened when Quirinius was governor of Syria.' Critics hasten to remark, correctly, that there never was a single census of the whole Roman empire. The assessment of the different provinces was undertaken at different and widely separated dates in the Principate of Augustus.[1] But Luke has been misunderstood. A census or taxation-assessment of the whole provincial empire (excluding client kingdoms) was certainly accomplished for the first time in history under Augustus. Now it was the way of Augustus to issue general explanations of the particular actions of the central government. For example in 4 B.C. an amendment to the extortion law was issued to all provinces with the introductory formula: 'That it may be plain to all those who dwell in the provinces what care we take that none of those who are subject to us should suffer harm, we enact as follows.'[2] It is likely that Quirinius issued the instructions for the census of Judaea with an introductory edict of Augustus, explaining that whereas the welfare of the whole Empire requires that no man should pay more

(below, p. 171 n. 1), to link the birth of the last Messianic prophet with that of the Messiah himself, in a milieu of Judaic Christianity. The connexion may, as Braunert argues, be due to the source rather than to the author of 'Luke'.

[1] For a full discussion see Braunert, art. cit. He rightly rejects recent attempts to suggest that there was a single census of the whole Empire, and correctly separates the Augustan *census populi Romani* from the assessments of the provinces. The Augustan *breviarium imperii* may be taken to imply the completion of the census of the whole provincial area in some form, but not by a single act. Cf. ibid. 203 f.

[2] E–J, no. 311, v. 77 f. Braunert, art. cit. 201 f., less probably supposed that the edict of the legate, on the model of those concerning the census in Egypt, was popularly regarded as the edict of Augustus.

than his due, and that the census should be completed throughout all the provinces, this is now to be undertaken in Judaea at the same time as the revision of the census in Syria,—or words to that effect.[1] The supposed weakness in Luke's formulation may turn out to be the best proof of his accuracy. His whole statement means that the general policy of Augustus was carried out piecemeal in Judaea in A.D. 6 by Quirinius.[2]

A word may be said about the alternative version derived from Tertullian.[3] He substitutes the name of the consular Sentius Saturninus for Quirinius, as the legate of Syria presiding over the census taken at the birth of Christ. There is copious evidence in Josephus to show that this Saturninus governed Syria in the years preceding 6 B.C., though he cannot then have been conducting a census in Judaea.[4] If

[1] *ILS*, 2683, proves that Quirinius conducted a census in Syria during his legateship. The genuine character of this inscription, or of this part of it—which has been doubted—was demonstrated by F. Cumont, *JRS* (1934), 187 f.: 'Q. Aemilius Secundus . . . sub P. Sulpicio Quirinio legato Caesaris Syriae . . . iussu Quirini censum egi Apamenae civitatis, &c.' This is likely to have been at least the second census taken in Syria under Augustus. Possibly its predecessor was taken by Sentius Saturninus *c.* 9 B.C. Braunert does not consider this possibility, art. cit. Similarly the census was taken in the three Gauls in 27 B.C. (Dio, 53. 22. 15, Livy, *Per.* 134), in 12 B.C. (Livy, *Per.* 138. *ILS*, 212, ii. 36), and in A.D. 14–16 (Tac. *Ann.* i. 31, 33, ii. 6).

[2] Braunert, art. cit. 206 f., defends the probability of Luke's account of the return of travelling workmen and absentees to their place of nativity for the census, alleging the Egyptian parallel where an edict ordered just such a return εἰς ἰδίαν. But Egyptian parallels should not be invoked too freely, as Egyptian procedure is often abnormal for the rest of the Empire. Braunert might have invoked the Ptolemaic substratum in the administration of Judaea in support, cf. p. 127.

[3] *Adv. Marcionem*, iv. 19. The wording is more than a passing allusion. Cf. *RE*, (2) ii. 1, 1520 f.: 'sed et census *constat* actos sub Augusto tunc in Iudaea per Sentius Saturninum.'

[4] *Ant.* 16. 9. 1, 10. 8, 17. 1. 1, 5. 2; *BJ*, i. 27. 2, 29. 3. The date is after 13 B.C., *Ant.* 16. 3. 3, and after the twenty-eighth year of Herod, ibid. 5. 1, and in Olympiad 192, ibid. He evidently succeeds Titius, ibid. 16. 8. 6, and is commonly assigned to 9–6 B.C., preceding Varus.

Tertullian is to be taken seriously he must be repeating a version which aimed, already in antiquity, at removing the contradiction posed by Luke. How Tertullian or his source acquired this information can only be guessed. There is a notable absence of any evidence that formal lists of past governors were published or preserved in provinces.[1] It would be extremely hard to discover at Carthage in Africa a list of the former legates of Syria in the Roman east. But Tertullian is well informed about Sentius; he also knows, less surprisingly, that he had been proconsul of Africa. Sentius was a notable statesman and general of the Augustan period who features quite large in the brief history of Velleius.[2] His biography may have been included in some lost history of the early Principate. The version of Tertullian is intelligent, but it should not be used to suggest that Luke—or his source—was making an unconscious error. The Saturninus date has its own difficulties for the chronology of the nativity. Sentius was certainly not legate of Syria after 6 B.C., when Quintilius Varus replaced him, and he cannot have been conducting a census of Judaea, though he might have been in charge of an earlier census of Syria, in 9–6 B.C.[3] For a nativity of Christ in the last years of Herod the legate should have been Sentius' successor—Varus—or the unknown successor of Varus.[4] Quirinius is preferable to Sentius. He did not have to be dug out of books. He was the first of the Jewish bugbears of the Empire period. To return

---

[1] Above, p. 105.

[2] Tert. *De Pallio*, 1, Velleius, ii. 92, 105, 109. 5, 110. 1. Cf. *RE*, (2) ii. 1 s.v.

[3] Above, p. 166 n. 3, p. 169 n. 1. A Saturninus date cannot be combined, for example, with Luke's statement that Christ was 'about thirty years old' if this is dated literally to the 'fifteenth year of Tiberius'. Cf. p. 166 n. 2.

[4] Cf. p. 166 n. 3. It is a possible hypothesis that Tertullian has confused Sentius Saturninus with his namesake Volusius Saturninus, who as legate in A.D. 4–5 might well have initiated the taking of the census in Syria. Sentius cannot have been assisting Quirinius—though such consular assistants are known—because in A.D. 6 he was in Illyricum; Velleius, ii. 109, 5.

to the starting-point, Luke called the governor of Syria Quirinius, *Κυρήνιος*, using the *cognomen*. It is precisely the form used by Josephus in the text of the *Antiquities*. Luke should mean what he wrote.[1]

[1] Those who do not wish to dispute the alternative chronology may welcome the theory of Braunert, art. cit. 213 f., that the synchronism of Christ's birth with the census of A.D. 6 was intended to link the birth of the Messiah with the origins of the Zealots. But he seems to weaken his own case by his argument that the Zealot movement in fact began at the death of Herod. If so, the Matthew chronology already connected the two, and alteration was not necessary.

The argument of the Note in this lecture tends in the same direction as Braunert's article, but by a different road. It was, I may add, worked out independently before reading his article, a fact which may add somewhat to the value of both.

I have no space to bother with the more fantastic theories, such as that of W. Lodder (*Die Schätzung des Quirinius*, 1930), who regards the attribution of the census of Q. to A.D. 6 as due to Josephus' misunderstanding of his source. This kind of reasoning, without supporting evidence, destroys the value of all sources. Equally, F. W. Heichelheim's (and others') suggestion (*Roman Syria*, 161) that *πρώτη* in Luke iii. 2 means *πρότερον* could only be accepted if supported by a parallel in Luke himself.

LECTURE EIGHT

Aspects of Roman Citizenship, and the Question of Historicity

ASPECTS OF ROMAN CITIZENSHIP AND THE QUESTION OF HISTORICITY

THE general importance attributed to the Roman citizenship in Acts fits the early period. Enough has been said earlier about the technicalities of *provocatio* and the qualified immunities from personal punishment of the Roman citizen in the provinces. Here what calls for attention is the tone, the indignant tone, in which these things are mentioned, and the alarmed reaction of those who find that unwittingly they have maltreated a Roman citizen. Paul at Philippi declaims like Cicero on Verres. 'They have given us a public beating without the formality of a trial. We are citizens of Rome and they have thrown us into prison. Now they are trying to send us away without any fuss. It won't do'—οὐ γὰρ ἀλλά—'They had better come in person and escort us from the gaol.'[1] Not so differently did Cicero phrase it. 'Along comes the gaoler, the governor's butcher, the death and bugbear of Roman citizens, the lictor Sextius.' 'The crosses that Verres set up for condemned slaves he kept in hand for Roman citizens who had been given no trial.' 'A Roman citizen, C. Servilius, was beaten and cudgelled at your tribunal, at your very feet. Is there any legal reason why this should happen to any Roman citizen?' Such are the more moderate passages from Cicero's great effusion on the rights of Romans.[2] Style, circumstance, detail, even the legal situation, differ. But the tone, the approach,

[1] Acts xvi. 37.   [2] *II in Verr.* v. 12, 118, 140–1.

is the same. There is a climate of feeling about this topic—the sacrosanct quality of the Roman overseas—which extends from the last century of the Republic, the age of the master race, down into the Empire. The force of this feeling ultimately petered out with the large extension of the citizenship through the provinces, just as the privileges of Romans came to be whittled down at a similar rate.

Acts breathes the climate of the earlier phase. Fifty years later the literary Pliny, though steeped in Cicero, when he comes to deplore the savagery of a proconsul towards Roman citizens forgets to dwell on their privileged status as citizens, and characteristically for his generation, concentrates on the social status of a victim who was a Roman knight, instead of his legal status as a citizen.[1] The dramatic date of Acts belongs to the period when the spread of Roman status in the provinces was still on a small scale. The scale of extension was a matter of great debate at Rome in the time of the emperor Claudius. There was still organized opposition at Rome to the over-rapid extension of Roman privileges in the provinces at that time.[2] In the half-century after Claudius the tide of extension flooded fast and high, though, as will presently appear, not so fast or so high in the eastern provinces as in the west. In references to the citizenship, Acts gets things right both at the general level, in its overall attitude, and in specific aspects such as were discussed in the last lecture—the type of names of the centurions, the prevalence of bribery in this context under Claudius.

Something has already been said of the emergence, in the later second and third centuries, of the classes known as

---

[1] Pliny, *Ep.* ii. 11. 8: 'exilium equitis Romani septemque amicorum eius ultimam poenam, . . . unius equitis Romani . . . plura supplicia arguebatur emisse: erat enim fustibus caesus, damnatus in metallo, strangulatus in carcere.' Cf. ibid. 2. Contrast the apologetic tone of the Augustan edict on the arrest of certain Roman citizens cited above, p. 60.

[2] See Sherwin-White, *RC*, ch. viii.

honestiores or *curiales*, the municipal aristocracies. In the late Empire the distinction between *honestiores* and *humiliores*—the masses—replaces the earlier distinction between *cives Romani* and *peregrini*.[1] Hints of the future trend can first be distinguished in the time of Trajan and Hadrian. Pliny advises a proconsul on the importance of maintaining the distinctions between the classes—'discrimina ordinum dignitatumque'—and of showing due respect to the men of influence, the *potentes*, in his province. Pliny himself, in Bithynia, preferred to recruit civic councillors from the 'sons of the well born', *honestorum hominum liberi*, rather than from the common folk.[2] Hadrian was the first emperor to discriminate in favour of the curial class in the matter of criminal punishment.[3] This led to the doctrine that normally the member of a magisterial family was not liable to capital execution or to humiliating punishments, a doctrine general in the late Empire.

Acts is remarkable for the absence of these social and legal distinctions which became increasingly rigid in the late Empire. In Acts a man is either a Roman or a provincial. There is no privileged and recognized Third Estate, though naturally the municipal upper classes, the men of substance and authority, who later became the *honestiores* and *curiales*, appear in the appropriate situation. These may be the First Men of the City, and the 'ladies of good estate', αἱ εὐσχήμονες, as at Antioch and Beroea, or the Asiarchs as at Ephesus. The ladies of good estate, with the implication

---

[1] The development of the *honestiores* has long been the theme of the great books on the later Empire, e.g. M. Rostovtzeff, *Soc. and Ec. Hist. of the Roman Empire*[2], ch. viii. But the precise significance of the term in legal contexts has been developed more recently by G. Cardascia, art. cit. (p. 69 n. 1), and briefly by A. H. M. Jones in relation to Roman citizenship and the right of appeal, 'I appeal', 929 f.

[2] Pliny, *Ep.* ix. 5. 3; x. 79. 3, 112. 3.

[3] Cardascia, art. cit. 305 ff. Cf. above, pp. 69 f.

of a propertied class, reappear at Thessalonica.[1] But, as appeared from the detailed analysis of the civic situation at Philippi and Ephesus, the stress in Acts is on the actual magistrates in office, and the mass of the population plays some part in affairs: the demos is active both at Ephesus and at Thessalonica.[2] The city councils, so predominant in the later period, are conspicuously absent from the story. Even at Athens there is no word of the council which administered the city, and it is very questionable whether the meeting 'on Areopagus' is a meeting of the council of Areopagus. Paul addresses his assembly as 'Men of Athens'.[3]

Provincial Romans in the eastern Empire lived in a different legal and social atmosphere from their fellow citizens in the western provinces. In the latter, Roman material and cultural civilization dominated the life of the communities, and technical Roman status was being steadily granted to whole communities in increasing numbers. The Mediterranean provinces in the west were becoming an extension of Italy, and the term *provincia togata* was coined to indicate this massive extension of Roman rights and Roman ways.[4] Hence the individual Roman citizen circulated against a background of Romanism or Latin civilization. In the eastern provinces the predominant civilization was Hellenistic

---

[1] Acts xiii. 50, xvii. 4, 12, xix. 31.

[2] Above, pp. 83 f. For Thessalonica, Acts xvii. 5–10.

[3] Acts xvii. 19. Simply ἐπὶ τὸν Ἄρειον πάγον ἤγαγον ibid. 22. ἐν μέσῳ τοῦ Ἀρείου πάγου. In s. 21 'all the Athenians and the resident aliens' are in question. The reference in s. 34 to Dionysius the Areopagite has led to the hasty inference that Paul addressed the Council of Areopagus. Athens had two councils in this period, the Areopagus and the Six Hundred. See P. Graindor, *Athènes de Tibère à Trajan* (Cairo, 1931), 62 ff., 117 ff., who admits that the phrase in Acts does not technically refer to the Council, but notes that the Hill was a very odd place for any purpose save an inquiry before the latter, while admitting that this was not a trial.

[4] Pliny, *NH*, 3. 112. Mela, 2. 4. 59, 'Gallia togata'. Strabo uses the Latin word *togati*, in Greek spelling, to describe the provincials of Spain, iii. 2. 15, p. 151.

and the predominant language Greek. There were no roman-ized communes of provincial origin, no cities which had acquired Roman citizenship *en bloc* and so become what were called *municipia civium Romanorum*.[1] There was, how-ever, a small number of Roman military colonies founded mostly by Julius Caesar and Augustus, at a time when they had to provide land for an unusually large number of veterans and civilian settlers in a period of crisis. There was also a group of three or four military colonies in southern Asia Minor around the highlands occupied by the turbulent Pisidian mountaineers; these had been established by the generals of Augustus. It happens that the direction of Paul's travels took him remarkably often through these Roman settlements. He visits Antioch and Lystra in Asia Minor, though Acts does not mention their status, and also two Roman colonies in Macedonia and Achaea, Corinth, and Philippi—where they were more frequent than in Asia Minor—and one of the three colonies on the long coasts of the province of Asia, Alexandria Troas.[2] This recurrence of the colonies in Acts, largely due to the Roman habit of placing their colonies at centres of communication, gives a misleading impression of the part played by colonies in the

[1] Cf. Sherwin-White, *RC*, 174, 236 ff.

[2] For the colonies cf. Jones, *Cities*, ch. v, 135; *Greek City*, 61 f. M. Grant, *From Imperium to Auctoritas*, 238 f., 264 f. Iconium was not a Roman *colonia* at this date. Its title Claudia indicates only some municipal benefit re-ceived from Claudius, or the desire to honour him, as also at Derbe and Laodicaea. *Cities*, 136 and n. 21. Momigliano, *Emperor Claudius*, &c. 117 n. 71. Troas is always taken to be Alexandria Troas, another Augustan colony, Jones, *Cities*, 86 and n. 98. But properly it was a large district, not a single city. Jones, op. cit. 40 f., 85 f. Cf. Strabo, pp. 581-2. 586, xiii. i. 1, 3, 4, 9, 23. But Pliny, *NH*, v. 124, uses Troas as the city-name, as in Acts: 'ipsaque Troas Antigonia dicta nunc Alexandria colonia Romana.' Troas was the only colony on the west coast: Parium and Lampsacus lie on the north, or Propontic, coast of Asia. All these colonies were genuine veteran settlements. In the later Empire the title was given even to Greek cities, without actual colonization, as to Claudiconium by Hadrian.

East. It is precisely because the Roman colony was exceptional that Acts notes the colonial status of Philippi, which
was relevant to the story because the disturbances at Philippi
involved a point of Roman custom.[1]

The population of Roman settlers maintained themselves
with some vigour in the eastern colonies, but they formed
only a small proportion of the total local population, sometimes constituting a city within a city. The Roman class
formed an enclave of which a passing stranger might not be
aware in the smaller settlements, though the government
was in its hands. In Acts, Antioch, Lystra, and Corinth
have as many Hellenes and Jews in their streets as Romans.[2]
Elsewhere in the hundreds of Greek and half-Greek cities,
large and small, the Roman citizen was a somewhat rare
bird. Tribal lists of inhabitants and even lists of annual
magistrates from the Greek cities in the Julio-Claudian
period frequently contain the names of no recognizable
Roman citizens.[3] The individual inhabitant of a great Greek
city who happened to possess the Roman franchise could
make effective use of it, if he was a proletarian, only by
entering the Roman army, or if he was a magnate, by securing admission to the Equestrian order and thence into the
public service as an officer. Such promotion required great
wealth and considerable personal influence in the right
quarters at Rome. There are perhaps a dozen Roman citizens, in the Julio-Claudian period, from the eastern provinces, who are known to have made a career in the
Equestrian service as military officers and procurators of the
emperor.[4] This was the way of few among the few provincial

[1] Above, pp. 78 f.

[2] Acts xiii. 14, xvi. 2, xviii. 4.

[3] Above, p. 91. A–J, no. 68, Istria, 1, 50 ff. Cf. ibid., no. 52 in A.D. 51. some
Rhodian emissaries, all *peregrini*. Ditt. *Syll.*[3] 799–800. But cf. *SEG*. xvi. 415.

[4] Cf., e.g., Sherwin-White, *RC*, 190 n. 4, to which list add at least
Gessius Florus, procurator of Judaea, from Clazomene, Jos. *Ant.* xx. 11. 1.

Romans from Greek cities of the East, though members of
the Roman colonies from the East might make more active
use of their status.

It was natural that the Hellenistic Roman, as one may
call the type for convenience, tended to regard his citizenship as a kind of honorary degree, which was of little
practical use to him unless it was joined with other, separate
privileges, such as immunity from taxation and compulsory
services. The Hellenistic world was familiar with the notion
of *isopoliteia*, the exchange of honorary citizenships, which
became effective if one changed one's domicile. Men of
substance tended to collect citizenships in that style. This
is very apparent in the inscriptions of notables from Lycia.
They like to list their citizenships in a sequence, e.g. C.
Iulius Demosthenes, citizen of Rome, citizen of Patara, and
citizen of Xanthus. The Roman status appears as merely
the highest of a list of civic dignities, though from time to
time particular Lycian magnates materialized their Roman
status by successfully pursuing a career in the Roman public
services.[1]

Dio of Prusa in his discourse 'To the Senate of Apamea
on Concord', delivered about A.D. 100–5, casts a curious
light on the attitude to Roman status in the Asiatic provinces.[2] Apamea was one of the veteran colonies of Julius
Caesar, like Alexandria Troas where Paul left his cloak.
Dio indicates that there was a flourishing Greek community
mixed up with the Roman colony, and apparently identified
with it in many respects. Intermarriage, exchange of citizenship, exchange of magisterial appointments, are all proceeding merrily between the Roman colony and Prusa, as

Ti. Claudius Balbillus, prefect of Egypt under Nero, and probably Nymphi-
dius Sabinus, pretorian prefect under Nero; cf. *BSR*, xv 25, nn. 98–100.

[1] *RC*, 242 f., e.g. *IGRR*, iii. 603, 628, 634, &c.

[2] Dio Chrys. 41.

between any two Greek provincial cities. 'Senators of Apamea', says Dio, 'You have made many men of Prusa citizens and senators of Apamea, and have given them a share in the solemnities which belong to the state of Rome.'[1] But Dio is cheating a little, for the one thing that the Senate of Apamea could not do was to make outsiders, *peregrini* from other cities, into Roman citizens. Dio lets that slip out in another passage, admitting that his own family received the franchise of Apamea without having Roman status.[2] So, even at the colony of Apamea, the personal status of the *coloni*, the descendants of the Roman settlers, as Romans, if not submerged, has retired into the background, and the pattern of Greek city life prevails. Being Apameans was of greater practical importance than being Romans.

Still more in an ordinary provincial community, a man who happened to have Roman status, such as Paul at Tarsus, would tend to look for an active political life in the municipal affairs of his own city. Thus in Lycia, in the early Principate, the magistracies of one's own city, and the headship of the Lycian provincial council, or *koinon*, are the ordinary limit of political ambition even of those who are Roman citizens.[3] It is not surprising, then, that there is a certain ambiguity in Paul's references to his personal status as represented in Acts. He thinks of himself first and foremost as a citizen of Tarsus, and only refers to his latent Roman status when it is expedient to do so. To Claudius Lysias, the ex-provincial Roman officer, he identifies himself as ἄνθρωπος Ἰουδαῖος Ταρσεὺς τῆς Κιλικίας and repeats this identification to the Jewish mob.[4] The addition, 'a citizen of no mean city', is a very characteristic Hellenistic

[1] Ibid. 9–10.
[2] Ibid. 6. He distinguishes the acquisition of Roman citizenship from the grant of Apamean franchise.
[3] Sherwin-White, *RC*, 242 f.
[4] Acts xxi. 37–39, xxii. 3.

addition, and touches the theme, with the help of an erudite quotation from the classics, of half the municipal orations of Dio of Prusa. Tarsus is Paul's city, and he takes pride in it. For Tarsos, as Strabo's description shows, was the first city of Cilicia, not merely in material wealth but in intellectual distinction, as one of the great university cities of the Roman world.[1] His Roman franchise was only a personal privilege to be invoked if and when necessary. Just so did the Lycian dignitaries regard their Roman status.

This touch, as with so many other details, is part of the pattern of the earlier Empire, the first century and a quarter A.D., when there was something exceptional about Roman status. In the third century, after the *Constitutio Antoniniana*, all the inhabitants of the *oikoumene*—except slaves—became Romans, and the distinction ceased to have validity. The word *Romanus* came to be used in a different sense, for the generality of the inhabitants of the Roman empire. This usage can first be discerned in Tertullian's *Apology*, at the end of the second century A.D., in such passages as: 'Our enemies will not allow that we Christians are Romans.' 'We are reckoned non-Romans because we do not worship the god of the Romans.' 'Those who used to be counted as Romans have been found out to be enemies.' Tertullian also uses *Romanus* in its specific historical sense, but this loose usage is characteristic.[2] It led to the identification of the Greek-speaking half of the Empire, and ultimately of the Byzantine empire, with the term 'Ρωμαῖοι—Romani. But this usage is quite alien to the author of Acts. For him ἄνθρωπος 'Ρωμαῖος or 'Ρωμαῖος alone means *civis Romanus* in the technical sense of the early Empire.[3] This would be remarkable in the writer of a popular novel in the third or

[1] Strabo, xiv. 5. 10–15 with Dio Chrys. 34, for the material aspects.
[2] Tertullian, *Apol.* 24, 35, 36. Cf. *RC*, 266 f.
[3] Acts xvi. 21, 37, 39, xxii. 25, xxiv. 27–28.

fourth century A.D. The great catalogue of the Peoples of the World at Pentecost in Acts, may represent, as Dr. Wein-stock demonstrated, the utilization of a list of peoples ori-ginally composed for astrological purposes.[1] But it has been adapted by the author of Acts in a manner interesting for the present inquiry. He introduces 'the Romans visiting Jerusalem', οἱ ἐπιδημοῦντες ῾Ρωμαῖοι, and contrasts them with the inhabitants of the various provinces, Judaea, Cappa-docia, Pontus, Asia, &c.[2] This is a nice contemporary touch from the Julio-Claudian age.

There is a preliminary question about the Roman citizen-ship that has attracted a good deal of attention in recent years. In the Republican period the Roman citizenship was incompatible with that of any other State. The provincial who became a Roman ceased to be a member of his native community, and to exercise any rights or to be required to perform any duties there. This was certainly the standard rule or custom in the time of Cicero—though as with all customs there were differing interpretations of its effects.[3] It is an important consideration in dealing with the eastern provinces, where the cities continued to rate as *civitates iuris peregrini* and were not incorporated as communities into the Roman State, as in the western provinces, where the com-munes tended to become Roman municipalities. The in-compatibility of two citizenships would be a serious limita-tion on the local political life of enfranchised persons in the eastern provinces. It can be seen from the speech of Dio at

[1] S. Weinstock, 'The Geographical Catalogue in Acts II 9–11', *JRS*, xxxviii. 43 ff.

[2] Cf. Acts ii. 17, 21. Ἀθηναῖοι δὲ πάντες καὶ οἱ ἐπιδημοῦντες ξένοι.

[3] The development of dual citizenship from the Republic onwards is discussed in Sherwin-White, *RC*, 54, 69, 134, 189 f., 213 f. F. de Visscher, at length, in *Les Édits d'Auguste* (Louvain, 1940), 108 f. For a summary of recent discussions see H. F. Jolowicz, *Historical Introduction to . . . Roman Law*[2] (Cambridge, 1954), 542 ff.

Apamea that this incompatibility had certainly ceased to exist by the end of the first century A.D., so much so that the former position had almost been reversed. The Roman status had become a titular dignity, except for the small number of persons who entered the Roman public service. The characteristic oriental Roman citizen lives out his life with his local community as its focus. Just such a one is that magnate of Ephesus, Claudius Aristion, a local magistrate and an Asiarch too, who was involved in a political charge in A.D. 106, and like Paul exercised his right of appeal to the emperor Trajan. His trial and acquittal are described briefly in a letter of Pliny.[1]

Roman historians have been much exercised as to the stages and dates by which the change in the rule of incompatibility was accomplished. For the study of Acts the only concern is whether the change came about early enough to fit the attitude of Acts or of Paul to the citizenship. This is not in serious doubt. The rule of incompatibility was beginning to waver, even in the late Republic, when different opinions were held about it in the fifties.[2] A few years earlier it had been taken for granted by Pompeius as a basic principle and applied, rather oddly, in his organization of city life in the new province of Bithynia, though it was alien to Greek practice.[3] One consequence of

---

[1] Pliny, *Ep.* vi. 31. 3.

[2] Cicero, *Pro Balbo*, 28–31, gives the prevailing rule—'duarum civitatum civis noster esse *iure civili* nemo potest', and notes certain violations of it. Cf. Nepos, *Atticus* 3. 1. The italicized words indicate the difficulty—that a Roman's property depends on the Roman law, and confusion would arise if it became subject to different legal systems.

[3] Pliny, *Ep.* x. 114. 1, noted originally by Hardy, ad loc. The rule was modified slightly to fit Hellenistic conditions. Cities might grant their franchise only to members of communities outside Bithynia; i.e. a Bithynian might not hold active citizenship in two Bithynian cities, but might hold the honorary citizenship of more distant cities in other provinces. The rule was neglected in the time of Pliny and Dio Prusensis.

the rule of incompatibility was that the provincial Roman enjoyed immunity from local municipal taxation and other civic obligations. This automatic exemption was whittled down in the time of Augustus and finally abolished altogether by a series of specific edicts referring to particular persons and areas.[1] Probably there was no general rule, but the cumulative effect of the various documents suggests that citizenship and *immunitas* had ceased to be coextensive. In and after the last decade of Augustus it is unlikely that any fresh grant of Roman franchise conferred automatic immunity of any sort, and previous grants were circumscribed to some extent. Hence the enfranchised πολίτης of a Hellenistic city remained a πολίτης.

It remains to inquire, at what date did such men begin to hold magistracies as a matter of course in their native cities. The probable answer is that they never altogether left off despite the nominal rule—they would make the most of both citizenships, enjoy the honours of their cities as native citizens and escape its burdens as Romans. There is a dearth of evidence about Roman citizens in Hellenistic cities in the early Julio-Claudian period. However, two Romans appear holding city priesthoods at Ephesus in an inscription of A.D. 19–23.[2] In the documents collected in the *Sylloge Epigraphica* and subsequent volumes of the *Supplementum Epigraphicum*, which are representative, though not exhaustive, it is not till the period after Tiberius that Hellenistic Romans appear to be holding city magistracies with any regularity, and even then they are not very frequent.[3] The long document known as the genealogical tree of Oenoanda, which

---

[1] Above, p. 181 n. 3. Cf. the third edict of Augustus from Cyrene (E–J, 311. iii) and the Volubilis inscription, which shows the abnormality of *immunitas* in a provincial municipality by the time of Claudius (*Inscr. Lat. Afr.* 634 or Charlesworth, i. 36).

[2] *SEG*, iv. 515.

[3] Cf. *DS*, ii. 796–7 (A.D. 35 and 37), 802, 804–5.

gives the complete civic history of a Lycian family over a very long period, shows that the highest civic dignitaries were already apt to be Roman citizens in the early Julio-Claudian period.[1]

It would seem that the compatibility of Roman and non-Roman citizenship became an established practice before the *floruit* of Paul and the dramatic date of Acts. There is one development of the dual citizenship which plays a large part in the political thought of the second and third centuries but leaves no trace in Acts. This is the doctrine summed up as *communis patria Roma*, which the orator Aristides elaborated in his famous panegyric of Rome. The doctrine itself has a respectable ancestry in a text of Cicero. Thinking in terms of the unification of Italy after the Social War, he formulated the doctrine that within the Roman State each man has two *patriae*, that of his local city or *municipium* and the Roman State itself.[2] This notion was applied in later times to the relationship between Rome and the civic communities of the whole empire. There is no trace of this in the Acts, very much the reverse. Rightly. It should not be there. The idea in its Greek form took shape in the age of the Antonines. It is barely foreshadowed in Dio of Prusa's speech to the Senate of Apamea, when he speaks of Apamea, the Roman colony, in terms suitable to Rome herself, sharing her citizenship and laws and benefits with all peoples, and taking to herself anything external that was worthy, and so forth: οὐδὲν ἀλλότριον ἡγουμένη τῶν ἀξίων.[3]

Cadbury was tempted to find an echo of the theme of *communis patria* in the well-known phrase of Philippians iii. 20: ἡμῶν τὸ πολίτευμα ἐν οὐρανοῖς ὑπάρχει, 'Our community

---

[1] *IGRR*, iii. 500.

[2] Cic. *De legibus*, ii. 2. 5. Cf. *RC*, 134 f.

[3] Dio Chrys. 41. 9. This echoes the thought of the Tacitean version of Claudius' *Oratio Lugdunensis*: 'transferendo huc quod usquam egregium fuit', &c. *Ann.* xi. 24. Cf. *ILS*, 212, c. ii.

is in heaven.' This will not do. πολίτευμα is not πόλις or πολιτεία: it is community not citizenship. Tertullian alluding to this passage uses the term *municipatus*. The metaphor is in terms of the city-state, but no wider. Paul is contrasting Christians with the men of this world: οἱ τὰ ἐπίγεια φρονοῦντες ὧν ὁ θεὸς ἡ κοιλία καὶ ἡ δόξα ἐν αἰσχύνῃ. Technically the term πολίτευμα was used in connexion with the great cities, metropolitan in size, such as Alexandria and Seleucia on Tigris, to denote self-sufficient and self-governing communities of non-citizens, especially of Jews, who form a city within a city. Josephus uses the term—in a verbal form—of the subordinate element of Syrians at Seleucia, who were under the general authority of the citizen body, but organized their own internal affairs.[1] The Jewish synagogues and Sanhedrins were such *politeumata* in some cities.[2] The metaphor would come naturally to the mind of a travelled Jew, who had seen the Jewish *politeumata* of half Asia. The point of the metaphor in Philippians is that the Christians are not citizens but resident aliens in the cities of the world, and their colony has special rules. The idea of Roman status—or a unitary status—as the general condition of mankind fails to occur in the very passages where one would most expect it. One notes the great passage in Colossians: 'where there is neither Hellene nor Jew . . . neither barbarian nor Scythian, neither free nor slave'. The category 'Roman' is absent.[3] At this date and in this context, of Paul to men of Colossae, this absence is not astonishing. The characters of Acts and Epistles lived in a world that was Greek not Roman, and where the persistent contrast, as in both sets of writings, is between Jew and Hellene.

[1] Jos. *Ant.* xviii. 9. 8–9.

[2] Cf. L–S⁹, s.v. iv. 2. It is used of the Jews at Berenice, in *SEG*, xvi. 931 (*CIG*, iii. 5361. 21), which shows the organization of this organ.

[3] Col. iii. 11.

THE HISTORICITY OF THE GOSPELS AND
GRAECO-ROMAN HISTORIOGRAPHY

So much for the detailed study of the Graeco-Roman setting of Acts and Gospels. But it is fitting for a professional Graeco-Roman historian to consider the whole topic of historicity briefly and very generally, and boldly to state a case. Though for two short periods of our history we are lucky enough to have two major contemporary historians of remarkably objective character in Thucydides and Polybius, we are generally dealing with derivative sources of marked bias and prejudice composed at least one or two generations after the events which they describe, but much more often, as with the *Lives* of Plutarch or the central decades of Livy, from two to five *centuries* later. Though connecting links are provided backwards in time by series of lost intermediate sources, we are seldom in the happy position of dealing at only one remove with a contemporary source. Yet not for that do we despair of reconstructing the story of the tyranny of Pisistratus or of the tribunates of the Gracchi.

Subtle techniques of source-criticism have been evolved for the detection and elimination of various types of bias and anachronism, whether of the intermediate or of the original source, or of the writer who actually survives and transmits his work to us. To judge by what is so freely published, we are satisfied with our methods, and believe that a hard core or basic layer of historical truth can be recovered even from the most deplorable of our tertiary sources—be it Diodorus or Florus or even the *Epitome de Caesaribus*. The refinement of source-criticism has not led to the notion that knowledge in ancient history is unattainable, or that the serious study of ancient politics is nothing but the history of rival propaganda. The basic reason for this confidence is, if put summarily, the existence of external confirmations, and the working of the synoptic principle. From time to time external contemporary evidence of a sort less warped by the bias of personalities—e.g. the texts of laws and public accounts—confirms the conclusions drawn from the critical study of literary sources. Hence we are bold to trust our results in the larger fields where there is no such confirmation. Equally the criticism of sources tends to reveal the existence of a basic unitary tradition beneath the manifold divergences of detail in rival narratives, which is often the product of their particular bias.

So, it is astonishing that while Graeco-Roman historians have been growing in confidence, the twentieth-century study of the Gospel narratives, starting from no less promising material, has taken so gloomy a turn in the development of form-criticism that the more advanced exponents of it apparently maintain—so far as an amateur can understand the matter—that the historical Christ is unknowable and the history of his mission cannot be written. This seems very curious when one compares the case for the best-known contemporary of Christ, who like Christ is a well-documented figure—Tiberius Caesar. The story of his reign is known from four sources, the *Annals* of Tacitus and the biography of Suetonius, written some eighty or ninety years later, the brief contemporary record of Velleius Paterculus, and the third-century history of Cassius Dio. These disagree amongst themselves in the wildest possible fashion, both in major matters of political action or motive and in specific details of minor events. Everyone would admit that Tacitus is the best of all the sources, and yet no serious modern historian would accept at face value the majority of the statements of Tacitus about the motives of Tiberius.[1] But this

---

[1] Save perhaps Professor Syme, whose great book, *Tacitus*, aims at a very general rehabilitation not only of the factual but of the ideological accuracy of Tacitus. But, e.g., F. B. Marsh, *The Reign of Tiberius* (London, 1931), is more characteristic, or G. Walser, *Rom, das Reich,* &c. (Baden-Baden, 1951).

does not prevent the belief that the material of Tacitus can be used to write a history of Tiberius. The divergences between the synoptic gospels, or between them and the Fourth Gospel, are no worse than the contradictions in the Tiberius material.

Another example. The internal synoptic divergences, such as arise in the narratives of the trial of Christ, are very similar to those that Roman historians meet in the study of the tribunate of Gaius Gracchus. We have two or even three contradictory versions, for instance, of the content of the most important of the legislative proposals—a central point in the story—and there are three divergent versions of the way in which the riot began in which Gaius lost his life. The four accounts of the trial of Christ are not more troublesome. The two cases are rather similar in terms of analysis. The three versions of the death of Gaius aim at attributing the blame for the great riot to different persons or groups.[1] So, too, the mildly divergent versions of the scene before Pilate and the Sanhedrin may aim, as has often been suggested, at transferring the blame for the condemnation of Christ, in varying degrees, from the Romans to the Jews.

The objection will be raised to this line of argument that the Roman historical writers and the Gospels belong to different kinds of literature. Whatever the defects of our sources, their authors were trying to write history, but the authors of the Gospels had a different aim. Yet however one accepts form-criticism, its principles do not inevitably contradict the notion of the basic historicity of the particular stories of which the Gospel narratives are composed, even if these were not shored up and confirmed by the external guarantee of their fabric and setting. That the degree of

[1] For a detailed narrative of the rival sources for the tribunates of Caius Gracchus on these lines see J. Carcopino, *Autour des Gracques* (Paris, 1928), ch. iv. For the three versions of the riot see Appian, *B.C.* i. 25. 4; Diod. 34, fr. 28 A; Plut. *Gaius*, 13. 3–4.

confirmation in Graeco-Roman terms is less for the Gospels than for Acts is due, as these lectures have tried to show, to the differences in their regional setting. As soon as Christ enters the Roman orbit at Jerusalem, the confirmation begins. For Acts the confirmation of historicity is overwhelming. Yet Acts is, in simple terms and judged externally, no less of a propaganda narrative than the Gospels, liable to similar distortions. But any attempt to reject its basic historicity even in matters of detail must now appear absurd. Roman historians have long taken it for granted.

What to an ancient historian is most surprising in the basic assumptions of form-criticism of the extremer sort, is the presumed tempo of the development of the didactic myths—if one may use that term to sum up the matter. We are not unacquainted with this type of writing in ancient historiography, as will shortly appear. The agnostic type of form-criticism would be much more credible if the compilation of the Gospels were much later in time, much more remote from the events themselves, than can be the case. Certainly a deal of distortion can affect a story that is given literary form a generation or two after the event, whether for national glorification or political spite, or for the didactic or symbolic exposition of ideas. But in the material of ancient history the historical content is not hopelessly lost.

Herodotus particularly comes to mind. In his history, written in mid-fifth century B.C., we have a fund of comparable material in the tales of the period of the Persian Wars and the preceding generation. These are retold by Herodotus from forty to seventy years later, after they had been remodelled by at least one generation of oral transmission. The parallel with the authors of the Gospels is by no means so far-fetched as it might seem. Both regard their material with enthusiasm rather than detached criticism. Both are the first to produce a written narrative of great events which they regard as a mighty saga, national or ecclesiastical and esoterical as the case may be. For both their story is the vehicle of a moral or a religious idea which shapes the narrative. For Herodotus the classical concept of 'koros-hubris-até' is no less basically influential than the notion of, for example, oblation in the pattern of the Gospels, affecting both the parts and the whole of the narrative. Yet the material of Herodotus presents no intractable difficulty to a critical historian. The material has not been transformed out of all recognition under the influence of moral and patriotic fervour, in a period of time as long, if not longer, than can be allowed for the gestation of the form-myths of the synoptic gospels.

Herodotus enables us to test the tempo of myth-making, and the tests suggest that even two generations are too short a span to allow the mythical tendency to prevail over the hard historic core of the oral tradition. A revealing example is provided by the story of the murder of the Athenian tyrant Hipparchus at the hands of Harmodius and Aristogeiton, who became the pattern of all tyrannicides. The true story was that they assassinated Hipparchus in 514 B.C., but the tyranny lasted another four years before the establishment of the Athenian democracy. Popular opinion created a myth to the effect that Harmodius and Aristogeiton destroyed the tyranny and freed Athens. This was current in the mid-fifth century. Yet Herodotus, writing at that time, and generally taking the popular view of the establishment of the democracy, gives the true version and not the myth about the death of Hipparchus. A generation later the more critical Thucydides was able to uncover a detailed account of exactly what happened on the fatal day in 514 B.C. It would have been natural and easy for Herodotus to give the mythical version. He does not do so because he had a particular interest in a greater figure than Harmodius or Aristogeiton, that is, Cleisthenes, the central person in the establishment of the democracy.[1]

All this suggests that, however strong the myth-forming tendency, the falsification does not automatically and absolutely prevail even with a writer like Herodotus, who was naturally predisposed in favour of certain political myths, and whose ethical and literary interests were stronger than his critical faculty. The Thucydidean version is a salutary warning that even a century after a major event it is possible in a relatively small or closed community for a determined inquirer to establish a remarkably detailed account of a major event, by inquiry within the inner circle of the descendants of those concerned with the event itself. Not that one imagines that the authors of the Gospels set to work precisely like either Herodotus or Thucydides. But it can be maintained that those who had a passionate interest in the story of Christ, even if their interest in events was parabolical and didactic rather than historical, would not be led by that very fact to pervert and utterly destroy the historical kernel of their material. It can also be suggested that it would be no harder for the Disciples and their immediate successors to uncover detailed narratives of the actions and sayings of Christ within their closed community, than it was for Herodotus and Thucydides to establish the story of the great events of 520–480 B.C. For this purpose it matters little whether you accept the attribution of the Gospels to eyewitnesses or not.

The impression of a historical tradition is nowhere more strongly felt than in the various accounts of the trial of Christ, analysed in Roman terms in the second lecture. Consider the close interdependence of Mark and Matthew, supplementing each other even in particular phrases, yet each with his particular contribution, then Luke with his

[1] Herod. vi. 123; cf. ibid. 109, 3; Thuc. vi. 53, 3.

more coherent and explicit account of the charges and less clear version of the activity of the Sanhedrin, finally John, who despite many improbabilities and obscurities yet gives a convincingly contemporary version of the political pressure on Pilate in the age of Tiberius.

Taking the synoptic writers quite generally as primitive historians, there is a remarkable parallel between their technique and that of Herodotus, the father of history, in their anecdotal conception of a narrative. Consider the great episodes of Herodotus such as the campaign of Salamis or the story of the rise of Athens and Sparta, before the Persian invasion, each of which is comparable to one of the Gospels in length. Each is composed of a series of small and disconnected but significant incidents or anecdotes.[1] It is notorious that Herodotus discarded even as a framework the famous account of Salamis provided by the eye-witness Aeschylus in his play, the *Persae*, and replaced it by what appears to be a hotch-potch of incidents. These turn ou when carefully considered to be the great actions of the major personalities—Cleomenes, Themistocles—whose activity decided the event. The parallel with the technique of the synoptic writers is apparent. It is as though this was the natural manner in which a primary innovator, with no models to follow, instinctively wrote history, especially when the narrative of events was controlled by an idea rather than the mere desire to explain what happened. The notions of form-criticism have not been applied systematically to Herodotus. His stories are obviously open to treatment of this kind. The investigation would cast much light on his literary method, but would not affect seriously the basic historicity of his material, which is sufficiently established.[2]

---

[1] Herod. v. 39–54, 66–98, vi. 48–84, for Sparta under Cleomenes; viii. 1–95, for the Salamis campaign.

[2] Mr. P. A. B. Brunt has suggested in private correspondence that a

INDEX

Roman citizens are listed under the part of their name in common use. References to notes are under page numberings.

INDEX OF SPECIAL PASSAGES

This is limited to texts of which the meaning is discussed in detail.

INDEX OF GREEK PHRASES